Digital Transformations in Contemporary Art and Media Practices

Murat Han Er
https://orcid.org/0000-0002-3896-2796
Ataturk University, Turkey

Basri Gençcelep
Ataturk University, Turkey

IGI Global
Scientific Publishing
Publishing Tomorrow's Research Today

Vice President of Editorial | Melissa Wagner
Director of Acquisitions | Mikaela Felty
Director of Book Development | Jocelynn Hessler
Production Manager | Mike Brehm
Cover Design | Jose Rosado

Published in the United States of America by
IGI Global Scientific Publishing
701 East Chocolate Avenue
Hershey, PA, 17033, USA
Tel: 717-533-8845 | Fax: 717-533-7115
Website: https://www.igi-global.com E-mail: cust@igi-global.com

Library of Congress Cataloging-in-Publication Data

(CIP Data Pending)
ISBN13: 979-8-2600-0944-4
Isbn13Softcover: 979-8-2600-0945-1
EISBN13: 979-8-2600-0946-8
British Cataloguing in Publication Data
A Cataloguing in Publication record for this book is available from the British Library.

Table of Contents

Detailed Table of Contents

New media has a unique communication feature in terms of providing multiple and fast interaction with instant text, photo, video and sound recording sharing. These interaction networks, which are widely used today and determine life, are very effective in presenting content such as chat, shopping, art, as well as easily preparing and sharing videos and images that are contrary to the moral understanding of society. New media has become an economic power where products with 'commodity' value are marketed through the bidirectional connections it provides in the preparation and consumption of content. The 'new media', which puts values in the background, has turned into a digital market with 5.5 billion users, providing continuity for the 'culture industry' by adopting a language that directs consumption. This new area, where billions of people meet, also reveals serious behavioural differences. This new form of communication was analysed through consumption-oriented posts consisting of millions of messages.

The aim of this study is to examine the presence of nature-human-technology culture in art, related to sound ecology, through digital tools that influence nature and humans, and to examine installations created with objects, movement, and sound that reference nature. Document analysis and content analysis, two qualitative research techniques, were employed in the study. The selected artists were selected and limited among those who focused on nature and human culture in installations created through the collaboration of technology, nature, sound, and movement. The use of nature sounds in sound installations, through artistic and scientific collaboration, revealed that it revives the ecological spirit of nature. In conclusion, the study revealed that sound plays a crucial role in healing nature and humans and restoring natural balance in sound installations that address nature-human relationships from a digital aesthetic perspective in art.

Although the term graphic design was first coined by typographer William A. Dwiggins in the early 20th century to define emerging professional practices, the origins of the discipline can be traced back to prehistoric times. Visual expressions such as those in the Lascaux Caves demonstrate that symbolic communication predates written language. Over centuries, graphic design evolved through major cultural and technological shifts, including the invention of writing, the development of typographic systems, the advent of the printing press, and the transformations brought by the Industrial Revolution. In the modern era, digitalization fundamentally redefined the field by enabling greater interactivity, flexibility, and creative experimentation. Today, artificial intelligence marks a new epistemological threshold, reshaping design methodologies, questioning authorship, and expanding the conceptual boundaries of visual communication.

This article explores the relationship between digitalization and accessibility in the art world. It highlights how digital technologies have transformed the creation, exhibition, and distribution of art, making it more globally accessible through online platforms. Digital tools like virtual reality and AI have expanded creative possibilities, while internet access allows people from diverse regions to engage with art. However, the digital divide still presents challenges to equal access. Overall, digitalization has made art more inclusive, innovative, and collaborative, reshaping how it is experienced and shared worldwide.

In contemporary society, rapid advancements in information and communication technologies have significantly reshaped social structures and individual lifestyles. As access to information has become a key priority, digital technologies have transcended traditional boundaries of time and space, making knowledge globally available. The integration of computer technologies into everyday life has led to an information-driven transformation, influencing how people communicate, work, and learn.Digital technologies have not only revolutionized traditional art forms like painting, photography, and music but have also given rise to entirely new genres such as internet art, NFTs, and virtual reality. Digital art has developed its own theoretical and aesthetic foundations, challenging conventional ideas of the artist, artwork, and audience. Artists can now create, share, and preserve their works more efficiently using digital tools, reaching global audiences and redefining the artistic experience in the digital age.

Since the beginning of life on earth, living beings have managed to communicate with each other in some way. The most notable of these creatures is humans. Humans, who have the ability to speak, have developed various communication skills in order to reach other people with whom they share a common life. Over time, verbal communication has developed and given way to communication methods. The internet and social media, which have developed along with the internet, have also made a great contribution to the communication adventure. Mass media, which have shown themselves in many areas of our lives, have not only strengthened the communication environment, but have also managed to play a leading role in many areas such as information exchange, entertainment or education. The most prominent of mass media are social media platforms. Social media platforms have also brought with them a number of problems.

Vera Molnár, who discovered computer art at an early stage in the 1960s and was one of the first female artists to work in this field, utilized algorithms and produced digital artworks. She developed a method called the "Molnárt System," which introduced a 1% degree of irregularity into her compositions. This method enabled her to incorporate deliberate distortions into her works, overlapping with the principles of Glitch art. This study will analyze how Molnár's digital works produced in the 1960s and 1970s intersect with Glitch art. Her works will be examined using visual analysis and literature review methods. The findings indicate that Molnár's works, created through deliberate distortion and randomness, can be regarded as early examples of Glitch art. In conclusion, it is observed that Molnár's works expand the boundaries between computer art and traditional painting, developing a new

Preface

INTRODUCTION

Digital Transformations in Contemporary Art and Media Practices examines the multilayered transformations brought about by digitalization in the fields of contemporary art and media from an interdisciplinary perspective. Comprising nine chapters, the volume begins by exploring the language of communication shaped by new media, consumption-oriented content practices, and forms of multiple interaction. It then addresses such contemporary issues as the relationship between nature, sound, and technology; the historical development of graphic design from cave paintings to artificial intelligence; digital accessibility in art; the theoretical and aesthetic foundations of digital art; and the desire for visibility and approval in social media environments.

The book also critically evaluates the early examples of glitch aesthetics through the works of Vera Molnár, the new expressive possibilities that emerge at the intersection of digital art and sculpture, and Refik Anadol's transformation of big data and artificial intelligence into artistic productions that reshape the perception of space and time. In this respect, the volume reveals not only the impact of technological tools on artistic production, but also how digital culture reconfigures the ways in which we think, perceive, produce, and communicate.

CHAPTER OVERVIEW

Chapter 1 by *Meral Güler & Kainat Özpolat.* Maps "digital market" dynamics through consumption-oriented content practices, along with the economic/cultural effects of instant and multiple interaction.

Chapter 2 by *Özlem Gürpınar.* At the intersection of sound ecology and the nature–human–technology nexus, evaluates—through qualitative methods—the restorative/ecological contributions of installations that use sounds from nature.

Chapter 3 by *Nurevşan Karaduman Başcı & Burcu Toğrul.* Offers a history of graphic design spanning from prehistoric symbolic communication to writing, typography, printing, and the Industrial Revolution, extending to how digitization and AI reconfigure authorship and methods.

Chapter 4 by *& Burcu Toğrul & Nurevşan Karaduman Başçı.* Argues that digital tools—including VR/AI—make production, exhibition, and distribution globally accessible, while also discussing inequalities created by the digital divide.

Chapter 5 by *Musafa Bulat & Serap Bulat.* Examines how information and communication technologies influence artistic genres within social transformation; addresses the theoretical/aesthetic foundations of forms such as internet art, NFTs, and VR.

Chapter 6 by *Ece Nur Yalçınkaya & Kainat Özpolat.* Investigates how social-media platforms reshape communicative habits and the problems that arise alongside these transformations.

Chapter 7 by *Melis Sucuoğlu Doğan.* Provides a historical/formal analysis of glitch through Molnár's "1% irregularity" approach; shows how early digital works propose a new aesthetic.

Chapter 8 by *Musafa Bulat & Gülümser Beyaztaş Özlütürk.* Discusses how 3D modeling, AR/VR, and digital production techniques transform material/expressive possibilities and the interaction between viewer and artwork.

CONCLUSION

The studies brought together in this volume demonstrate that digitalization has generated not merely a technical transformation in contemporary art and media practices, but also profound changes at aesthetic, intellectual, and social levels. These multidimensional discussions, ranging from the language of new media to digital art, from the history of graphic design to social media culture, and from glitch aesthetics to data-driven artistic production, reveal that art is being redefined today through its interaction with technology. The acquisition of new meanings by such elements as nature, sound, body, space, audience, and data within digital environments both expands the boundaries of artistic production and brings to the fore issues such as accessibility, inequality, visibility, and criticality. In this respect, the book provides a holistic framework for understanding the relationship between art and media in the digital age and constitutes a significant reference source that contributes both to theoretical discussions and to contemporary practices.

Murat Han Er

Atatürk University, Turkey

Basri Gençcelep

Atatürk University, Turkey

Chapter 1
New Communication Language With New Media

Meral Güler
http://orcid.org/0009-0009-7550-7061
Fırat University, Turkey

Kainat Özpolat
http://orcid.org/0000-0003-1377-5262
Fırat University, Turkey

ABSTRACT

New media has a unique communication feature in terms of providing multiple and fast interaction with instant text, photo, video and sound recording sharing. These interaction networks, which are widely used today and determine life, are very effective in presenting content such as chat, shopping, art, as well as easily preparing and sharing videos and images that are contrary to the moral understanding of society. New media has become an economic power where products with 'commodity' value are marketed through the bidirectional connections it provides in the preparation and consumption of content. The 'new media', which puts values in the background, has turned into a digital market with 5.5 billion users, providing continuity for the 'culture industry' by adopting a language that directs consumption. This new area, where billions of people meet, also

DOI: 10.4018/979-8-2600-0944-4.ch001

reveals serious behavioural differences. This new form of communication was analysed through consumption-oriented posts consisting of millions of messages.

INTRODUCTION

New media has reached a large number of users around the world with all the features of traditional media and even more. Digital networks, which are used by more than half of the world's population, have brought with them a wide range of dangers.

With the introduction of new media into human life, it has revealed a form of communication that affects people both mentally and physically with the shares they are exposed to instantly from all over the world. The more active form of communication of the new media is many times more active than other tools in terms of negative consequences on human behaviour. The new media, which is the most effective of the mass media in the last century, has created a completely different field of communication with a weak moral and ethical side. The rapid advancement of artificial technologies has shifted much more of the behaviour in consumer culture to this field.

These new media environments, into which children and adults are born, create an online danger environment for people of all age groups; moreover, it is easily shared in an environment where no ethical and moral values are ignored. One of the darkest sides is that every shared information is processed as ‘goods’ and easily reaches the whole world.

In this study, it has been tried to be done by using a descriptive language on the problematic effects of the new form of communication brought by sharing in new media environments on behaviours.

NEW MEDIA CONCEPT

New media, which we know as digital media, multimedia, interactive media, online, social media, unlike newspapers, radio and television, which represent the traditional press, is connected to multiple networks in the electronic environment and realises the interaction of all and more of the publications made by traditional media tools through a single area via the internet.

The new media is now a versatile tool that enables simultaneous information exchange with its users both individually and collectively over all internet connections. The most important effect that distinguishes this new communication option from other traditional media is the fast and wide flow created by instant sharing between users in the digital environment.

One of the most important features of the new media is that individuals can create their individual channels with the publications they prepare through their own social media pages and easily reach millions of people by sharing these prepared contents with other social media members. The internet journey, which started in ARPANET (1969) with the initiative of the Ministry of Defence of the United States of America, has developed with many technical infrastructures until today and has managed to become the most widely used means of communication in the last 50 years.

Electronic communication studies, which started with the aim of collecting data for the USA, progressed and gained its commercial identity after 1970. With the protocol connections between countries, other countries started to use this fast communication tool after the 1990s and after the 2000s, it has become the most widely used communication tool in the world.

The communication type of the new media, which is realised through fast texts, can provide mutual and very wide access by delivering the effects created by the heavy and one-sided publications of the traditional media to both the individual and the society through network environments. It is a very effective structure for communicating both because it contains a wide range of media content specific to one's own taste and because important information in the public sphere is immediately shared with the public. The unlimited flow of all kinds of information concerning the individual and the general public after it is shared through the network environment is a characteristic of new media environments. Another important reason for the new media to be at the forefront is that instead of the productions made by large media companies by allocating high sums of money, the content created by people with their own likes through their individual pages is watched over and over again by millions of people. The new media, which reveals the communication format of our age, is also due to the fact that the communication format created by millions of people by bringing all users together in the same environment mutually over the same space has a structure that facilitates people's shift to this field.

INTERNET USAGE IN THE WORLD

Since the existence of communication tools, it has been one of the most important concepts for countries with its power to shape political and social life, especially economic development (countries that know how to use communication tools well start all their economic initiatives from here). The social changes that affected the world population after the First World War brought along new political formations. The war of ascendancy between countries has developed in proportion to the mass media. The power struggles, which first started with radio broadcasts, continued with communication technologies with the improvement of the conditions brought by the age and left its popularity to television. The desire to possess communication technologies, which continued with television after radio, laid the groundwork for internet connections after the Second World War. Attempts to reveal the image of a strong country through communication tools have always produced results in favour of countries; radio, television and internet communication, which is today's digital communication tool, has always been a powerful concept that determines economic and sociological balances. 'Obtaining information', which is one of the most used discourses of communication tools, has a much more importance than "having fun", and the fact that it changes the course of events that affect the whole world has drawn attention to this field. The role of communication tools in every period has been to prepare a soft social environment that will contribute to their own interests (political and economic) through persuasion, apart from 'entertaining' and 'informing' the masses. In the last few hundred years, information and entertainment have always remained in the background, from magazines to radio, from radio to television, and even to the Internet, which determines today's way of life.

The social and economic events of the last hundred years are closely related to the mass media. After the two great wars, America started to concentrate its efforts on a new form of communication. These new searches led to the emergence of the first attempts of the Internet in 1969. The main reasons that led to the emergence of this new communication were to facilitate the collection of data by more reliable mass media as a result of the major wars. The US Department of Defence, which initiated the studies, was able to interact with the networks in a very limited way, and the uninterrupted efforts to establish new and faster interaction succeeded in gradually expanding the limited way of communicating and made it available to the masses through the protocols made at the end of the 90s.

The efforts to establish network communication, which started after the Second World War, with the improvement of technical infrastructure facilities and the development of mobile devices (computers, phones, tablets, wearable technologies), connections that all people can easily use have been realised and a media tool that provides multiple interaction has emerged. Internet-based communication networks brought an effective communication opportunity to human life in the late 90s and early 2000s. In the beginning, the internet-connected communication option, which was only one-way at first, has become more active as it has reached a level that allows information and documents to be easily edited and shared with web 2.0 based applications. Content preparation and content sharing activities through the programmes on the applications have prepared the environment for the proliferation of social networks and the increase in the interaction created by the users mutually. The difference in the interaction created by the masses has increased the orientation towards this field.

Social networks, which have so many users in the world, have led to the focus on technologies that provide faster interaction and have led to the emergence of web 3 studies. In the coming years, it is expected to be used more widely in many areas such as art, health, education and virtual money.

Thanks to the economic conditions and new technologies in developed countries, fast internet usage is more widespread. This reveals that new technologies are used more actively by the countries that first introduced them in every sense and that they are used more effectively both economically and socially.

Sociological and psychological factors in the new types of communication exhibited by the world population have been among the developments that have attracted the attention of people conducting scientific research on this field. New studies have also shifted to communication technologies and important data have been obtained. According to the results of a research on internet consumption behaviours, it has been determined that there are more than 5.5 billion social media users. The new media environment, which has such intensive use, has revealed its existence as a place that makes a significant contribution to the new economic areas of countries (Social, 2024).

The fact that the Internet is not only an economic power in itself has also revealed its impact in the market studies of other countries; especially countries that reveal this technological and economic power and use it actively are seen to be numerically ahead in the return of the market. As a result of a research conducted by a US-based research company (IAB), it has been determined that the Internet has an important area in the country's economy. The economic effects measured starting from 2008 have grown every year. By 2021, its economic growth has increased many times over, reaching 2.45 trillion from 300 billion (Danghad, 2021).

Although the mass media has the basic job of informing people, there is a strong consensus that all organs of traditional media from the past to the present need the economic assistance of sovereign powers in order to survive. The important issue here is that the media's semaya power, which was unilateral in the past, has revealed a double-sided and highly profitable economic value due to the active sharing (commodity value) of users on networks.

THE DIMENSION OF CONSUMPTION IN NEW MEDIA

New media realises all the functionality that exists in traditional media through a single space. Moreover, it does this without the need for huge televisions or radios. Thanks to the unbelievable communication skills of mobile devices, which are many times smaller, communication has become a much faster process. It is possible to interact with small mobile devices that can be carried as much as desired regardless of distance and time. New media also has a special importance in terms of actively publicising services in the public sphere through networks. This form of communication is a very functional tool that is frequently used in the promotion of new products, instant news, sharing the photo taken immediately, sending the prepared document to the other party instantly and announcing new-current information. In terms of reaching the economic and cultural dimension of all these activities to the society, new media is also a very preferred reason for being a preferred active form of communication.

The distinctive part of the new media here is that it is in a position to announce to large masses by realising the promotions provided by all media tools (radio, television, newspapers, television) in the most effective way against both the individual and the society through virtual networks.

Another important reason that makes the new media different from the beginning to the end is that it is a digital and economic media tool that transfers advertising products that determine production and consumption to both individuals and masses in the easiest and most effective way.

It will be easier to understand the importance of its economic dimension, especially when we consider the power created by the billions of users of social media platforms. If we accept that every message disseminated through messages is an explicit or implicit consumption-oriented message, we can grasp the basic logic of all media tools (McLuhan's 'the medium is the message'). On the basis of the broadcasts made by means of communication tools, it is shaped in order to prepare people for a new way of life and thinking through the advertisements published.

Consumption has become a way of life in itself: 'The more you consume, the happier you will be' is a subtle message in almost all adverts. In this way, content policies are processed that the reason for one's existence is not to produce but only to consume.

Among today's media products (which have economic value), people take their place as an object. In the content, people have ceased to be a subject and have become a mass that is valued as a 'commodity'. The person's own identity is of no importance; he/she tends to exist from this artificial list of needs with the needs created by the consumption culture.

Thus, the new communication language provided by billions of users takes the form of a field with an economic dimension, and the promotions that affect people both physically and mentally lead to consumption. ‘Consumption’, which we consider as a simple “concept”, is the main factor affecting all our thoughts (up to the lowest point of our minds) and behaviours, and this form of consumption is realised with a single media without being realised piece by piece with traditional media tools.

DIGITAL ADDICTION

Every age has its own problems. Digital addiction is one of the problems of our age. Virtual games, which have entered human life with computers, tablets and smartphones developed with the Internet, have reached visible levels with the rapid consumption brought by multiple networks. Although digital games played with groups are played to meet the daily entertainment needs of people, the fact of addiction created by the digital world results in the continuation of these games over time without being able to control oneself. Digital game addiction, which starts with friend circles and cultural changes brought about by the internet, also reveals life-threatening negative behavioural effects, especially among young people. The games played on the internet and the addiction created by the excessive amount of time spent on the internet reveal another negative aspect of communication tools.

‘In India, a 16-year-old boy addicted to gaming died after playing games for days without eating food or drinking water.‘ (’ Gaming addict boy dies of starvation’, 2020).

The consumption behaviours of people all over the world are similar to their relationships on mobile devices. Looking at the age of users, whether in a developed or developing country, it is seen that those on the addiction side of the scale exhibit the same behaviour.

Compared to young people who spend one hour a day with electronic devices, young people who spend five hours or more a day are 71% more likely to exhibit suicide risk factors. 47 per cent of the children surveyed believe that they are addicted. In addition, more than 40 per cent of young mobile device users say they are overwhelmed by constant notifications ("44 Smartphone Addiction Statistics for 2024 [INFOGRAPHIC]", 2019)

The pandemic period, which started in 2019, has brought consumption habits that will radically change the lives of both the individual and the society with its impact on the whole world. In order to reduce the risk of the epidemic, the heavy restrictions of governments on not going out have resulted in an increase in time and product consumption in this area by directing people to shop in the digital environment.

With this risky addiction created by networks, consumption behaviours have emerged in proportion to each other. With the time spent, consumption behaviours have revealed a global addiction form that flows by revealing new habits.

In Bauman's words, we live in a world 'dominated by fluidity'. Everything flows, it flows without the need for a constant. In my opinion, the internet platform and these structures formed through the internet internalise this fluidity so seriously that they can adapt to every new development (Coronavirus Triggered Digital Addiction', 2020).

The new media, which provides the fast and easy interaction of the age we live in, causes the negative side effects of the age we live in on the world to spread just as easily.

DATA BREACHES OF NEW MEDIA

Mobile mobile phones, which people cannot put down, have become almost a part of our body. Digital use, whose frequency of use is increasing day by day, is not as ordinary as we think; especially in the virtual world! The connections we make with search engines on a daily basis with the mobile devices we take in our hands at every opportunity are realised on a data structure that also accumulates information about our identity. When we use search engines for a new product or news about a subject that we have previously researched verbally or in writing, all the information in the old searches appears before us again. Even if we do not search, the fact that mobile devices perceive sound and visuals (such as the digital pages you use immediately after talking about your dental problem with your friends, offering content about dental health, etc.) and record our behaviours reveals that we are an important ‘object’ for this environment. The world is now shaped through networks, and the complex structure of this world in new communications is victimising the people who surf the networks the most. In a virtual environment where billions of data are stored, the use of individuals' banking, health, security, personal information without complying with ethical rules results in the easy realisation of big data breach in these complex network societies.

There have been negative developments related to the fact that social media pages, especially the companies that produce mobile devices, do not protect personal information sufficiently, and that the new media environment is open about data privacy. These and similar incidents that reveal data privacy reveal that photographs and other private information are also taken without authorisation, especially in digital environments. ‘Malicious actors continue to devote a lot of time and resources to finding more creative and effective ways to steal consumer data, and we continue to work relentlessly to stop them,‘ said Craig Federighi, Apple's chief executive, showing that the danger is proportional to technological progress (’ Report’, 2023).

Mostly new generation technologies, especially communication technologies, always strive to gain profit by aiming for more consumption for the market that dominates production. The reason that makes the means of communication important in itself is that the whole chain of production and consumption (our political views, what we listen to, what we eat or drink, what we eat or drink, who we like or which brand we follow more, etc. behaviours) that concern human beings can quickly reach everyone through a certain policy (laws sometimes provide opportunities for consumption). They are trying to control and direct people through artificial technologies that even design how people should think and behave from head to toe. The new intelligent technologies that have emerged in the age of communication now determine both the behaviour of human beings in consumption and the new form of consumption in production through these areas.

Whether individually or in the form of communities, these network environments appear as a communication problem that is dangerous with the fact that large groups can be easily controlled. This global market, which has a mass of billions (a large part of solid matter), has emerged as a powerful consumption tool that affects people all over the world both materially and spiritually, and has a complicated structure in itself.

Instead of the behaviours that reveal each society's own identity, in a multicultural and very complex environment, people are exposed to everything good or bad, resulting in people accepting these behaviours as normal without realising it. The new media, which is more active than radio, newspaper and television, has turned into a structure that is much more dangerous than all traditional media tools. The fact that one-way interaction tools such as television and radio did not have the function of storing the information of the viewers or listeners could partially protect people. However, in the digital environment, it is a dangerous way of communication in itself for people to share their private information on their pages (with the specific purpose of collecting data) through media tools and to be seized by others and used as 'property'. The unauthorised use of information both harms people individually and causes an increase in the economic and social damages of countries. New generation technologies have a structure that is far from ethical values that badly affects the security of both the individual and the society, with large gaps in data breaches (down to the smallest detail of the research that people do with search engines from where they sit).

PUBLICATIONS CONTRARY TO GENERAL MORALITY IN NEW MEDIA

The most basic thing that constitutes society is undoubtedly the concept of 'morality'. From the first primitive societies to the present day, morality has maintained its importance as the most fundamental concept that ensures the order and security of society. In the past periods, it is morality that is unwritten and reveals good behaviours such as trust, respect and peace between people.

Mass media and morality are two important concepts to maintain reliable communication. The moral weakening of the behavioural disorders emerging in our age is due to the detachment from ethical values in virtual communication.

Z. Bauman, one of today's thinkers who evaluates sociological events with his own studies, has focused on the consequences of the negative factors brought about by modern life that reveal social segregation. Stating that the erosion of morality in the age we live in has taken the form of a flesh and blood structure, he stated that modern life plays an important role in the formation of such precise lines between ‘right’ and ‘wrong’ for the first time. While explaining that human behaviour has moved away from tradition and taken on a new and standard form, he states that the most important reason for human existence is morality. While focusing on the place of the concept of morality in society with its factors in our age, Bauman also says that changing values are a negative consequence of modern life. He also underlines that ethical values have become ambiguous in modern times and that it is practically impossible to speak of a morality ‘based on objective foundations’ in modern life (Öztürk, 2020).

While emphasising the importance of values, I. Kuçuradi, another contemporary intellectual professor of philosophy who focuses on morality, states that the behaviour of people that makes them forget humanity is rooted in the fact that they are disconnected from morality and ethical values. He says that the most important thing in human relations is trust, love and respect, and the most important source of this is morality: ‘There is no interest in real value judgements; because there is morality.’ (Kuçuradi Philosophy and Human Rights Foundation, 2019).

Countless people can perform an action by connecting to the internet anywhere in the world with a phone, tablet or an ordinary mobile device. Whether the behaviour exhibited is ‘good’ or ‘bad’ is decided by the general rules of life of the society we were born into. For a communication that makes people feel safe, respecting people and their values is the most basic requirement. Assuming that the new media constitute a worldwide community and that all kinds of communication can be easily carried out from here, we need to underline that morality should be the most valid here. Since the virtual environment is open to everyone and billions of people are in the same place, it is an inevitable reality to build a more reliable communication.

We call the age we live in communication. But it is necessary to examine whether we can communicate in the real sense of communication. With the new communication language of the new media, for the sake of 'clicks', many content with a weak moral side is shared. Pornographic images and obscene behaviours, which have international criminal sanctions, reach people easily and quickly in the virtual environment. People of all age groups can easily access the images prepared illegally in the virtual media. This situation with negative effects has brought serious dangers especially for children and people who avoid obscene content. The blood relationship between communication tools and sex has continued from yesterday to today. However; with the new media, this situation has moved towards another uncontrollable phase by using all kinds of new technologies (especially in creating realistic nude content).

Making this situation more problematic with new media, intelligent technologies do not exclude nudity. Pornographic images are broadcast in an increasingly professional format through artificial media. So much so that the moral confusion created by erotic and nude videos has recently become the most discussed topic of the countries. American singer Taylor Swift came to the agenda with a serious nude video in 2023, creating a controversy in the world. The singer was later informed of her nude images, and although this video was unauthorised and banned, Twitter (X) was removed after 19 hours. In a short period of time, it reached nearly 27 million views. Discussions started again to organise new laws on the prohibition of these images prepared using clever technologies in the virtual

At the last point, it has been revealed that all people have a dangerous interaction in the digital field with the artificial intelligence technique. Children suffer the most. This community of networks, into which children are easily immersed, causes major problems for their future that they do not realise.

As a result of a study conducted in the UK (IWF), it was stated that abuse images created with artificial intelligence were used together with real images. It was revealed that these images were images of sexual intercourse classified as Category A ('Artificial intelligence', 2023).

Social moral values, which provide the world's thousands of years of life adventure, are the most important concepts that prepare the ground for that society to live in trust and peace. It is a serious detail to protect these values in order to leave a healthy society to future people. The disappearance of moral behaviours that keep people together means the disappearance of peace and trust in the society. As a matter of fact, this communication age we are in, one of the most important reasons for the emergence of deteriorating human behaviour has been as a result of the break from values. The right and good behaviour, which is called morality in society, is also referred to as ethical rules in law; these rules have been shaped both in society and in law in order to secure the values of people. The mass media cause the degeneration of society and the breakdown of human relations with their content that puts both morality (the values of society) and ethics (a philosophically abstract way of thinking, a form of behaviour with sanctions) values in the background.

Thanks to the phones, tablets, wearable digital devices that are always in our hands, we spend time intertwined with web-based publications from all over the world and all kinds of good, bad and all kinds of shares of individuals on social networks. Each message shared has a purpose; people usually take action for a good or bad purpose. In order to understand 'what' this purpose serves, social ethical values emerge. It is not a realistic way of thinking at this point to say that the information that every person shares in these environments represents completely correct and good behaviour.

Tik Tok, Youtube, Instagram, WhatsApp, Facebook, X etc. Sharing content contrary to general morality in environments has become a commonplace in recent days. The viewing rates of videos appealing to all age groups are increasing day by day on these platforms. Increasing video sharing behaviours have also affected daily life and created an understanding of consumption that adopts virtual life.

The form of communication with the world in general shares various contents on lifestyle from every culture and society. The shared content also reveals different forms of consumption dimensions that mostly occur with new communication tools. Any video content that is liked by another content producer on the other side of the world (whatever media organisations have done before) or even more is spread very actively from here. Moreover, it goes beyond the borders of the country where it is located and realises it with all its negative sides.

In some studies on the prohibition of this application, it has been decided to be abolished in some countries due to its bad effects on general morality and bad effects on people.

'TikTok, which has been closed in many parts of the world from Australia to the UK, from Canada to India, was finally tried to be out of use in America.' ('Why TikTok is Banned in Which Countries?', 2025).

In the discussions that arose after the users objected to this situation, the dominant side ensured the continuity of the closure decision due to the negative content. Again, conflicts arose between the country and company authorities due to unethical and unlawful content through these platforms.

As in almost every part of the world, there have been some incidents in our country that have come to the agenda with the display of behaviours contrary to general values ('The woman who made obscene broadcasts for money on TikTok was released').In fact, although countries change, behaviours and ways of sharing content show similarities. It has become a very possible job to encounter many content that is not accepted in general morality regarding the content of the broadcasts.

In the behaviours that take place in the virtual environment, people do not fail to set a bad example even in live broadcasts. In live broadcasts, it is sometimes seen that young children are also exposed to this virtual violence. In a similar example, an adult woman's negative behaviour towards her children during her broadcast on social media caused a reaction and the children were taken under state protection.

'The violence that Merve C., a woman with 177 thousand followers, who opened a broadcast on TikTok under the name 'Karagül' in Bursa, infuriated citizens with the violence she inflicted on her children during her broadcasts. ('Investigation into TikTok disgrace! Children are under state protection', 2024).

THE PROBLEM OF UNAUTHORISED SHARING IN NEW MEDIA

'New media', which is accepted as the field with the most interaction among mass communication tools, has brought negative consequences in the public sphere with the situations created by instant news, photographs, texts, videos, graphics, audio and video sharing. Again, as every information shared in the 'new media' environment is copied from hand to hand, information enters into a rapid circulation, and this out-of-control information spreads to large masses. This information, which cannot be controlled, creates an environment for information pollution in the social sphere both financially (copyright, tax) and morally (unauthorised photos and documents; content that does not reflect the truth).

In the field of art, unauthorised use of works also takes place through virtual networks. Right holders who put a work or a product on the market have problems with the loss of rights with illegal publishing policies in the new medium. Laws exist to prevent this unauthorised form of virtual sharing, albeit partially.

> *The right to rent, lend, put up for sale or otherwise distribute the original or reproduced copies of a work exclusively belongs to the author. The right to bring into the country copies reproduced abroad with the authorisation of the author and to benefit from them through dissemination shall exclusively belong to the author. Copies reproduced abroad may not be imported under any circumstances whatsoever without the authorisation of the author and/or the owner of the right of dissemination who has the authorisation of the author. Provided that the authorisation to rent and lend to the public remains with the author, the resale of certain copies after their first sale or distribution within the borders of the country by transferring ownership as a result of the right holder's exercise of the right of dissemination does not violate the right of dissemination granted to the author.('4630 Amendment of Certain Articles of the Law on Intellectual and Artistic Works... - Original Text', n.d.).*

Some sanctions are imposed to prevent this situation legally. However, it is not yet possible to talk about the effect of a sufficiently protective legal regulation to stop the copied products of the authors.

DANGEROUS WEBSITES

Dark Web, Deep Web, Deepfake network connections are web usage areas with deeper layers. Illegal transactions (perhaps the most problematic area of new media) are also carried out here. While anonymity and encryption are needed for the Deep web, Tor Project and similar search engines are needed in the Dark web; the sharing of illegal publications in this area is quite commonplace. The dark web is another dangerous layer of the internet. It belongs to the subset of the Deep Web and functions anonymously. It is known as the web area of illegal work. It carries out activities on the sale of child abuse images, the sale of addictive drugs, arms trade, the commission of cybercrimes, pirated publishing. Dark web, which cannot be accessed by normal networks, creates its own interaction area where the connection is provided through the tor network (hiding information in the virtual environment). Careful use is required to protect such sites from dangerous content.

Deepfake publications also enable the publication of unwanted nude photographs thanks to the interaction over internet networks. A photo you share can be visualised as nude thanks to the skill of artificial intelligence. This situation reveals a situation that is open to re-discussion about how secure personal data is on social media. The owners of obscene images published illegally also face a difficult situation. The famous US singer Taylor Swift has been on the agenda of social media with her photos created by artificial intelligence ('Taylor Swift's deepfake porn sparked AI debates', 2024).

The right to be forgotten, also known as content removal (deslisting), means requesting the removal of unwanted images in the digital domain from the internet as a result of interference with the private rights of the person and removing the content through legal means. In our country (BTK, 1 October 2020; enacted by Law No. 7253) and in some other countries, the right to be forgotten is legally granted to individuals on the grounds that it violates the right to privacy.

The fact that every age group can access inappropriate images and that no legal control is preventive enough creates an unsafe communication area. Another unsafe communication aspect is the sharing of nude images (which do not actually belong to you) without the owner's knowledge of these banned images. Images copied in the new media environment easily reach network users. Even if they are blocked on networks, it is possible to store images on normal devices. There is also the possibility of copying and reproducing banned images outside of interactive environments.

TIME IN NEW MEDIA

Time is one of the most needed concepts these days. The new media, which is a marvellous digital showcase, aims to keep its users in this space as much as possible by offering them an endless world of content when they dive into individuals with bright and vivid design. In doing so, it does this by mobilising the desires of the person.

Thanks to the magic used with countless products and product promotions, the individual almost never realises how time passes. The more it keeps users in this area, the better economic income it means. For this reason, no expense is spared and it is to keep the audience here by using perfect visuals as much as possible. The new media, with its unique infinite network connections, serves to keep the person in this virtual world until he/she disappears. New media environments, which are widely used with this form of communication, have made it difficult to understand how time passes by including all forms of entertainment so that people never get bored.

Social media, where time consumption is at least as important as product consumption, also has a structure that is at the forefront of time loss. The issue of spending time on social media has an important place in the change of behaviours in society.

New media, which has a large number of users in all segments of the society, is seen to have high usage rates, especially among young people and children. In particular, it is revealed that young people use it more intensively for games and videos on online sites, which are very effective in losing time ('TÜİK Corporate', 2024).

This situation has led to a result that reveals the consumption of consumption. 'Time enters this system in the same way as it enters any other system. As an object of time calculation, it must and must be exchanged for any commodity (especially money). Moreover, the concept of object/time has a reversible value' (Bauldrillard, 2023, p.197).

With the infrastructure works carried out in all countries of the world, the number of internet users exceeds 5 billion. The vast majority of this number of users use network communities effectively on a daily basis. Interaction with many mobile applications such as Facebook, WhatsApp, Instagram, X (Twetter) is uninterrupted. The digital environment, which is increasingly used every day (one million new participants per day), has managed to become an indispensable part of daily habits.

In this case, both economic and cultural change has been inevitable. The virtual environment, which also brings excessive consumption, has brought along problems that need to be solved. With the proportional development of new media and technological infrastructure, a new consumption habit has emerged in the global arena. The easy interaction of people and the fact that products with 'commodity' value (electronic devices, clothing, food, accessories, public content, books, films, programmes, series promotions, etc.) are constantly in front of the eyes, it comes to the forefront as the most efficient network in the advertising field of communication. This fast network society, which is realised through new media, has the feature of being a high-budget market for countries (especially China and the USA) that want to establish digital superiority. Due to its effects on individual and social behaviour, it is necessary to answer the question 'what are we doing with the media' instead of 'what is the media doing with us'. For these reasons, a serious situation arises that requires a solution for awareness on the negative (excessive consumption and addiction) effects on social, economic and social behaviour. The data collection adventure of the Internet has developed over time and has become the most used area for mass communication and has also adopted a structure that adopts excessive consumption. It has also managed to become a problematic and complex communication network that can easily violate individual rights (protection of artworks and private life). In order for communication to take place in a healthy and safe environment, an environment that appeals to all people through trust should be offered.

NEW COMMUNICATION WITH ARTIFICIAL INTELLIGENCE

Our involvement with artificial technologies has brought along some problems. Those who attribute a positive meaning underline that advanced technologies with artificial intelligence are a defence power for countries and that these technologies have an important place in perceiving the risks in the field of health, especially in education. On the other hand, those who criticise this new technology think that it is likely to be a very dangerous innovation (especially about ethical values) for humanity both morally and ethically.

While underlining that the devices coded on a system produce results according to the commands determined according to the area in which they are used, and that they do not have the ability to reason, they explain that the fact that these technologies, which are soulless and serve only a specific purpose, are so visible may have many drawbacks for people. One of those who criticised this negative speed of modern technologies was Ioanna Kacuradi. While criticising the giving of human characteristics such as identity and name to robots, she stated that it is a wrong point of view to attribute personal concepts to artificial technologies by using the expression 'if you open my chest, you will see blood, but if you open his chest, you will see a cable' ((DW Türkçe, 2020)).

As a result, they emphasise that it cannot think like a human and that the reactions of a human can only be shown with certain commands. While those who are on the logical side of positivist science are optimistic that the innovations advocated by those on the logic side of positivist science will bring conveniences for human life, those who interpret it critically express their concern that the technological age of the modern period, the technological age of the modern period, the actions carried out by the codes of the machines, having commands that override the intelligence of man, will bring the individual and social disaster of man. Because they believe that in order to preserve the importance of human relations, a truly beneficial result will emerge through behaviours that are unique to human beings (primarily having emotions).

Artificial technologies, as always, are one of the most important factors in the orientation towards this field due to the power that the most useful technical infrastructures add to the economy (the pioneers benefit the most from this). Countries that want to be at the top allocate large budgets in order to provide political (to publicise the political decisions taken) and social benefits that communication tools have added to their structure in the last hundred years. In this new era, the aim is to succeed in staying in a technically stronger position than other countries with all kinds of artificial means.

The most important part of the new generation of connections through communication tools is the determination of the advertisements followed according to personal use and determining a new consumer identity under the name of 'personalisation'. This occurs due to an attempt to ensure some kind of user control. Another important detail is that all forms of communication in digital network connections bring along a deceptive dimension. It has a problematic structure related to sharing false and misleading information, exploitation of personal data, discrediting the person or governments (the most common method used by political powers with all kinds of communication from the past to the present).

New generation technologies, which contain a deceptive and false structure, create a complex structure by intertwining reality and fiction. This new form of communication that emerges with the blurring of borders constitutes the dark side of these spaces.

Mariarosaria Taddeo, in her research on digital ethics, 'Why do we need the philosophy and ethics of cyber warfare?' used these expressions: 'Cyber attacks are rarely out of the headlines. We know that state actors, terrorists and criminals can use cyber tools to target the digital infrastructure of our societies. We have also learnt that as our societies become more dependent on digital technologies, they become more vulnerable to cyberattacks'. At the International Humanitarian Law (IHL) meeting in 2021, it was agreed that ethical and cultural values should be emphasised. In order for this to happen, they focused on a common agreement on the necessity of proper cyber security for society and the state ('Why we need philosophy and ethics of cyber warfare | University of Oxford', 2022).

Cyber-attacks, in addition to the benefits they provide for those who are inclined to technology around the world, also reveal a structure that is more harmful than unethical weapons. Every protective operation performed on the international network connections of countries means that cyber-attacks can take place in new media environments. The uneasiness created by the fact that all important data of countries are accessible in this environment damages daily human life at least as much as bloody wars. The vital importance of two basic elements such as war and economy in the digital environment reveals how important security is for this field.

The emergence of damage in cyber attacks means that everyone who uses this area is in danger. Recently, increasing digitalisation has had consequences that are expanding the field of cybercrime more and more.

While states such as Russia, China, Ukraine and the USA are leading the way, global attacks are increasing over networks from all over the world. ('World's first "Cybercrime Index" ranks countries according to cybercrime threat level | Oxford University', 2024).

New technologies enable unauthorised surveillance of people, and the most important aspect of data breaches is that they create an environment that is insecure in terms of unauthorised processing of people's information. In new media environments, the possibilities of tracking or being tracked on mobile devices cause both private and public information to be easily obtained. In this collected data, people's thoughts and tendencies are processed and used with the intention of creating an object of consumption again.

Ethical values and secure communication are indispensable for the whole world for cyber-attacks, which are among the new problems of nations. A virtual environment with little harm is what both individuals and governments need most to build a peaceful society.

THE MODERN STATE OF CONSPICUOUS CONSUMPTION

Product promotion, which was discovered by the mass media in the 20th century, still continues its effect without slowing down despite the intervening years (the main reason for this is the cycle provided by the strong economic relationship between the production and consumption rings); moreover, it realises its power much faster through phenomena whose number of followers exceeds hundreds of millions without the need for production companies or the budgets of major television channels in new and much more effective new media environments.

With the shift of their famous names to new media areas, they add fame to their fame and make huge monetary gains. 'Did you know that some of the richest people in the world are Instagram influencers?' ('The annual earnings of social media influencers are jaw-dropping', 2025).

Product promotions are renewed with each new means of communication, making it an extension of new consumption technologies by trying to convince people again. The new marketing method that emerges with new generation communication forms is realised with celebrities who use the new media very actively. The names who become famous in the virtual environment and gain a large number of followers earn a large income economically with the rate of viewership of content such as videos and photographs. For example; a football player earns big money by advertising the brand of shoes he wears. Another example is that a famous woman can earn a high amount of money by establishing a cosmetics company thanks to her publications with make-up and daily care products.

The social life experiences that we were born into in time have common similarities with the past. People have made similar attempts to reveal their social positions from the past to the present. The main reason for this situation is that it is preserved with a type of behavior that contains the distinctive features of other people's positions in terms of class. Beyond this common behavior, the effort to reveal a lifestyle that adopts people's consumption for the sake of gaining economic and social status is an important detail.

Through the works of T.B. Veblen in the 20th century, the theories of "leisure class" and "conspicuous society" lead us to understand today's behaviors. In the behaviors that Veblen tried to analyze sociologically, he focused on the main reason for the inequalities that emerged while consumption and conspicuousness built the status of an upper class without any effort. Veblen's views, which still maintain their importance today, also contain their own unique realities in the new media environments we are in.

The conspicuous behaviors of that period continue today with social media tools and are done with a much more effective method. In traditional life, people were only exposed to consumption when they met one-on-one on the street or in a social space.

In this period, influencers at the top of the ostentation are presenting a new form of "leisure class". The interaction they create on social networks with video content based solely on consumption rather than production is returned as income to the influencers. Although we cannot include all those who produce digital content in the group of idlers, it is possible to include those who produce content solely on ostentation and luxury living without working hard. Some names with millions of followers on virtual media try to stay on the agenda by sharing many things about their family life and daily work. Here, the form of ostentation that Veblen emphasizes continues under a different guise. Not only the upper-income people of the consuming group, but also a certain segment of the middle-income group exhibits "ostentation" and "consumption"-related behaviors. The expansion of consumers to the lower classes through media has also brought new sociological problems. This is due to the fact that internet networks with billions of users have brought consumption to a dominant position.

Social media users, especially in the West, earn large amounts of income from these networks. There is a two-way consumption style here; first, celebrities manage to attract millions of people to their pages while presenting a lifestyle focused on consumption. Second; these ostentatious and abundant consumption-based lives return to content producers as financial resources. Countries that use advanced internet technologies put the large economic income from these networks into their country's coffers with this method. Those who control the production conditions have created a new class of conspicuous and consumer through new media broadcasts.

With the new media containing a wide variety of content, the people being followed are also exposed to more consumption styles due to this diversity. This area, which is at one's fingertips and allows for unlimited interaction with all people, is leading to the person becoming alienated from their own thoughts and physical appearances (trying to resemble them with aesthetics) and focusing on the world of phenomena. Followers who are curious about this imaginary life, as a result of their interest in the private lives of the people they admire, start to consume like them and see themselves as a part of this ostentatious world.

Celebrities who try to impress people with posts that are far from the real world's living conditions (focusing only on the flashy and consumer side) draw people into this area by editing their beautifully shot images. Followers sometimes forget that these contents are fictional and accept them as if they were real. They even reject the physical appearance of their bodies in order to resemble them and do not hesitate to spend anything to resemble the person they follow.

Products that reshape the perception of beauty, especially in women, are marketed here. "Kim Kardashian's body-shaping clothing brand Skims has reached a value of $4 billion after raising $270 million in a new round of financing."("Kim Kardashian's Skims is now worth $4 billion", 2023)

This situation, since the behavior of being carried away does not coincide with real life, negatively affects the perception of reality of both celebrities and those who constantly follow them. Because; while the economic value of the house a celebrity lives in or the cars and belongings he uses are more than covered by sponsorships, the main aspect of the problem begins to emerge because the fans who follow them day and night do not have a budget to buy these. The problem does not only arise from an economic structure, but also results in the disruption of people's physical and emotional ties to their own lives and the people around them, and the person's separation from his own essence.

"The age at which young people perceive themselves as sexual objects has fallen considerably. They now define their existence with their sexual identities at a younger age," says psychiatrist Kemal Sayar. Girls are more attractive at an early age, while boys are trying to appear impressive. The main reason for this is the feeling of emptiness. Those who cannot find permanent values to express themselves are forced to make do with superficiality. According to Sayar, today's culture increases narcissistic structuring: "This way of thinking says that young people only exist to the extent of their visibility. If someone else pays attention to you and sees you, you exist, otherwise you are 'nothing.'" Therefore, those who can inspire admiration around them feel more valuable. The most important evidence of this is screens: "All privacy is revealed on television, thus confirming their existence." The examples on screens also come into being in social life after a while. In Baudrillard's words, "You see America on the screen, and when you go out on the street, you see the screen." (Tarhan, 2000).

People's addiction to consumption and ostentation maintains its importance even though hundreds of years have passed. The adventure of building consumption ostentation began with the mass production form of the Industrial Revolution. The concept of "conspicuous consumption", which Veblen focused on in the 19th and 20th centuries, criticized people's attempts to gain status through continuous consumption without working hard, and revealed the economic and social separation brought about by this form of production. He stated that the ruling class was an exploitative group and that workers adopted a ostentatious life with their labor. According to him, he saw those who tried to gain superiority over ostentatious objects as a group that did not contribute to production and only tried to prove themselves with the remainder of the workers' labor. He also described those who exhibited such behavior as the "lazy class". The most important part he emphasized stems from the aim of protecting the social class revealed by the consumption behavior with objects through "ostentation". The same form of consumption continues today through objects (in this age where humans are also treated as objects). The behavior with the highest rate in new media environments today is based on conspicuous consumption.

Digital communities in the 21st century, which consume consumption unconsciously, have shifted their dependence on consumption to wider areas compared to the previous centuries. They do this by constantly seeing and placing it in their consciousness after seeing it, with the desire to obtain it.

Bauldrillard shares a common denominator with Veblen: sociological problems arising from consumption behaviour. While Bauldrillard (in The Society of Consumption) tries to explain all kinds of effects of the media on consumption from a holistic perspective, he focuses on the main reasons why people in the middle class (Veblen refers to the upper class) tend to consume both emotionally and physically. He emphasises that people's adoption of consumption based on needs is not a simple behaviour, but rather an effort to impose themselves on society through consumption. In our age, the negative effects of consumption, both mental (the idea of buying), emotional (the activation of desires) and physical (clothing, aesthetics, food, a fit body), have become much more evident than in the past, as all kinds of flashy content are easily presented through networks in a field that more than half of the world's population sees, hears and practices.

The behaviours that arise from people's instinct to have a nose that belongs to someone else, to wear branded clothes or to own objects that belong to someone else all express the 'consumer society'. Rather than complaining about this situation, the existence of people who give more than themselves for the continuation of this order makes the problem even more important.

CONSUMPTION CULTURE IN NEW MEDIA

The concept of consumption society is the name given to the sociological dimension of consumption-oriented behaviours that take place as a result of the deceptive and subconscious discourses of the broadcasting policies offered by the capitalist system that forms the production-promotion-consumption chain of the media, especially after 1970, in order to encourage people to use more than they need (no matter whether it is any goods or vehicles; as long as it has commodity value).

Although at first we only see the word 'consumption' as a simple form of behaviour, in fact, what a person individually 'prefers' is not his/her preference, he/she has only preferred something that he/she finds close to himself/herself from the available options. For example; we want to buy a car. In this car model, there are cars with the same features as white, grey and black options among the colour options. A car with red and slightly more features that the person wants is not among the vehicles offered. Here, the colours and features determined by the company must be preferred, not what the person wants. The same logic applies to the choice of clothes and food. Since the current production systems mostly make sales plans over the masses, the individual request of the person cannot come into play. This leads to the proliferation of stereotypical behaviours such as everyone should wear jeans and eat ready-made foods.

In short, everything that has 'commodity' value in the capitalist free market is packaged and offered to the masses, whether it is value or product.

THE CONTROL PROBLEM OF NEW COMMUNICATION

The uncontrolled side of the media in publishing all kinds of documents, information, sound, graphics, photographs in electronic media (the publications carried out by large media companies through a certain control order, including news editors, news managers, reporters, producers, etc., are quickly realised only by users through new media connections) has brought along consequences that question the quality of media content. The conveniences (?) brought about by people's instant connection to the common networks of the internet through smart devices and their wide-scale communication lead to the emergence of a situation that creates a drawback in making the information and value belonging to the individual known by all people.Social media, which is our means of communication, creates a negative return by narrowing the private areas. Sharing all intimate information for the sake of being liked and followed may cause situations that are not right for both the sharer and the followers (especially unethical use of threatening information).

The field, which practically realises the access of intimate information to millions of people through networks, also reveals bad results just as effectively.

'Private' sharing through these networks means a new "product" for those who use these networks for data collection. While sharing people's private information, they may also exhibit behaviours that may endanger their lives, perhaps without realising it. For example; if a person looks at you to the extent that it makes you uncomfortable, it means 'harassment'; but if a person watches you for hours on social media, it is not seen as 'harassment'. The difference is nothing but the existence of a screen between the content producer and the consumer. It is an indication of the complexity of the private and the general that the person preparing the content makes a nude video with his/her own consent and the consent of the person watching it is also an indicator of the complexity of the private and the general. This abnormal situation is something that is unlikely to be experienced in daily life. However, the existence of countless similar content platforms in the virtual environment emerges as a form of action that disrupts society both morally and ethically.

Especially this wide area of the new media, which is uncontrolled, brings serious consequences for people of all age ranges. New forms of communication, which cause the disappearance of almost all the elements that protect the privacy of private life in virtual networks, turn into a life in which everyone intervenes in the areas that belong to the human being, and prepare the environment for the emergence of a challenging psychological problem.

CONCLUSION

In the age we live in, the instant realisation of everything with just two fingertips means the instant destruction of everything with two fingertips. The means of communication, which have influenced societies in all the actions that have emerged in recent centuries, including wars, create a new and negative communication language with the content shared with new media today, realising a moral erosion that is at least as harmful to society as wars. Another serious point is that there is also the possibility that the information belonging to us can easily fall into the hands of bad, very malicious people (even to the extent of using images of young children) in new media environments without our knowledge.

The basic logic that constitutes the means of communication is the attempt to control people 24 hours a day by focusing only on consumption and to create a new consumer in the global sense. Today's digital media has taken over the culture of consumption from radio, television and other print media and has reached a much more active functionality for the realisation of all kinds of consumption. With mobile devices that we even go to bed with, the boundaries of consumption have expanded even further and it does not decide what we eat, what we wear or what we should choose; it even decides how our minds and emotions will be activated. The networks that gather more than 5 billion people in the world together with the new media have brought dangers with the open access environment for people. With the availability of the digital environment, all kinds of negative interaction forms, which are multiply harmful, appear as one of the biggest effects of the age we live in, which shows the moral weakness of the age we live in. This communication area, which goes so far that even children can be used in immoral content, also prepares the environment for irreparable social deterioration.

The danger that arises when every behaviour we perform as ordinary actions is processed on the digital network and offered for sale like a 'commodity' and all private information is included in the communication has turned into a structure that scares people.

The question of 'what' is in the content of the content produced by users of all kinds of cultures is an important detail. This communication language, which is very diverse, negatively affects the whole life of human beings by being far from values.

It is important to communicate in environments that give people confidence and protect their values. However, it is not a realistic attitude of thought to talk about trust and morality in the new media environment with its bad results today. Under these circumstances, it does not seem possible to believe that this complicated form of communication, in which countless messages reach us easily every day without being checked, will reach a solution.

REFERENCES

Baulrillard, J. (2023). *Consumer Society* (19th ed.). Ayrıntı Publications.

Coronavirus Triggered Digital Addiction [Corporate Site]. (2020). Received February 23, 2025, Sender Https://Www.Yesilay.Org.Tr/Tr/ Website: Https://Www.Yesilay.Org.Tr/Tr/Makaleler/Koronavirus-Dijital-Bagimligi-Teritikledi

Danghad, M. (2021). Study Finds Internet Economy Grew Seven Times Faster Than Total U.S. Economy, Created Over 7 Million Jobs In The Last Four Years. Received February 21, 2025, Posted by IAB Website: Https://Www.İab.Com/News/Study-Finds-İnternet-Economy-Grew-Seven-Times-Faster

Kuçuradi Philosophy and Human Rights Foundation (Director). (2019). ETHICAL VALUES AND EDUCATION Part 1. Received Date Sender Https://Www.Youtube.Com/Watch?V=İpmm5cydeyy

Öztürk, R. (2020). "Proteophobia" in the Context of Zygmunt Bauman's Understanding of Morality.

44Smartphone Addiction Statistics For 2024 [INFOGRAPHIC]. (2019). Received February 25, 2025, by Slicktext Website: https://Www.Slicktext.Com/Blog/2019/10/Smartphone-Addiction-Statistics/ 4630 On Amending Some Articles of the Law on Intellectual and Artistic Works…—Original Text. (T.Y.). Received March 04, 2025, by LEXPERA Website: http://Www.Lexpera.Com.Tr/Resmi-Gazete/Metin/Fikir-Ve-Sanat-Eserleri-Kanununun-Bazi-Maddelerini-Degistirilmesine-İliskin-Kanun-24335-4630-1

Social, W. A. (2024, January 31). Digital 2024. Received December 26, 2024, by We Are Social UK Website: Https://Wearesocial.Com/Uk/Blog/2024/01/Digital-2024/

Tarhan, P. D. N. (2000). YOUNG PEOPLE WHO RESEMBLE EACH OTHER WITH AESTHETIC SURGERY. Date of Arrival March 21, 2025, Posted by Nevzattarhan.Com Website: Https://Www.Nevzattarhan.Com/Estetik-Ameliyatla-Birbirine-Benzeyen-Gencler.Html

Taylor Swift Nude Deepfake Goes Viral On, X. Despite Platform Rules. (2024, January 26). Received February 24, 2025, Posted by Https://Www .Nbcnews.Com/Tech/Misinformation/Taylor-Swift-Nude-Deepfake-Goes -Viral-X-Platform-Rules-Rcna135669

Taylor Swift's Deepfake Porn Sparks AI Debate. (2024, February 1). Received May 05, 2024, Posted by Euronews Website: Https://Tr .Euronews.Com/Kultur/2024/01/29/Taylor-Swiftin-Pornografi-Deepfake -Goruntuleri-Abdde-Yapay-Zeka-Tartismalarini-Ilevlendir

Turkish, D. W. (Director). (2020). Philosopher Kuçuradi: Human Relationships Are Harder Than Going to Mars - DW Turkish. Received Date From Https://Www.Youtube.Com/Watch?V=SQ7soJHTZ9g

World's First. 'Cybercrime Index' Ranks Countries by Cybercrime Threat Level I Oxford University. (2024, April 10). Received March 16, 2025, From Https://Www.Ox.Ac.Uk/News/2024-04-10-World-First-Cybercrime -Index-Ranks-Countries-Cybercrime-Threat-Level

ADDITIONAL READING

Baudrillard, J. (2023). *Consumer Society*

Becker, H. S. (2013). *The Writing Ordeal of Social ScientistsVarol, S, F. (2016).* Temsil İdeolojik Kimlik.

Bourse,M. (2021) Kültürel Çalışmaları Anlamak

Hall, S. (2020). Analysis of Stuart Hall's Encoding/Decoding Erişim tarihi: 2.08.2025 https://literariness.org/2020/11/07/analysis-of-stuart-halls -encoding-decoding/

Kaçuradi, İ. (2019). Etik Değerler Ve Eğitimi 1. Bölüm. www.youtube .com/@kucuradifelsefeveinsanhakl9038

Kılıç, C. (2012). *Bilgelik Hikayeleri Atılgan, G., Aytekin, A. (2012).* Siyaset Bilimi.

Turner, G. (2015). British. *Cultural Studies.*

KEY WORDS AND DEFINITIONS

Dangerous Web Sites: the problematic form of communication created by illegal and dangerous network layers.

Data Breaches of New Media: It is the capture of information that will undermine the security of the country (social and economic) or the person (private status).

Digital Addiction: the name given to a personal or social disorder that occurs as a result of a person spending time uncontrollably on networks.

New Communication with Artificial Intelligence: It is the whole of the reactions that arise as a result of the association of intelligent technologies with the human mind.

New Media Concept: It is the form of interaction created by digital network communities.

Publications Contrary to General Morality in New Media: It is the whole of behaviours that are not accepted by the majority of the society.

Time in New Media: the situation arising from the excess of time spent in the interactive environment.

Unauthorised Sharing Problem in New Media: all the negativities caused by unauthorised sharing of private content in the social life of individuals.

Chapter 2
Nature and Sound in Art:
An Evaluation From the Perspective of Digital Technologies

Özlem Gürpınar
http://orcid.org/0000-0003-1771-2509
Ardahan University, Turkey

ABSTRACT

The aim of this study is to examine the presence of nature-human-technology culture in art, related to sound ecology, through digital tools that influence nature and humans, and to examine installations created with objects, movement, and sound that reference nature. Document analysis and content analysis, two qualitative research techniques, were employed in the study. The selected artists were selected and limited among those who focused on nature and human culture in installations created through the collaboration of technology, nature, sound, and movement. The use of nature sounds in sound installations, through artistic and scientific collaboration, revealed that it revives the ecological spirit of nature. In conclusion, the study revealed that sound plays a crucial role in healing nature and humans and restoring natural balance in sound installations that address nature-human relationships from a digital aesthetic perspective in art.

DOI: 10.4018/979-8-2600-0944-4.ch002

INTRODUCTION

Nature has taken place in the cultural-artistic sense as the foundations of life and the source of art. "Life is not separate from matter and a living nature; is a comprehensive one shaped by creativity and constantly developing. According to Schelling, human creativity represents the highest level of development of nature towards knowing itself" (Weeks, 2024, p. 268). Due to the change in the life of social change and transformation, there have also been changes in the practice of art. For example; The process that ended rapidly after the industrial revolution has significantly changed the material and approach of art.

The technology that the human mind imagines and creates has existed within art as an innovation. Technology, one of the structures that changes the representation and expression of art, has transformed and shaped the future of art. Art has rethought its own structure with technology and expanded its framework in this context. In our age, art finds direction according to the perception of technology and the audience. The audience and the artist with a technological perspective have not had difficulty in carrying out the artistic and technological context together. Therefore, the message to be conveyed is conveyed to the receiver without any problems. In this context, the intellectual structure that art wants to convey is presented within the scope of technology and aesthetic values. Today, art, which is within a technological structure, is not alien to the relationship between nature and technology, and they have also dealt with and fought against the problems of nature together. In line with this logic, art has made room for technology and accepted it as an indispensable tool. This relationship, which forms a cycle within each other, expands the range of human perception visually and auditory. Appealing to more than one emotion in art affects the impressiveness of art. "Multi-layered image compositions, structures with auditory and visual content, layered structures that can be created with digital image-sound transform into hybrid forms and provide artists with endless opportunities" (Avcı-Tuğal, 2018, p. 67). Electronic technology is a successful breakthrough that has given a new form, shaped and changed the 1900s. The system that structures the 21st century society is entirely an electronic technology system. This electronic technology has taught the artist to look at the age from a new perspective, reinterpretation, structuring and a broad perspective. Electronic systems have also brought concepts such as digital network technology, communication, control mechanism, sound, light. Since 1990, communication, intercommunication, and the dissemination of information through digital means are seen as a message of today's digital media tools. These developments create communication between technology in the art environment. The first uses of technological tools in art date back to 1900 and 1967. This period has formed the cornerstones and data of the art-technology relationship of 21st century art. Technological tools are seen as a medium in terms of being the material of art or creating the work of art (Avcı-Tuğal, 2018). Being in art as a tool has led the artist to question the relationship between technology and nature. The widespread use of the media regarding the state of nature and the demonstrations of its destruction has directed awareness towards nature. The destruction of nature in this developing age has mobilized artists and scientists. According to S. Avcı Tuğal (2018), the scientific examination of the structural events and characteristics of nature has emerged and developed as one of the fundamental starting points of techno-ecological art (p. 44). The great concern of Engels and Marx, who are among the founders of Marxism, is the use of human actions against permanent and continuous nature, and they have tried to find a solution on the condition that they focus on nature. Humans are seen as the main factor of developments and changes affecting nature. If humans continue to be both the subject of nature and a part of nature, they will be the subject of changes and developments (Turner, 2019, p. 203). Marx and Engels' concerns have legitimate aspects; disrupting the ecological structure of nature with human actions means disrupting and destroying our own living space. In this context, the concept of ecology was put forward by Ernst Haeckel in 1850. This concept means house in Greek and includes all organisms in motion. In the 1960s, environmentalist and scientist James Lovelock placed this definition in theoretical logic with the Gaia Hypothesis, which defends the world as a self-regulating form and interaction. When viewed in the Lovelockian sense, ecology is a unique structure. As Williams and Jackson put it, the unique universe has been seen in the past as well as in the greenhouse world, which has a warning feature in the future, and will continue to be seen. It is claimed that there is no other example of technological advancement in the digital age, which creates a virtual universe in a universe where nature, ecology and humans exist. When we look at Plato, he is of the opinion that technology can both improve an individual's understanding and comprehension of the world and restrict their behavior, and this view dates back to Ancient Greece (Hassan & Sutherland, 2024, pp. 17-21). With the awareness that nature is the home of humans, as well as all living things, artists take action to create awareness about nature and try to direct attention back to nature. This orientation was made using technology and nature's sound data. The sounds obtained from geophony and biophony sounds within the soundscape ecology are presented to nature again by artists with digital, kinetic and technological works for the healing of nature. This presentation is an approach made for the healing of nature.

In this context; the study examining the relationship between art, technology and nature aims to reveal the effects and relationships of sound data resulting from technological developments on art and nature through artist works. The purpose of this research is to reveal the reflection of sound-based artistic practice on art and nature and to draw inferences about future trends. In this research, content analysis and document analysis methods, which are qualitative research techniques, were used. A literature review was conducted by reviewing national and international sources such as books, articles, and websites/blogs, and visual data was obtained.

Sound Perception in Art within a Technological Context

When we look at the concept of sound in its general sense, it appears as a means of communication in the simplest sense. Sound takes place in all areas in a multifaceted way and acts as the counterpart of a substance. Sound creates itself when it is produced by something or belongs to something. In order for sound to continue, it must be recreated with breath and the vibration of matter. The gathering of spatiality, corporeality and sonority together with sound causes materiality to constantly reveal itself. The fact that a sound has linguistic data without any denotative data shows that it has a characteristic feature. Thanks to sound, no matter what is being called, the physical existence of the sound occurs in the place it is being called or in the person who hears it. That sound allows two different spaces to merge into one. The being that makes its voice heard communicates with the one who hears the sound and touches it (Fischer-Lichte, 2016, p. 222). Sound provides communication between living beings. Living beings have understood time with sound; they have felt in danger or safety according to sound. They have used sound as a tool for their own safety. When a living being is attacked or feels a dangerous moment, they announce it with their sound. Sometimes humans have announced their rebellion by shouting; sometimes they have made their fun heard by laughing and again with sound to their surroundings and themselves. The fact that humans represent themselves with sound is not limited to themselves. As a living being, 'nature' also announces what they feel with their own voice within the same logical framework. After all, nature includes humans; humans came to the world as an extension of nature. For this reason, nature and humans have been one with nature since creation and have continued their lives. In the process of continuing this life together; environmental pollution brought by human life and greenhouse gases released into the atmosphere are damaging nature and the atmosphere, and therefore these situations are associated with the concept of Anthropocene, which means the human age. The developing industrial revolution, machines and technologies have accelerated the realization of this action. The concept of nature, which is constantly at the center of art, has been addressed with exhibitions, artistic projects and different aspects within art, especially after 1950, on nature and ecological problems, and attempts have been made to raise awareness in individuals.

In art, the nature-art relationship initially began on the canvas; later, in the 1960s, approaches based on nature such as environmental art, land and earth art emerged (Antmen, 2012). These environmental movements moved the space of art from the gallery space to the space of nature. In today's art, environmental and nature problems have been tried to be expressed using technological tools; this has changed the practice and method of art. When ecological problems such as environmental pollution, greenhouse gases, overheating, and melting glaciers emerged and alarm bells began to ring, art and science began to act together. Today, artists who address the relationship between nature and humans try to express this relationship with the methods and tools offered by the age. The artist has always been inspired by nature and has never broken off his connection.

If we look at the artist's connection with nature in art; from ancient times to the present day, discussions on art have always been about the relationship between nature and humans. When we look at the paintings from the Chinese, Byzantine and Gothic Periods, there are natural phenomena in all of them. However, nature is included in each of them with different visual expressions and explanations. For example, if the tree figure is taken as a basis, its representation is different in all of them. While civilizations continue to analyze nature through art, some philosophers put forward the idea of ideal nature. By the mid-18th century, art was seen as an imitation of the ideal of nature. The perception of nature changed between 1780 and 1830; science replaced ideal nature. The science here is the science of weather. Here again, there is a departure from nature, but on condition that it is addressed with the reality seen... For example; the paintings made by artists such as Constable, Courbet and Delacroix are seen as sensational for that period. The weather science that Constable worked on has now left the past behind with impressionism. Cezanne, on the other hand, reached the essence of nature with an analytical method that can be considered a scientific technique. In these artistic periods, nature was addressed differently and the state and problems of nature were examined. Again, as the painter Reynolds said, the artist believes that nature can be corrected through nature. The damaged aspects of nature are covered by the beauties of nature. The alternative solution to the problems of nature is again nature (Read, 2020). The perspective and medium of art change within the developing and changing society. The occurrence of World Wars played a major role in the change of the idea of artists. For example; The Futurism movement, which started in 1909 and ended with World War I, set out with technological developments and made new searches and thoughts heard with tools such as light, sound and electricity. Luigi Russolo, who was a part of the movement, caused the emergence of "Noise Art" in 1913; It was claimed that shouts, calls, protest sounds and tool and machine sounds could be the sound and music of the innovative age by recording them (Antmen, 2012, p. 69). Thus, Futurism appears as a movement that uses sound in art and moves with different approaches. In the Dada movement, which emerged in 1916 as a rebellion against the values of society and art, shows with songs, poems and performances took place in the nightclub called Cabare Voltaire opened by Hugo Ball.

For example; Hugo Ball wore a costume created with cubist forms and shapes (Figure 1) and read his abstract poem (Dachy, 2014). Ball tried to express his thoughts through sound.

"gadji beri bimba
glandridi lauli lonni cadori
gadjama bim beri glassala
glandridi glassala
glandridi glassala tuffm i zimbrabim
blassa galassasa tuffm i zimbrabim..." (Dachy, 2014, p. 27).

Figure 1. Hugo Ball, Cabaret Voltaire in Zurich, 1916

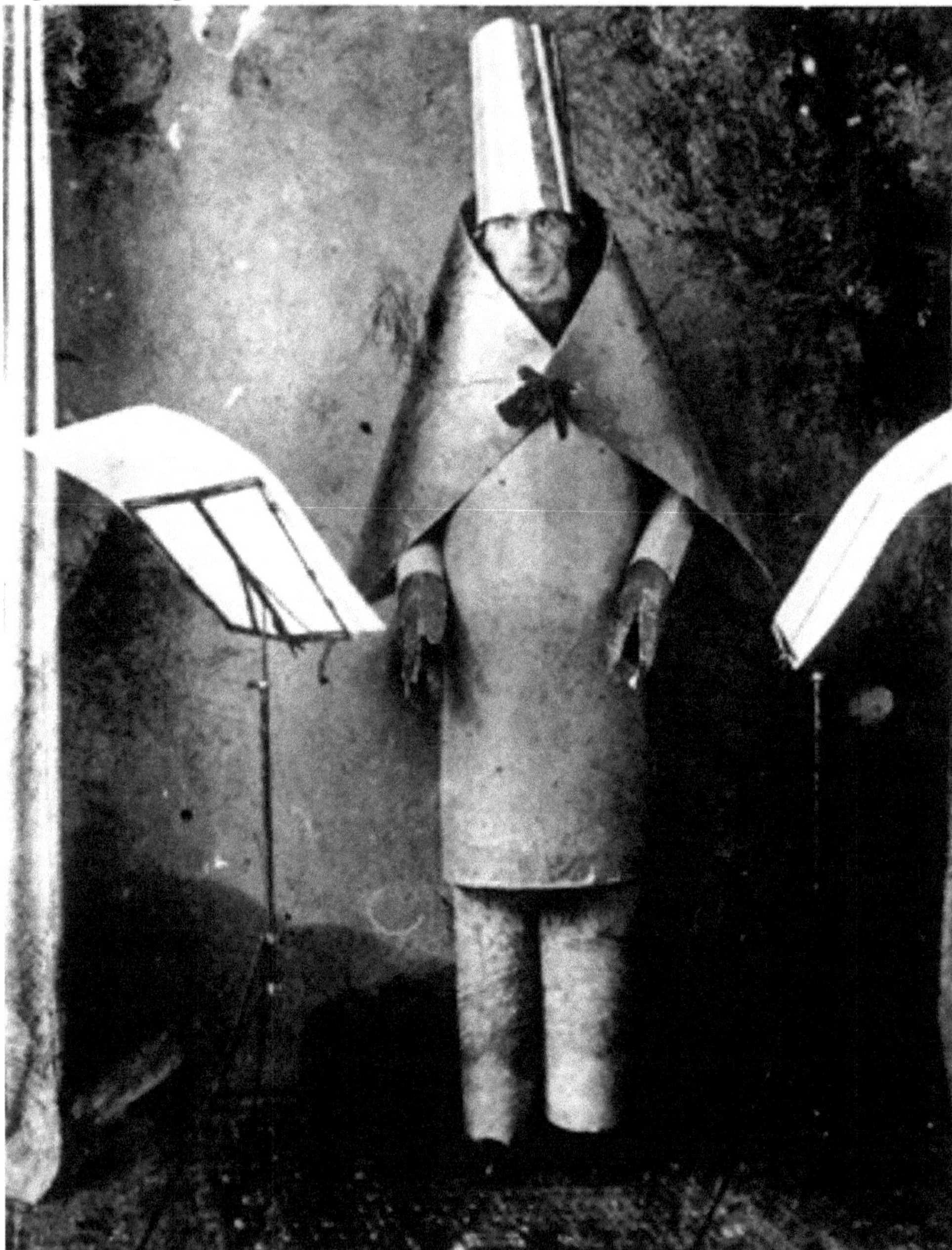

(Ball, 1916)

In the 1950s, technology, computers, and communication tools developed, and with these tools, the language of art began to transform. Technology, which has developed in different dimensions in every era, has integrated with art, developed and continued to evolve. The material of art is no longer limited to the canvas; music, sound, computers, TV, and screens have become the material of art and have taken on different forms. These have been used as the main material of art. "Each period creates its own technology, and progress is achieved with the products of the technology created. Discoveries, inventions, and thought systems created in past periods have been developed by being associated with each other over the centuries" (Avcı-Tuğal, 2018, p. 15).

In addition to these technological approaches seen in art movements, groups established in the context of technological and scientific thought also attract attention. For example; in the EAT (Experiments in Art and Technology) movement, which emerged in the 1960s, artists and engineers came together in the context of art and technology and produced works that included techno-art in an eclectic structure. This group includes artists such as Yvonne Rainer, Jean Tinguely, Andy Warhol, Jasper Johns, and John Cage. During this period, new works of art were created using new art ideas using sound data and technologies that were products of the media. For example; artist John Cage's interest in using sounds and sound data caused his perspective on art and his artistic actions to change (Bozkurt, 2012, p. 215). John Cage, one of the representatives of kinetic art and who used music and sound in Fluxus actions, explained that "one can give up the desire to control sound, purify musical consciousness, and find ways to allow sounds to be themselves, instead of being tools for human-made theories or expressions of human emotions. Hearing sounds only as sounds leads the theoretical mind to institutionalize immediately. And people's emotions are constantly stimulated as they encounter nature" (Fineberg, 2014, p. 166). This affects people physically, spiritually and emotionally. Duchamp's 'ready-made object', which is a part of the Dada movement, has turned into a 'ready-made sound' in John Cage. Cage's work 4'33" is a silent music performed in the hall in front of the audience. For four minutes and thirty-three seconds, no sound related to the music is heard by the audience; the piano waits to be played, and the hum of the audience and the whispering of the words spoken from ear to ear in the face of the inaudible silence constitute the sound of the action. Cage's action was realized with the audience voices emerging from the sound of silence. Also within Fluxus, the artist Allison Knowles' work called 'Newspaper Music' is a sound action created by reading newspaper articles given to each audience member in different languages (Yılmaz, 2013, pp. 332-333). Jean Tinguely produced his works with sounds created by using materials such as music, noise, machinery, horn, piano sound and light. The artist's installation work named "Homage to New York," (Figure 2) made in 1960 is a successful work known as self-destructive. He expressed his sarcastic attitude towards machines and technology in this way. The artist paints the constructive structure he creates from materials such as wheel sounds, complex sounds, engines and paper in white. When the opening ceremony takes place, the participants who are stylish and meticulously dressed start to hear the unplanned sounds created by the machines. After a certain period of time, smoke is seen and the work ends with the fire department extinguishing it. The artist's use of sounds here, the temporary nature of the activity and the work not being placed in a sacred space push the viewer to question. The work of art is not allowed to be evaluated within a specific context. The sounds and images at that moment made each participant think of different things due to the variability of the sounds; even though the action was temporary, the sounds were permanent in the mind. The need to question technology was announced to the recipient through the noise and sounds created by the machines. Here, the state of violence between seeing and hearing is emphasized with sounds (Fineberg, 2014, p. 216). Tinguely and other artists have inspired and formed the basis of today's sound art or digital sound arts with the mechanical sound aesthetics created by machines. The sounds created in these actions are the sound actions produced by human action or ready/produced objects. These are different angles in which sound is shown in the art practices considered within the scope of art. Whether the sounds are machine sounds, sounds produced by musical instruments or sounds produced by nature, they all create a musical rhythm.

Figure 2. Jean Tinguely, Homage to New York, 1960

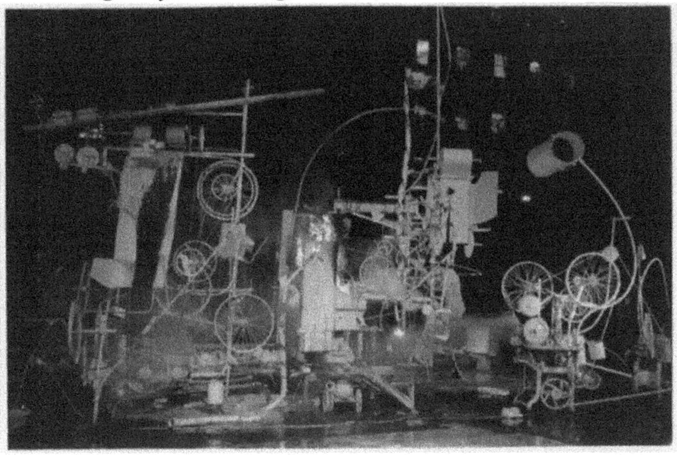

(Tinguely, 1960)

Music and sound continue to play a significant role in the contemporary art world. In their quest to engage and influence the viewer/participant, artists create environments that skillfully combine sound and visual elements and engage the viewer, as well as Internet-based projects that empower the user to shape sound worlds and works of art that feature sound. In practical terms, advances in technology have given artists access to music and sound production environments, performance systems, user-friendly hardware, and software tailored to their specific needs, all of which enable them to develop their own creative options. In this way, once a work is completed, technology has enabled artists to distribute it widely, in the form of CDs, DVDs, MP3 files, and also through the internet, where audio and video content can be transferred. The phrase 'sound precedes video' aptly describes the process of technological advances in analog and digital hardware. For example, the ability to record audio material on tape preceded the invention of videotape. Since the computing power required to process audio data was considerably less than that required by video, the transfer of audio production to a fully digital medium was relatively rapid... (Wands, 2006, p. 123)

This speed experienced in the development process of sound production and recording has caused it to take place very quickly in the art world and to permanently store sounds. In this section, approaches to how the first foundations of sound were laid by artists in the technological age are discussed and shown with artistic examples and definitions. In this process, while some artists have suggested that sounds are an artistic object in themselves, some artists have addressed the technological relations or critical aspects of sound. In this context, sound has served as both an object and an object in art. In addition, artists have shown that sound can be an artistic phenomenon. The period and artist studies given as examples above have paved the way for the use of natural sounds in art and formed the basis.

Examples of Technological Artistic Expression through Nature and Sound

In this section, we will look at how sound is handled with technological tools as nature's cry for help and guide in today's problems and relationships. Music created by human hands and the symphony of nature created by nature are not the same. Although both sounds are musical sounds, they are separated as natural and artificial, and the artist's logic of handling is also separated here. Daily sounds created by nature's own tools and sounds expressing the deterioration of nature or sounds formed as a result of natural events are presented in the gallery space or again with the material of nature in the space of nature through technology. This presentation makes the existence and sound of nature heard; at the same time, it draws attention to the negative situations experienced by nature, nature exposed to wear and tear due to the human factor, and the careless use of nature and reconsiders it. The sounds of nature move with a certain rhythm within themselves. They convey information to us from time. "Music is the voice of time and an interrogation of the time of sound: This is the argument that makes music art" (De Bolla, 2012, p. 62). In this context, the music created by nature has taken its place in art as a sound in itself, and examples of the use of the healing sound of nature for nature have been studied in terms of the relationship between art and technology.

In this context; it is seen that technological developments have transformed the course and perception of art. Sound and data processing, which are a part of technological developments, emerge as a means of expression in the field of art. The focus of this section is the expression of the relationship between nature and technology in digital art with sound. The works are presented by interpreting them through artistic and scientific practices through installation examples. The natural sound environment is transferred to nature or gallery space through digital sound. Digitally collected sounds are used as a thin line in the healing of nature, ensuring ecological balance and raising human awareness and are used in art. The use of image and sound data together in art has an important position because it increases the power and interaction in the perception of the viewer.

Sounds in nature are used scientifically, musically and ecologically. Raymond Murray Schafer, a Canadian composer, musician, environmentalist and pioneer of acoustic ecology, first mentioned the concept of soundscape in his book Tuning of the World in 1977. Murray drew attention to the industrial revolution that took place in England between 1760 and 1840 among the technological factors affecting sound. According to him; the rapid development of the production of metals such as iron and steel, the use of these metals and new energy sources affected soundscapes. Murray sees the key to soundscape as climate and geography. These soundscapes are composed of sounds such as bird sounds, leaf sounds, water sounds, wind sounds, and sea sounds (Schafer, 1994). Bernie Krause, an American musician and ecoacoustic artist, has been recording sounds in nature since 1968, creating a large sound archive. He has recorded the sounds of more than 15,000 species in 40 years from untouched areas and archived them. The reason why it is considered an archive is that some types of sounds obtained in the wild no longer exist, and thc sound has disappeared due to human-induced sound and noise. That's why these sound data are archives that bear witness to the sound of nature (Vidal, 2012). Sounds obtained from nature constitute the sound ecology. The soundscape ecology consists of biophony, geophony and anthrophony. Krause's concept, biophony, is the sound created by animals; geophony is the sound of leaves, wind, etc. in nature; in other words, it is non-biological. Geophony consists of four subheadings of sound: Sounds formed by the effects of water, air, wind and geophysical forces. And finally, anthrophony is all sounds created by human voices. Sounds deeply affect nature as an auditory transformation of both spiritual and physical form. Sound data is an indication of the relationships between sounds and what the sound means as an expression. These sounds, which are the music of nature, are scientific data about the state of nature (Krause, 2008). A sound obtained from nature in the past may no longer exist today due to its destruction by itself or by humans. From this perspective, sound data remains to the present day as the sound of destruction. In fact, sound remains as a warning and announces this destruction to us.

In this context, Marco Barotti, who creates kinetic sound sculptures with his works that can be considered as examples of geophony and is a media artist, has used sound as an inseparable part of his art. The source of his use of sound comes from his musical education at the Siena Jazz Academy. The artist has constructed sound data with a visual language and combined it with his installations and kinetic works. The artist's works generally consist of kinetic sound that he creates using digital tools and installations that he places in nature and urban spaces. Barotti creates works that are activated by sound by using sound technologies, consumer objects and waste in his moving sculptures. The basic logic of the artist's artistic approaches is to create a "technology ecosystem"; the purpose of doing this is to reveal the common points in animals, plants and nature. Barotti's works are an anthropogenic analogy due to their existence and position in the universe. At the same time, they give people a message and raise awareness about environmental problems (Barotti, n.d.).

The artist's actions towards renewing nature, sustainability, protecting nature with technology and raising people's awareness are remarkable. The main reason why the artist chose clams in his kinetic installation named "Clams" (Figure 3) is that clams protect nature and living beings and also improve the sea by affecting the quality of the water. The nature-protective nature of mussels has been scientifically proven with the project named "Applicability of biological purification properties of mussels in Izmir Bay", which was carried out in partnership with Ege University Faculty of Fisheries, Konak District Directorate of Agriculture and Forestry and Izmir Development Agency. According to this project; mussels increase water quality with filtration method while also acting as a spatial and nutritional source for other underwater creatures. They improve water quality with their filtration feature. Thus, mussels protect the ecological balance of blue resources and provide benefits in preserving sustainability and biodiversity. This protection and sustainability are important for both nature and humanity. Mussels are so good at cleaning water that they have been described as "super-filters" (Sunlu et al., 2023). Marco Barotti used technological tools in his art to use these features of mussels on behalf of nature and carried out a healing movement towards nature. The artist has addressed the problems of the digital age with digital and technological solutions.

Figure 3. Marco Barotti, Clams, 2019

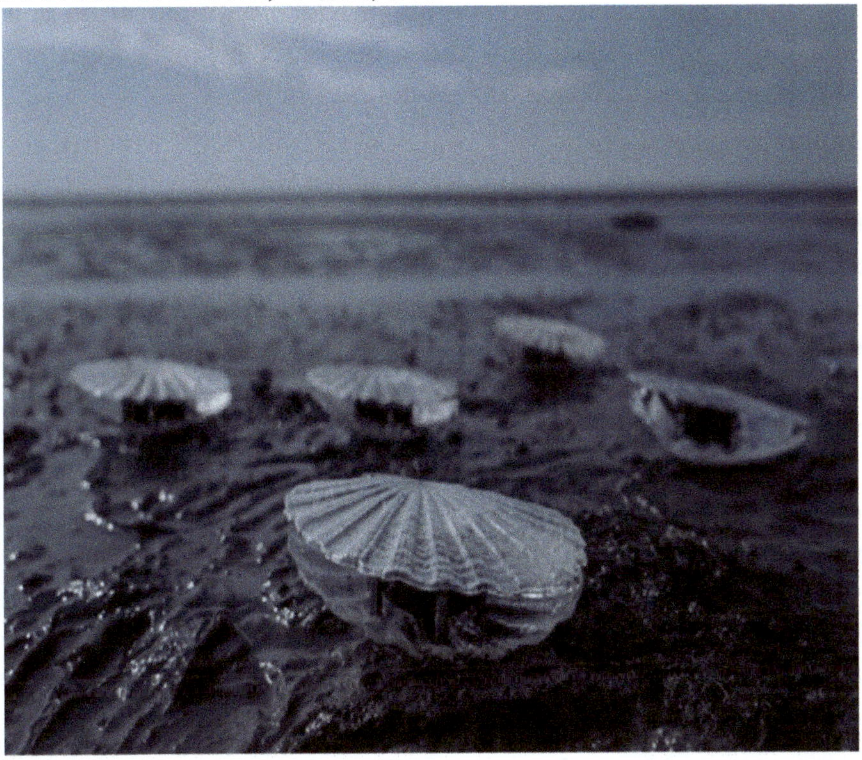

(Barotti, 2019)

Clams have become the artist's material and subject because they control pollution and act as detectors. These Clams that the artist placed in the sea are made of recycled material. They are shaped like real clams and made transparent from waste plastic. And speakers are placed inside these clams. The data received from the sensors placed in the sea that measure water quality is converted into sound; the converted sound causes these plastic clams to open and close by moving them. The sounds coming out of the clams come from the sound data received simultaneously from the sensor placed in the sea, and the sounds change as the water quality changes. There are differences in the movements of the clams according to the sound. These movements give an impression close to the natural movement of a clam. Due to the differences in the sound, a musical rhythm is created. Thus, the reflection of the sound created by nature by the technological data collection method of the clams conveys the connection between nature and environmental effects and ecology and sustainability to the audience (Barotti, n.d.). The transmitted sounds provide communication between humans and nature. Visual data and sounds create power together. The sound here is announced as a tool of nature's help.

Another work of the artist is "Coral Sonic Resilience", which deals with coral reefs that are subject to extinction in nature. Marco Barotti laid the foundations for the development phase of his Coral Sonic Resilience work in 2023 by coming together with Technische Universität, Berlin Science Gallery and 'BIfold', which deals with machine and data research. Barotti worked with data from Noaa, Copernicus and NASA in order to create "Techno Shamans", an algorithm optimized according to the shamanic music structure obtained from Japan, South Korea and South America. The logic behind this is to create healing sounds or rituals for coral reefs through art. The artist's artworks serve as shamans. The sounds he uses are healing mediums. According to Pelù's interview with Marco Barotti; The sounds obtained by the artist are sound data obtained after a period of 48-69 hours, through hydrophones, which are sound detection devices placed on healthy reefs on the Feridhoo Island in the Maldives (Pelù, 2025).

Since sound always attracts the attention of every living creature under all circumstances, Marco Barotti, an artist and musician, has also benefited from this feature of sound and used sound in a way that is beneficial for nature. Barotti, in order to protect coral reefs, recorded healthy coral sounds for corals that are affected by negative stress factors and bleached by using hydrophones on an island where there are undamaged and healthy corals. Healthy corals are ready to treat damaged corals with their sounds. The artist used sound like music to repair the worn-out structure of coral reefs and to relax and revitalize with the sound symphony created by nature. What is meant by nature sounds here are the sounds of healthy corals. Acting with this logic, the artist used previously recorded coral reef sounds in the sound sculptures he placed under the sea (Figure 4). These sounds obtained for underwater creatures have been listened to. Here again, natural sounds were used in natural life. Corals chat in their own language, sing songs, in short, they find the sound that will heal them. The sounds under the sea seem silent to those living on the surface of the land, but to those living under the sea, it is a loud song and a feast of sounds. The areas formed by corals provide a healthy living space, feeding and breeding environment for living organisms such as fish and larvae. For this reason, thanks to the audio data played, they were able to recover these lost living organisms. The artist combined the scientific data he obtained with the collaboration of NOAA and Copernicus with his art and drew attention to this situation by trying to stop the extinction of corals with the solidarity of science and art (Dusi, 2025).

In this study, the materials of the sound sculptures placed under the sea are ceramic and calcium carbonate. The textures of the sound sculptures are also shaped in accordance with marine life. Living things create symphonic sounds within their own organisms in the oceans and under the sea. In this blue space, sounds die due to reasons such as pollution, overfishing, and warming in the seas. Sound images and living organisms also disappear. Barotti brings vital ecosystems back to life by using sound and digital. Because healthy reefs under the sea are important for marine life. For example; fish larvae instinctively turn towards these sounds and these places become their places. At the same time, this return ensures the revival of the ecosystem. The power required for the continuous operation of thc sound sculptures under the sea is obtained from solar panels mounted on the buoy above the sea (Figure 5). Even the power obtained comes from nature, namely the sun. This power source ensures the uninterrupted sound playback for the protection and continuity of the reefs. (Artconnect, n.d.).

Figure 4. Marco Barotti, Coral Sonic Resilience 2025

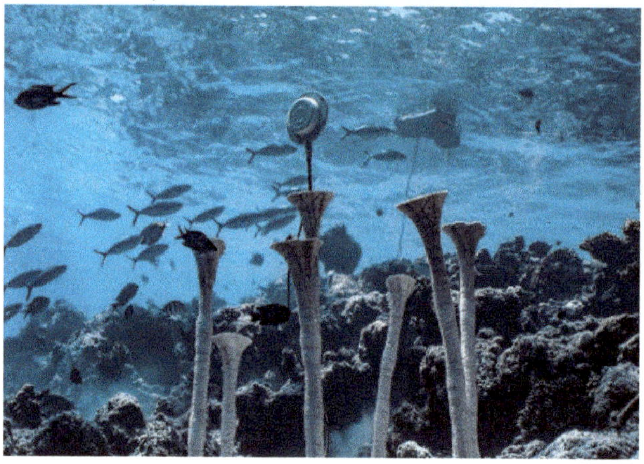

(Barotti, 2025)

Figure 5. Marco Barotti, Buoy, 2025

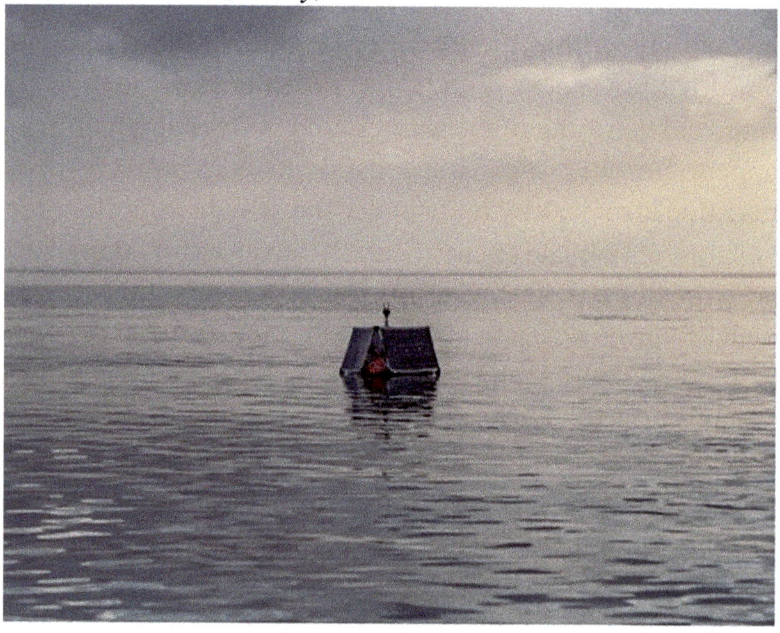

(Barotti, 2025)

German composer Richard Wagner uses sound and video together and "sees himself as a magician or prophet who tries to heal people through concerts consisting of simultaneous flow of sound and image" (Yılmaz, 2013, p. 327). In this work, where science and technology come together and are seen as healing just like Wagner, these reefs that have been damaged by sound and science are transitioning to a healing process. Underwater sound rituals take place as a healing medium. Barotti's sound installation shows the resistance of humans over the destruction in the seas.

David Bowen, an artist and educator at the University of Minnesota, has also created installations consisting of kinetic and robotic sculptures that combine science and technology. The installation work called Tele-Present Wind (Mars Wind Version), which was made in partnership with David Bowen and NASA Jet Propulsion Laboratory, is a work where science, art and technology come together. Mechanical devices attached to 126 dry grasses placed in the gallery space (Figure 6) are bent in the x/y direction. The direction of this wind is determined by the data received from the wind sensor in the Perseverance rover (Figure 7) located on the planet Mars; the wind, sound and movements transmitted from the space space to the gallery space are used simultaneously (Bowen, n.d.).

Figure 6. David Bowen, Tele-Present Wind, 2024

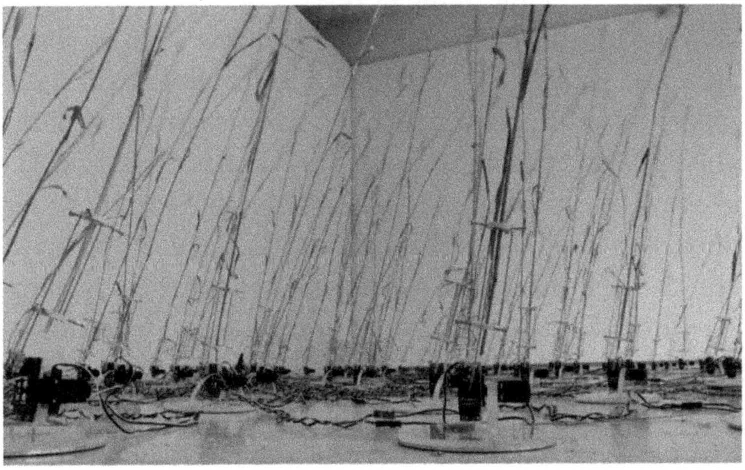

(Bowen, 2024)

Figure 7. David Bowen, Wind Sensor on the Perseverance Rover, 2024

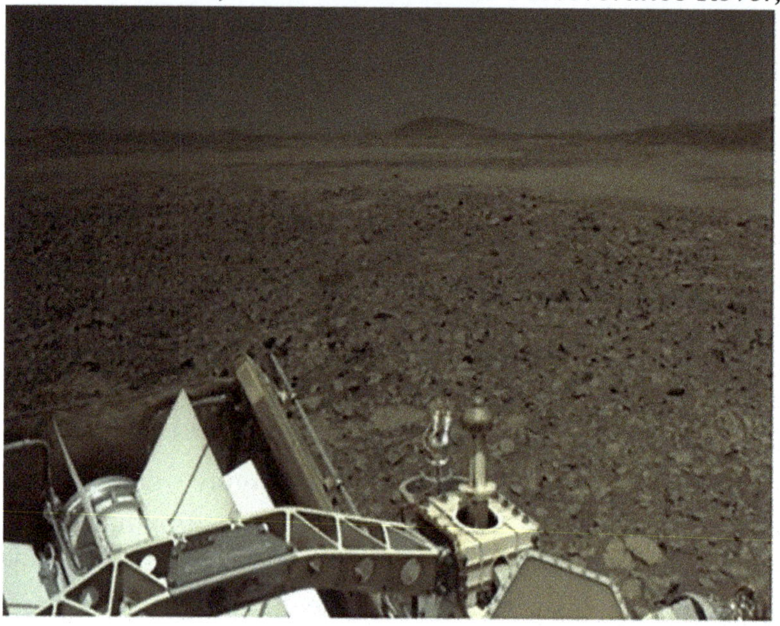

(Bowen, 2024)

The state of space is felt in the atmospheric space. Thanks to technological tools, those who cannot sense or feel this state of space feel and perceive it in the gallery space. Thanks to technological data, humans have the opportunity to approach such impossible situations. David Bowen used 13 white plastic bags in his work "Wilderness" (Figure 8). The data was collected by the artist on the Schmidt Ocean Institute Research Ship Falkor, which went from Astoria to Hawaii in 2019. While in the middle of the ocean, the fact that nature has never been touched by human hands, being alone with pure nature, the magnificent beauty of nature in its own state is occasionally spoiled by man-made waste floating in the ocean. During this journey, the up and down movements of the ship caused by the ocean waves were collected thanks to the accelerometer measuring the Z movement on the ship. The Z movement data obtained (movements on the vertical axis) is connected to the movement of the bags with technological connections in the gallery space. Thus, the perception that the ocean wave movements are suspended by the bags is created. In this study, sensory sensation is emphasized with material appearance (Bowen, n.d.). The representation of these ecological situations is the technological display of nature's movements and sounds.

Figure 8. David Bowen, Wilderness, 2021

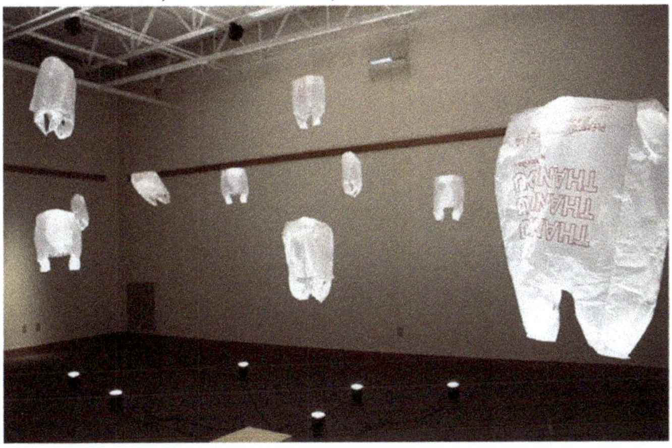

(Bowen, 2021)

The artist's use of these shopping bags is a conscious approach. Today, shopping bags have become a basic consumer product that people use a lot. Using too many bags causes environmental pollution. In addition, since they do not dissolve in nature, they cause the ecological order to deteriorate. The main material of plastic bags is made of cheap, light and durable polyethylene. 'Ethylene gas' obtained from natural gas and oil forms the raw material of 'polyethylene'. Polyethylene is difficult to dissolve in nature; although it breaks down physically, it takes decades to biodegrade. Not only that; the visual appearance of the bags in the environment also disrupts the natural beauty of the environment. This is also an environmental problem. It also poses a danger to the natural life of animals. Some administrations have taken social measures to reduce these serious problems. For example; The Selangor state government in Malaysia has declared every Saturday as "No Plastic Bag Day" since January 1, 2010. The aim of this declaration is to reduce the use of plastic bags, raise awareness and remind people of these negative problems (Kamaruddin & Mazila, 2012, p. 206). In addition to the social-cultural and scientific studies aimed at solving ecological problems, the visual, auditory and technological relations of art also make this process more effective. Artists become the guides of society by constantly reflecting social and cultural problems to the tongue, ear and eye. That is why David Bowen also makes the cry of nature heard with his technological works. The flying sounds of the plastic bag in the gallery space are equal to the waves. Because these are the wave data of the real ocean. These sounds make us feel the sounds of the ocean and nature as if we were in the space itself and visualize them in our minds. Baudelaire says, "colors, smells and sounds are evoked there" (Akay, 2017, p. 278). The ocean wave data is also evoked in the gallery space. The mechanical tools in this gallery are the live embodiment of the obtained nature sounds with technological data connections. When looking at the installations, the following questions come to mind: Can humans act in harmony against technology and nature? Can nature be controlled through technology? Can technology reduce environmental problems? Questions like these open the human mind and make people think. In a way, the artist opens the way for the viewer to think about these questions and invites them to question and think about how nature and technology are combined.

Olafur Eliasson's first exhibition in Türkiye, "Your Unexpected Encounter", opened at Istanbul Modern between June 7, 2024 and February 9, 2025, consists of works that offer the opportunity to perceive, experience, hear and think about concepts such as light, sound and nature. The focus of his works is generally on nature and ecology. He technically and scientifically constructs images and materials of nature (such as stone and water) within the framework of art. In the installation titled "Model for a Timeless Garden" (Figure 9), which is included in the exhibition, the viewer who enters a room closed on all four sides is greeted by a pitch-black area; the viewer is confronted with briefly flashing lights and the sound of water.

Figure 9. Olafur Eliasson, A Model for a Timeless Garden, 2025. Istanbul

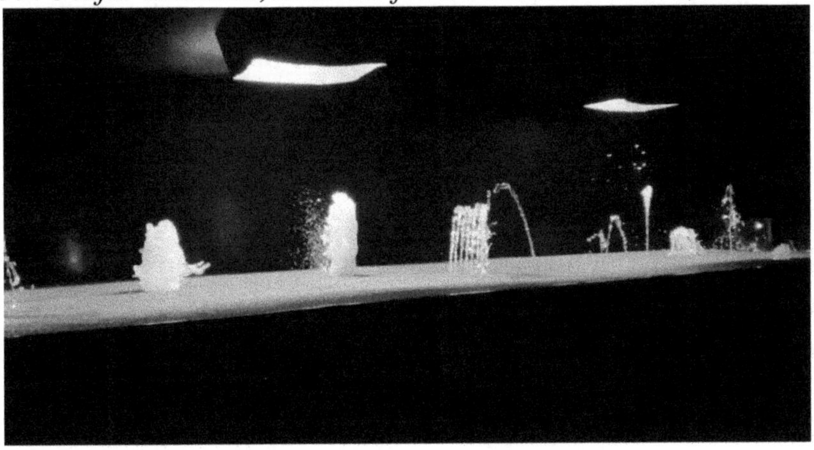

(Photograph Ö. Gürpınar, 2025)

While the continuous flashing of the flash lights prepared with the help of technological and technical tools in the space disturbs the viewer, on the other hand, the viewer tries to analyze the fountain mechanism created with the sounds of water. However, the flashing of the flash light on the water fountains disturbs the viewer in some cases. It is not possible for some viewers to stay in the space for too long. The fact that the water rises and falls again in that short period of time leaves a photographic frame in the mind along with the permanence of that moment in the human perception. It is perceived as a liquid sculpture. It is recorded in the mind like a momentary time slice taken by the camera. The sound of water heard in the space imprisons the viewer in that space. Perhaps the artist wants to emphasize the following here: The discomfort in the feeling and perception that that light leaves on the body has in a way prevented touching the water. In this context, it can be interpreted as a statement that we should not touch nature in the same way. The discomfort our body feels in that space is ironically a physical representation of nature's discomfort. The important thing is to be able to demonstrate this sensitivity by establishing a connection between nature, humans and technological culture, and at the same time to show the same sensitive thought to nature in its real space.

In the society we live in, everything is a technological extension. Technology is present in communication, transportation, health, in short, in every area of our daily lives, and we need technology for the continuation of life. Technological developments are a tool in organizing social order, nature, and ecology; they are an idea. These problems can be answered and solved with technological needs. Artists and scientists have worked in cooperation by using technology and have sought answers to problems with technological power. Technology is a war tool for ecological problems. Because the problems of this digital and technological age cannot be solved with traditional methods. Returning is an escape from the future. This means not being able to solve the problems. Artists have solved this logic with artistic and scientific works and thought that working together is more powerful. Both David Bowen, Marco Barotti and Olafur Eliasson have drawn attention to environmental and ecological problems by using their knowledge in fields such as science and engineering, and have advanced in terms of raising people's awareness.

CONCLUSION

The thought and voice of a person have a plastic structure in an abstract sense. Because these two situations have a formable and changeable content. The moment a person starts to think, their structure changes and their thoughts are expressed through voice. This voice is evaluated within a conceptual structure in artistic actions and artistic expressions. When a person speaks, the silence in the space is broken; on the other hand, nature creates the natural texture of the space with its voice and constant presence. The voice is invisible but acts as a sculpture in a plastic structure (Yılmaz, 2013, p. 345). With the development of technology and industry in art, it is seen that sound has become the material of art. In the first half of the 20th century, artists consider music as a part of art. The fact that artists use noise, metal sounds, and city sounds that they create with materials such as machines and metal has expanded the context of art, as in Futurism and Dada art. In art after 1950, with the development of technology, these sounds turn into the real sound of nature and the sounds obtained from nature as data are used in mobile installations. Artists have combined their installations with sound by using objects reminiscent of nature and the real material of nature together with technology. Thus, artists have brought a questioning approach to the relationship between nature and technology. In the works, attention is drawn to the problems of nature with nature's own sound. Sound emerges as the one that heals nature and makes its cry heard. Because a real sound has a greater effect on the viewer and makes them think. In installations made in nature, the viewer's perception is constantly reshaped and changed according to the interaction of space, sound and nature. Nature has a more dynamic spatial structure.

When the artist works examined are examined, it is seen that nature, science and art come together to draw attention to the perception of nature and its problems. The basis of the artist installations is sound data obtained from nature. Digital sound representations that include nature in the installations are experienced by the artist and the audience, creating a new and questioning impression about the future of technology and nature. The research reveals that art is open to technological innovations, how it can contribute to nature through digital innovations and how this contribution can harmonize nature with a sustainable ecological balance. The study provides social awareness about nature through the relationship between nature and technology. At the same time, this perspective, where technology and soundscapes in nature are used together in the kinetic installations examined, offers the reader an in-depth and analytical approach by addressing nature from a healing perspective.

REFERENCES

Akay, A. (2017). *Sanat bizi seviyor*. Doğu Batı.

Antmen, A. (2012). *20. yüzyıl Batı sanatında akımlar*. Sel Press.

Artconnect. (n.d.). Sounds of Survival: How Art and Science Are Reviving Coral Reefs. https://www.magazine.artconnect.com/editorial/coral-sonic-resilience

Avcı-Tuğal, S. (2018). *Oluşum süreci içinde dijital sanat*. Hayalperest.

Ball, H. (1916). Cabaret Voltaire in Zurich. [Photograph] https://arsenaldeletras.com/2014/06/22/hugo-ball-interpretaciones/

Barotti, M. (2019). Clams. [Photograph]. https://www.marcobarotti.com/Clams

Barotti, M. (2025). Buoy. [Photograph]. https://www.corriere.ca/sculture-sonore-per-rigenerare-i-coralli-e-lartescienza-di-marco-barotti/

Barotti, M. (2025). Coral Sonic Resilience. [Photograph]. https://www.corriere.ca/sculture-sonore-per-rigenerare-i-coralli-e-lartescienza-di-marco-barotti/

Barotti, M. (n.d.). Marcobarotti. https://www.marcobarotti.com

Bowen, D. (2021). Wilderness. [Photograph]. https://www.dwbowen.com/wilderness

Bowen, D. (2024). Tele-Present Wind. [Photograph]. https://www.dwbowen.com/telepresent-wind

Bowen, D. (2024). Wind sensor on the Perseverance rover. [Photograph]. https://www.dwbowen.com/telepresent-wind

Bowen, D. (n.d.). Dwbowen. https://www.dwbowen.com/

Bozkurt, M. (2012). Medya sanatı. Yılmaz, M. Sanatın günceli güncelin sanatı (pp. 214-256 in).

Dachy, M. (2014). *Dada sanatın başkaldırısı* (Türkay, O., Trans.). Yapı Kredi.

De Bolla, P. (2012). *Sanat ve estetik.* Ayrıntı.

Dusi, E. (2025, March 6). Ricreato il suono della barriera corallina: aiuterà a rifiorire i fondali marini degradati. https://www.repubblica.it/esteri/2025/03/06/news/suono_barriera_corallina_marco_barotti_universita_padova-424046626/#

Eliasson, O. (2025). Model for a timeless garden. [Photograph]. Istanbul Modern Art. (Photograph by Özlem Gürpınar, 2025)

Fineberg, J. (2014). *1940'tan günümüze sanat* (G.E. Yılmaz & S. Atay-Eskier, Trans.). Karakalem Kitabevi Press. Fischer- Lichte, E. (2016). *Performatif estetik* (T. Acil, Trans.). Ayrıntı Press.

Hassan, R., & Sutherland, T. (2024). *Medya felsefesi* (Mousavi, S., & Törenli, N., Trans.). Ütopya Press. (Original work published 2023)

Kamaruddin, R., & Mazila, Y. (2012). Md. (2012). Selangor Government's "No plastic Bag Day" Campaign: Motivation and Acceptance Level. *Procedia: Social and Behavioral Sciences, 42*, 205–211. DOI: 10.1016/j.sbspro.2012.04.183

Krause, B. (2008). Anatomy of the Soundscape: Evolving Perspectives. *JAES, 56*(1/2), 73-80. https://www.researchgate.net/profile/Bernie-Krause/publication/257943187_Anatomy_of_the_Soundscape_Evolving_Perspectives/links/00b4952668ef8dfbf5000000/Anatomy-of-the-Soundscape-Evolving-Perspectives.pdf

Pelù, M. (2025, March 18). Sculture sonore per rigenerare i coralli: è "l'artescienza" di Marco Barotti. [Rapporto]. Corriere Canadese. https://www.corriere.ca/sculture-sonore-per-rigenerare-i-coralli-e-lartescienza-di-marco-barotti/

Read, H. (2020). *Modern sanatın felsefesi* (Kök, E., & Orgun, H., Trans.). Hayalperest.

Schafer, M. R. (1994). *Our sonic environment and the soundscape the tuning of the world.* Destiny Books. (Original work published 1977)

Sunlu, U., Lök, A., Küçükdermenci, A., Kırtık, A., & Kurtay, E. (2023). *Midyelerin biyolojik arıtma özelliklerinin İzmir Körfez'inde uygulanabilirliği projesi raporu.* İzmir Kalkınma Ajansı 2022 Yılı Teknik Destek Programı, İzmir. https://izka.org.tr/wp-content/uploads/pdf/midyelerin-biyolojik-aritma-ozelliklerinin-izmir-korfezine-uygulanabilirligi.pdf

Tinguely, J. (1960). Homage to New York. [Photograph]. https://www.moma.org/calendar/exhibitions/3369

Turner, B. S. (2019). *Beden ve toplum sosyal teoride arayışlar* (Kaya, İ., Trans.). Nobel.

Vidal, J. (2012, September 3). 'A great silence is spreading over the natural world'. The Guardian. https://www.theguardian.com/environment/2012/sep/03/bernie-krause-natural-world-recordings#comments

Wands, B. (2006). *Dijital çağın sanatı* (Akınhay, O., Trans.). Renk Ayrımı.

Weeks, M. (2024). *Dakikalar içinde felsefe* (Özeren, M. M., Trans.). Kronik.

Yılmaz, M. (2013). *Modernden postmoderne sanat.* Ütopya Press.

ADDITIONAL READING

Arslan, C. (2023). *Dijital dönüşümün kültür ve sanat üzerindeki yansımaları.* Nobel.

Bakker, K. (2022). *The sounds of life: How digital technology ıs bringing us closer to the worlds of animals and plants.* Princeton University Press.

Brown, A. (2014). *Güncel sanat ve ekoloji* (Gözgü, E., & Adam, Y., Trans.). Lal Yayınları.

Lynton, N. (2015). *Modern sanatın öyküsü* (Çapan, C., & Öziş, S., Trans.). Remzi Kitabevi.

Pijanowski, B. C. (2024). *Principles of soundscape ecology: Discovering our sonic world.* University of Chicago Press. DOI: 10.7208/chicago/9780226824284.001.0001

Pijanowski, B. C., Villanueva-Rivera, L. J., Dumyahn, S. L., Farina, A., Krause, B. L., Napoletano, B. M., Gage, S. H., & Pieretti, N. (2011, March). Soundscape Ecology: The Science of Sound in the Landscape. *Bioscience*, *61*(3), 203–216. DOI: 10.1525/bio.2011.61.3.6

Schafer, M. R. (1969). *The new soundscape*. Associated Music Publishers.

Sezgin, E. (2022). *Sanat ve ekoloji sanat/yaşam/üretim*. İletişim.

Shanken, E. A. (2012). *Sanat ve elektronik medya*. Akbank.

KEY TERMS AND DEFINITIONS

Digital Technology: They are electronic devices and systems produced to store, process and produce data.

Ecological Art: They are artistic nature actions and thoughts that artists carry out in order to act together with nature, create nature awareness and protect nature.

Installation: From an artist's perspective, it is the placement of objects in closed or open spaces.

Nature: It is a structure that changes, transforms and renews itself and contains all living and non-living beings.

Sound Data: It is the recording and processing of a sound using digital tools.

Sound Ecology: It is the field that examines the effects of nature, animal and human sounds on the ecological balance.

Technology: It is the totality of knowledge, experience and methods used to produce tools, equipment and machines for a purpose.

Chapter 3
Digitalization and Graphic Design From Lascaux to Artificial Intelligence:
The Emergence of Visual Thinking – Lascaux and Symbolic Communication

Nurevşan Karaduman Başcı
http://orcid.org/0000-0002-6354-190X
Atatürk University, Turkey

Burcu Toğrul
http://orcid.org/0000-0003-1962-7543
Ağrı İbrahim Çeçen University, Turkey

ABSTRACT

Although the term graphic design was first coined by typographer William A. Dwiggins in the early 20th century to define emerging professional practices, the origins of the discipline can be traced back to prehistoric times. Visual expressions such as those in the Lascaux Caves demonstrate that symbolic communication predates written language. Over centuries,

DOI: 10.4018/979-8-2600-0944-4.ch003

graphic design evolved through major cultural and technological shifts, including the invention of writing, the development of typographic systems, the advent of the printing press, and the transformations brought by the Industrial Revolution. In the modern era, digitalization fundamentally redefined the field by enabling greater interactivity, flexibility, and creative experimentation. Today, artificial intelligence marks a new epistemological threshold, reshaping design methodologies, questioning authorship, and expanding the conceptual boundaries of visual communication.

INTRODUCTION

Since the earliest periods of human history, the need for self-expression has manifested through various forms of visual representation. From the prehistoric paintings in the Lascaux Caves to the digital images generated by artificial intelligence today, this process demonstrates that visual representation constitutes one of the fundamental ways through which humans produce meaning and communicate their experiences. Within this long historical trajectory, graphic design has emerged not merely as a field of aesthetic production but also as a system that organizes visual thinking, structures meaning, and enables cultural communication. In this sense, the history of graphic design is directly related to the formation of humanity's visual memory. The early visual narratives found in prehistoric cave paintings are not only artistic productions but also symbolic expressions of the relationship between humans, nature, experience, and the unknown (Clottes, 2008).

Throughout history, technological ruptures such as the invention of writing, the development of the printing press, and the emergence of typography have played a decisive role in transforming practices of visual communication. These developments fundamentally altered the ways in which visual knowledge was produced, organized, and disseminated. Particularly during the twentieth century, the emergence of modernist design, the Bauhaus approach, and the Swiss Typography School made significant contributions to the formation of graphic design as a systematic discipline. During this period, graphic design began to be considered not only as an aesthetic activity but also as a communication system capable of organizing knowledge and participating in ideological meaning production (Meggs & Purvis, 2016).

One of the most radical transformations in the history of graphic design emerged with the process of digitalization. The integration of computer technologies and digital software into design processes transformed graphic design from a field of static visual production into an interactive, participatory, and multilayered communication environment. Within digital media environments, visual production increasingly operates through data structures and algorithmic systems. The modular, variable, and reconfigurable nature of digital media fundamentally reshapes the structure of visual production (Manovich, 2001). From this perspective, graphic design can no longer be understood solely as the arrangement of visual forms but rather as a dynamic communication system in which meaning is produced through data, interfaces, and user interaction.

With the development of digital technologies, the integration of artificial intelligence systems into design processes has further accelerated this transformation. AI-supported visual production tools are capable of generating numerous visual variations within a very short period of time and transforming many stages of traditional design processes. At the same time, this situation reopens fundamental design concepts such as creativity, originality, designer identity, and ethical responsibility to renewed debate. Images produced through technological apparatuses represent a new stage in the historical development of visual culture (Flusser, 2000). In contemporary contexts, artificial intelligence systems can be interpreted as the most recent manifestations of this form of technical image production.

The ways in which communication technologies reshape cultural perception and modes of thinking have long been the subject of scholarly debate. Communication media are not merely tools that transmit messages; they are also structures that shape the cultural environments within which meaning is produced (McLuhan, 1964). Within this context, digital media environments and algorithmic systems can be interpreted not simply as technical tools but as cultural infrastructures that reconstruct the epistemological foundations of visual communication.

From this perspective, the development of graphic design can be understood as part of a long process of transformation extending from prehistoric cave paintings to contemporary digital interfaces. Forms of visual representation have continually evolved alongside technological and cultural changes, with each historical period generating its own visual language. Therefore, the development of visual culture can be interpreted as a historical continuity in which symbolic forms of expression evolve through technological mediation (Şan, 2024). In this respect, graphic design should be understood not only as a field of visual production but also as a cultural practice shaped by symbolic thinking, technological transformation, and processes of social communication.

This study aims to examine the historical development of graphic design from the perspective of visual thinking and to investigate how digitalization and artificial intelligence technologies transform the epistemological foundations of design practice. Within this framework, the study focuses on the following questions: Through which technological ruptures has the historical development of graphic design been shaped? In what ways has the process of digitalization restructured practices of visual communication? How do artificial intelligence systems transform the production processes and conceptual foundations of graphic design?

In order to address these questions, the chapter approaches the history of graphic design from a chronological and theoretical perspective. It first examines the emergence of visual thinking and the early forms of symbolic communication. It then discusses the invention of writing and the abstraction of graphic thinking. This is followed by an analysis of the impact of the printing press on visual order and the institutionalization of modern design practices. Subsequently, the effects of industrialization and postmodern critical thought on design are discussed. Finally, the transformation of graphic design in the age of digitalization and artificial intelligence is analyzed. Within this historical framework, graphic design is considered not merely as a field of visual production but as a multilayered cultural system shaped by technological developments, intellectual paradigms, and evolving forms of cultural communication.

THE EMERGENCE OF VISUAL THINKING: LASCAUX AND SYMBOLIC COMMUNICATION

This section examines how the symbolic thinking capacity of Homo sapiens was shaped through visual representations and analyzes the multilayered functions of the paintings found in the Lascaux Caves. The drawings on the cave walls are not merely aesthetic productions; they also function as mechanisms for the construction of collective memory, the transmission of ritual practices, and the symbolic encoding of cultural memory. The placement of these lines in the darkest and most inaccessible parts of the caves suggests that these images were produced within sacred, ceremonial, or intuitive contexts rather than for everyday use. Animal figures, abstract symbols, and the rarely depicted human forms reveal traces of early graphic thinking and demonstrate the complex structure of visual communication. In this respect, Lascaux may be considered not only a threshold at which visual thinking emerged but also a cultural site containing the earliest traces of meaning-making practices that would later constitute the historical foundations of graphic design.

Figure 1. Animal representations in the Hall of Bulls, Lascaux Cave, France (ca. 17,000 BCE).

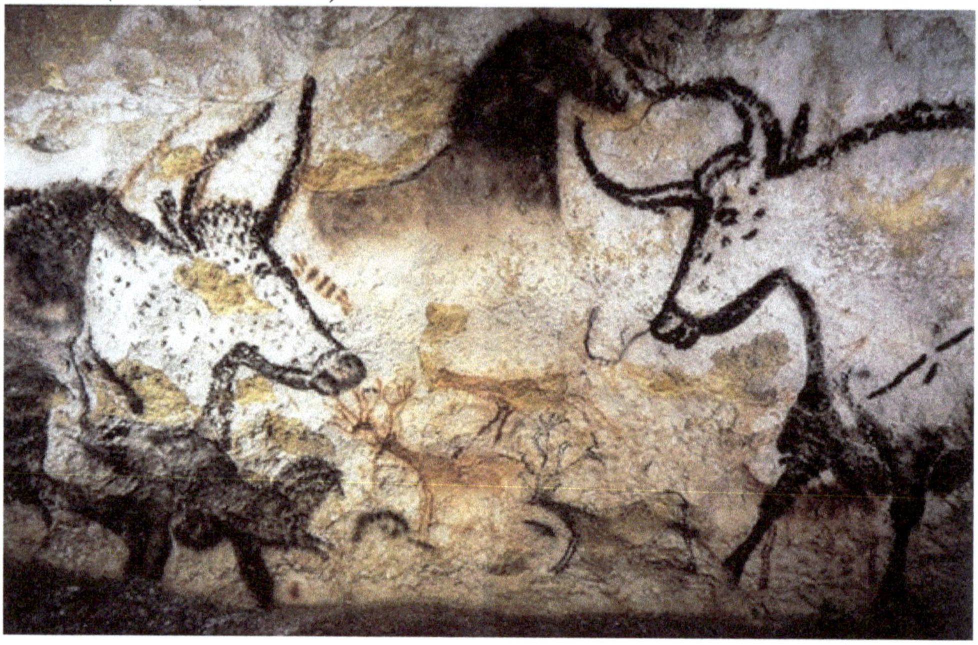

Retrieved from Wikimedia Commons.

It is not known with certainty when and where Homo sapiens—beings capable of conscious and symbolic thought—first appeared. Nevertheless, within the evolutionary process, forms of expression developed in response to communication needs gradually expanded beyond spoken language and enabled thought to be expressed through visual symbols. As humans began to communicate ideas through symbols, drawings, and signs, the graphical representation of thought became possible. These visual traces offered a form of expression that aimed for permanence in contrast to the ephemerality of speech. Before the emergence of writing, humans transmitted experiences and knowledge through images imprinted on surfaces, thereby fulfilling their need to leave lasting traces (Meggs & Purvis, 2016).

This symbolic production does not merely serve the transmission of knowledge. It also involves the encoding of relationships with the surrounding environment, the visualization of collective experiences, and the formation of cultural memory. In this context, visuality functions not only as a representational medium but also as a cultural environment in which social meaning is produced (Mirzoeff, 1999). As prehistoric societies grew in population and their social structures became increasingly complex, the transmission of accumulated knowledge across generations became a vital necessity. The animal figures, geometric shapes, and symbols drawn on cave walls are therefore not only aesthetic images but also visual codes that carry educational, ritualistic, and symbolic meanings.

These images likely served multiple functions, such as educating younger members of the group, establishing symbolic relationships with nature, or facilitating communication within the community. Early visual productions functioned as visual memory units that shaped not only individual memory but also collective memory (Assmann, 2011). The fact that many of the drawings are located in the darkest and most difficult-to-access areas of the caves suggests that these productions were evaluated within ritualistic or ceremonial contexts rather than everyday life. In this sense, the line should not be understood merely as a static mark; rather, it represents a carrier of layered meanings accumulated through rhythmic movement over time (Ingold, 2007).

The paintings in the Lascaux Caves do not merely depict animals; they also construct a complex visual language through abstract symbols, geometric forms, and nonfigurative elements. In addition to animal imagery, the rarely depicted human figures are often represented in fragmented, surreal, or caricatured forms. The presence of these figures deep within the cave suggests that they carry intuitive and ritualistic meanings rather than functioning as direct narrative scenes (Siyanbola et al., 2021).

When the development of such drawings is examined over time, it becomes evident that images gradually evolved from direct representations into structures that encode knowledge in abstract ways. Some of these processes of abstraction later contributed to the development of symbolic systems that eventually paved the way for the emergence of writing (Geneste, 2017).

The role of visual representation in human cognition extends beyond mere depiction. Visuality can also be understood as a distinct mode of thinking. From this perspective, prehistoric visual productions are closely related to the development of the human mind's capacity for symbolic thought. The ability of the human mind to construct symbolic systems has long been considered one of the fundamental components of cultural evolution. Therefore, cave paintings should be interpreted not only as artistic productions but also as early manifestations of the human capacity for abstraction.

Understanding the historical origins of graphic design cannot be limited to the development of printing technologies or the emergence of modern design theories. A deeper perspective requires the analysis of the earliest forms of visual thinking. In this context, wall paintings in prehistoric environments such as the Lascaux Caves should be evaluated not merely as aesthetic practices but also as early examples of symbolic communication. These visual narratives prepared the mental and cultural foundations for the later emergence of writing and typographic systems. For this reason, cave paintings can be regarded as one of the earliest points in the history of graphic design and as one of the first conceptual grounds in which visual thinking acquired social meaning (Mullen, 2008).

From this historical perspective, graphic design should not be understood solely as a discipline that emerged in the modern period. Rather, it can be interpreted as a cultural form of expression that evolved through the continuity of the human mind's capacity for symbolic production. Visual symbols have functioned as communication strategies that encode and transmit the shared experiences of human history, and within this long historical process visual thinking gradually became one of the fundamental instruments of cultural production.

THE INVENTION OF WRITING AND THE ABSTRACTION OF GRAPHIC THINKING

This section approaches the emergence of writing not merely as a technical development but as a fundamental conceptual transformation in the abstraction of graphic thinking. The traces left on surfaces during prehistoric times gradually evolved into systematic symbols and written language. This transformation reveals that graphic design has historically functioned not only as a carrier of information but also as a mechanism that organizes and constructs meaning. Writing, as the graphical representation of abstract thought, enabled the transition from individual memory to collective memory and played a crucial role in the formation of cultural memory and social organization. In this context, visual productions spanning from the Paleolithic to the Neolithic periods should be evaluated not merely as aesthetic artifacts but as indicators of cognitive, symbolic, and technological transformation.

Since prehistoric times, the human tendency to leave traces has constituted one of the earliest manifestations of graphic expression. A handprint left on a cave wall or a line drawn on sand represents a direct externalization of human cognition and identity. Over time, such traces gradually transformed into symbols carrying systematic meaning and eventually became the basis of written language. The symbolic nature of early visual production enabled thought to be expressed at an abstract level and formed the earliest stages of graphic thinking. Cultural stages commonly defined as the Paleolithic, Mesolithic, and Neolithic periods therefore represent not only chronological developments but also transformations in symbolic production and visual communication practices. Visual artifacts produced during these periods functioned as tools for constructing cultural memory, organizing social knowledge, and transmitting symbolic meanings across generations (Drucker & McVarish, 2009).

Human perception, particularly vision, has historically played a fundamental role in the process of meaning-making. Visual perception enabled individuals and communities to interpret their environment and translate experience into symbolic representation. Cave paintings dated to approximately 15,000 BCE can therefore be considered among the earliest systematic examples of visual communication. These images did not merely transmit practical information related to survival; they also reflected how humans interpreted and conceptualized the world around them (Uçar, 2004). Over time, these visual expressions evolved into increasingly abstract systems of representation, eventually leading to the development of writing. Writing, in this sense, is not simply a communication system composed of symbols. It is also an epistemological tool that enables knowledge to be structured, stored, and transmitted across generations (Jean & Başer, 2008).

The historical emergence of writing is closely linked to the cultural and economic developments of early civilizations in Mesopotamia. The region known as Mesopotamia—derived from the Greek term meaning "between rivers"—refers to the fertile lands between the Tigris and Euphrates rivers. Throughout history, this region hosted major civilizations such as the Sumerians, Akkadians, Assyrians, and Babylonians. Around the fourth millennium BCE, the Sumerians organized themselves into city-states and developed complex temple-centered economic systems. Within these administrative structures, particularly those associated with temple economies and ziggurats, the need to record economic transactions and manage resources became increasingly necessary. This administrative necessity created the conditions that led to the invention of writing (Becer, 2015).

Before the emergence of written symbols, early accounting practices relied on small clay objects known as tokens or calculi. These objects were used to represent specific goods or quantities and functioned as a primitive system of economic record keeping. In many cases, these tokens were enclosed within clay envelopes known as bullae, which sometimes bore markings representing the contents within them. Over time, instead of enclosing tokens inside the bullae, symbols representing these objects began to be inscribed directly onto the surface of clay tablets. This transition marked a crucial moment in the history of visual communication, as meaning could now be represented on two-dimensional surfaces through abstract signs (Albayrak, 2016). At this stage, symbols no longer functioned merely as substitutes for physical objects but as conceptual representations that encoded meaning within a visual system.

Figure 2. Proto-cuneiform clay tablet, Uruk III period (ca. 3200–3000 BCE), food ration record (British Museum).

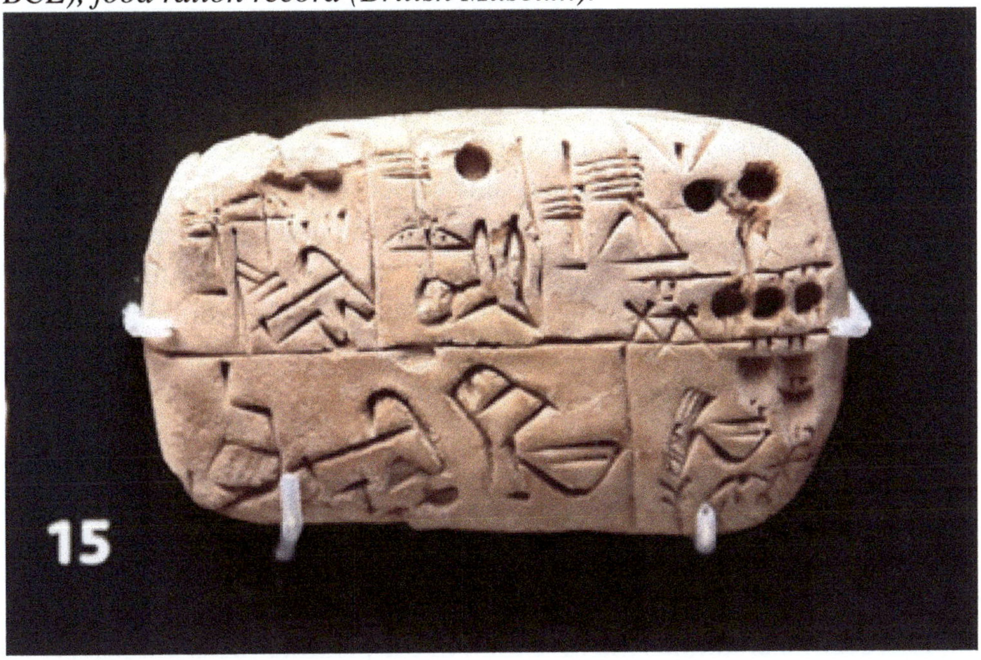

The development of writing thus represented a significant step in the abstraction of graphic representation. Meaning was no longer transmitted solely through speech or direct visual depiction but through structured systems of signs governed by visual and syntactic rules. In this context, writing introduced a new regime of meaning production in which visual form itself became a fundamental organizing structure of knowledge.

Over time, early writing systems continued to evolve and diversify. The transition from cuneiform writing to alphabetic systems occurred gradually across centuries in the Ancient Near East. During the 7th century BCE, Assyrian administrative systems often used both cuneiform writing and the Aramaic alphabet simultaneously, combining logographic and phonetic systems within the same cultural framework. Around 800 BCE, the Phoenician alphabet spread to Greece, where it was further developed through the introduction of vowel sounds and adapted into a more phonetic and flexible writing system (Schmandt-Besserat, 2014).

The development of alphabetic writing systems introduced new possibilities for visual organization and graphic structure. Greek inscriptions reflected not only linguistic representation but also an emerging aesthetic awareness emphasizing order, symmetry, and proportion. These developments demonstrate that the evolution of writing was not solely a linguistic transformation but also a visual and graphic one. As writing systems evolved, the relationship between function and visual form became increasingly significant. In this context, graphic design can be understood as the formal organization of knowledge through visual structures. Writing therefore represents one of the earliest moments in which graphic thinking became systematized. Visual marks were transformed into structured carriers of meaning within human culture.

THE INVENTION OF THE PRINTING PRESS AND THE MODERNIZATION OF VISUAL ORDER

This section examines the invention of the printing press not merely as a technical development but as a critical transformation in the organization of visual order within the history of graphic design. The emergence of printing technologies fundamentally altered the ways in which knowledge was produced, structured, and disseminated. The transition from manually reproduced manuscripts to mechanically printed pages introduced a new visual regime in which graphic layout, typographic hierarchy, and page composition gradually became standardized. In this sense, printing did not simply enable the multiplication of texts; it also reshaped the visual architecture through which information was organized and communicated. As a result, graphic design began to evolve from an aesthetic mode of representation into a systematic structure capable of organizing knowledge visually.

The origins of printing can be traced back to woodblock printing techniques developed in China during the seventh century. In this method, entire pages of text were carved onto wooden blocks and transferred onto paper through ink impressions. Although this technique allowed multiple copies of texts to be produced, the carving process was time-consuming and limited flexibility in editing or rearranging textual elements. Later developments in movable type printing during the eleventh century introduced a modular system in which individual characters could be reorganized and reused. This principle of modularity significantly accelerated production and introduced a structural logic that would later become fundamental to typographic systems.

A decisive transformation occurred in fifteenth-century Europe with the work of Johannes Gutenberg. Gutenberg's printing press, developed around 1439 and inspired by mechanical wine presses, enabled the rapid and consistent production of printed pages. The mechanical reproduction of texts made it possible for written knowledge to circulate beyond monastic scriptoria and elite intellectual environments. The spread of printing technology across Europe gradually increased literacy rates and facilitated broader access to knowledge. The introduction of printing to England by William Caxton in 1476 marked another milestone in this transformation, contributing to the expansion of printed literature and the wider dissemination of information across social groups (Nomonov, 2022).

Figure 3. Gutenberg printing press (15th century).

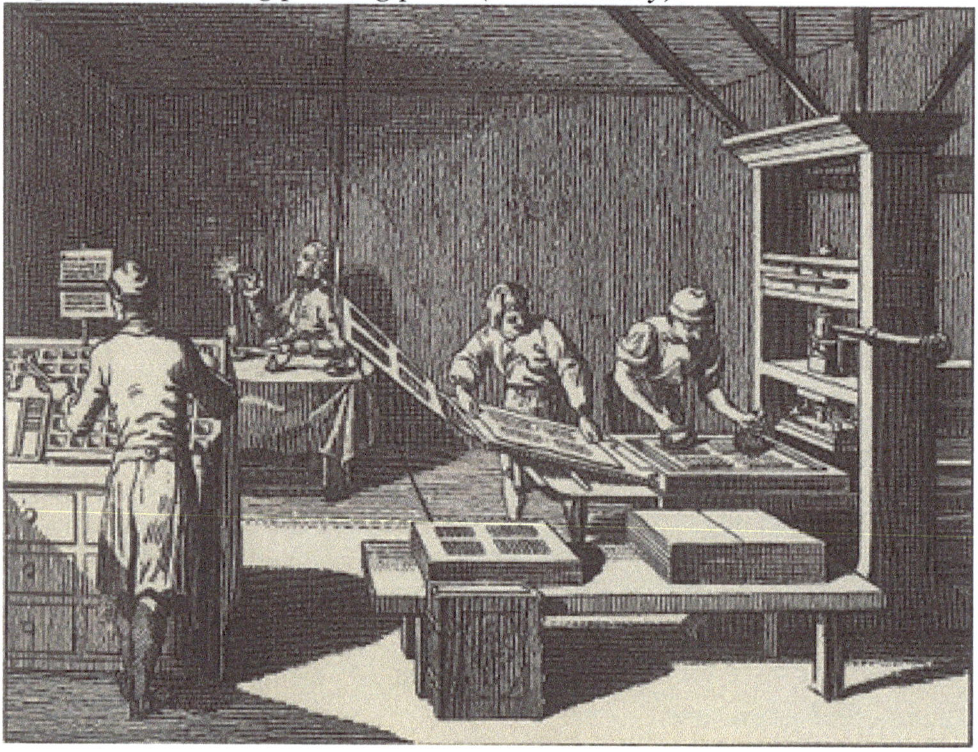

Beyond its cultural impact, the printing press also introduced a new system of visual organization. The reproducibility of printed materials required the stabilization of graphic elements such as margins, typographic hierarchy, spacing, and page composition. These structural decisions were no longer determined solely by aesthetic considerations but were increasingly shaped by the technical conditions of mechanical production. As a result, graphic layout evolved from the relatively fluid arrangements of manuscript culture into a more systematic visual order designed to enhance readability and clarity.

From the perspective of graphic design history, the printing revolution represents one of the most significant transformations in the development of visual communication. The mechanical reproduction of text encouraged the standardization of typographic structures and visual hierarchies, enabling information to be organized in consistent and repeatable formats. Principles such as alignment, modularity, and compositional balance gradually became essential tools for structuring visual information. These developments laid the groundwork for many of the visual systems later associated with modern graphic design, including typographic grids and modular layout structures (Meggs & Purvis, 2016).

The principle of repeatability introduced by printing technologies also reshaped the epistemological foundations of visual communication. Printed pages enabled visual information to circulate consistently across different geographical and cultural contexts, transforming visual communication into a reproducible system rather than a singular artifact. This structural logic would later influence the development of modern graphic design methodologies and continue to inform contemporary digital visual production. The production logic that today operates through digital software and algorithmic systems can therefore be understood as an extension of earlier graphic thinking shaped by mechanical reproduction technologies (Moran, 1971).

Consequently, the invention of the printing press should be understood not merely as a technological innovation but as a transformation in the relationship between visual form and knowledge organization. The visual order that emerged through printing technologies established new standards for structuring information and transmitting ideas. In this context, the printing revolution laid the conceptual foundations of a design epistemology that continues to shape graphic communication today, extending from early typographic systems to contemporary digital and algorithmic visual environments.

INDUSTRIALIZATION AND POSTMODERN GRAPHIC DESIGN

This section examines how graphic design evolved from the visual order established in Renaissance print culture into a modern discipline shaped by industrial production, modernist principles, and later by postmodern critique. Following the structural transformations introduced by printing technologies, the Renaissance initiated a period in which visual communication began to be organized through systematic aesthetic and intellectual principles. During this period, typography, page composition, and the relationship between text and image were reorganized according to ideals of proportion, clarity, and humanist scholarship. These developments laid the foundations for understanding graphic design as a structured visual practice rather than merely a decorative craft.

Renaissance humanism contributed significantly to the reorganization of visual culture. The rediscovery of classical Greek and Roman knowledge encouraged printers and scholars to rethink the visual architecture of books. In fifteenth-century Italy, printers began to design page layouts that combined classical typeforms with balanced spatial organization. Typography and page composition therefore became tools that structured the transmission of knowledge rather than simply containing it. In this context, graphic composition began to function as a strategic medium for organizing information and guiding intellectual interpretation (Ivins, 1953).

As print culture expanded throughout Europe, graphic layout increasingly influenced how knowledge was perceived and structured. Elements such as typographic hierarchy, margins, and the use of white space guided the reader's navigation of information and shaped the interpretation of texts. These visual decisions were not purely aesthetic; they also functioned as mechanisms that organized discourse and facilitated the circulation of knowledge within early modern societies (Burke, 2001). Through this transformation, graphic design gradually evolved from a physical carrier of text into an active component in the production of meaning.

The development of industrial production during the nineteenth century further transformed the function of graphic design. Mechanized printing technologies, mass production, and the growth of advertising industries expanded the reach of visual communication into everyday life. Posters, newspapers, packaging, and advertising materials introduced graphic design into public and commercial spaces. As a result, visual communication became closely intertwined with the economic and ideological structures of industrial society. Graphic design began to operate not only as a transmitter of information but also as a medium that reflected the values and cultural narratives embedded in consumer culture.

In the early twentieth century, modernist design movements emerged as a response to the communicative demands of industrial society. Modernist graphic design emphasized clarity, order, and functional efficiency. Geometric structures, typographic reduction, and systematic visual hierarchy became defining features of the modernist visual language. The Swiss Typography School exemplified this approach by organizing typography according to principles of rational structure and visual neutrality. Typefaces such as Helvetica became symbols of modernist ideals of clarity, objectivity, and universality within graphic communication (Eskilson, 2012).

Figure 4. Herbert Bayer's universal type experiment developed at Bauhaus

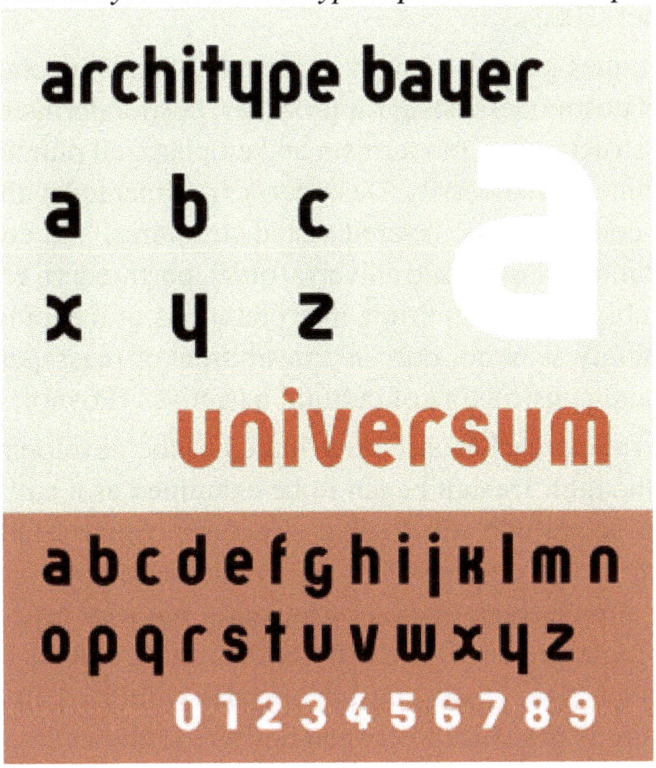

(Eskilson, 2012)

One of the most influential institutions shaping modern design was the Bauhaus School, founded in Germany in 1919. Bauhaus sought to integrate art, craft, and industrial production into a unified design philosophy. Typography, layout, and visual composition were treated as components of a rational visual system capable of organizing communication within modern society. Through its educational experiments and theoretical programs, Bauhaus played a decisive role in transforming graphic design into a modern institutional discipline grounded in functional and social principles.

Despite its significant influence, modernist design eventually faced criticism for its claims of universality and neutrality. Critics argued that the standardized visual language of modernism often suppressed cultural diversity and subjective expression. Within broader critiques of industrial modernity and mass culture, theorists began to question whether graphic design could truly function as a neutral medium of communication (Adorno & Horkheimer, 2002).

These critiques gained strength in the late twentieth century with the emergence of postmodern design approaches. Postmodernism rejected the rigid formal structures of modernism and emphasized plurality, interpretation, and contextual diversity. Designers experimented with fragmented typographic compositions, layered visual structures, and eclectic visual references. Rather than seeking universal order, postmodern graphic design embraced ambiguity and multiple interpretations of meaning. Designers were increasingly seen not only as transmitters of messages but also as interpreters and constructors of cultural narratives (Poynor, 2003).

Postmodern approaches also contributed to the development of critical graphic thought. Design began to be examined as a cultural practice embedded in social and ideological structures. Stuart Hall's encoding and decoding model demonstrates that visual communication does not operate as a simple transmission of meaning but as a process in which messages are interpreted within different cultural contexts (Hall, 1980). From this perspective, graphic design operates within a dialogical field in which meaning is negotiated between designers, audiences, and cultural frameworks.

As theoretical perspectives expanded, graphic design increasingly came to be understood as a cultural and ideological practice rather than merely a formal discipline. Victor Margolin emphasized that design should be evaluated in relation to its social, political, and ethical dimensions rather than being confined to aesthetic production alone (Margolin, 2002). Similarly, Johanna Drucker highlighted how design structures influence the interpretation of knowledge and shape visual discourse within cultural systems (Drucker, 2014).

Technological developments during the late twentieth century further transformed design practice. Desktop publishing technologies and personal computers expanded access to design production and enabled experimentation beyond traditional industrial environments. The introduction of the Macintosh computer in 1984 and the rapid development of digital design software allowed designers to produce work independently of large printing infrastructures. These changes contributed to the democratization of graphic design and opened new possibilities for experimental and critical practices (Blauvelt, 2011).

The gradual transition from print-based communication to digital media environments reshaped the structure of visual communication. Screen-based interfaces introduced interactive systems in which users actively participate in the creation and interpretation of visual content. Graphic design increasingly involves dynamic visual systems that integrate data, interaction, and user experience rather than static printed compositions (Galloway, 2004).

Within this historical trajectory, graphic design evolved from Renaissance print culture into a complex discipline shaped by industrial production, modernist rationality, and postmodern critique. The discipline increasingly moved beyond the organization of visual form toward the interpretation and construction of meaning within broader cultural and technological systems. Graphic design thus emerges not only as a visual practice but also as an intellectual framework through which societies organize knowledge, construct cultural identities, and negotiate the dynamics of communication.

DIGITALIZATION AND ARTIFICIAL INTELLIGENCE IN GRAPHIC DESIGN

Graphic design has historically functioned as a cultural practice through which societies construct visual meaning, transmit knowledge, and organize symbolic communication. From prehistoric visual narratives to the typographic systems developed after the invention of printing, the discipline has evolved alongside technological transformations that shape visual culture. In the contemporary era, digitalization and artificial intelligence have introduced a new phase in this historical trajectory. These developments have transformed not only the technical processes of visual production but also the epistemological foundations of graphic design. As a result, design is increasingly understood not merely as a visual communication practice but as a cultural and intellectual field that negotiates the relationship between technology, knowledge, and social responsibility.

The integration of artificial intelligence into graphic design has significantly reshaped the design process. AI-supported systems are now capable of generating visual alternatives, assisting in layout organization, and analyzing aesthetic patterns through data-driven processes. These capabilities reduce the time traditionally required for iterative experimentation and enable designers to explore multiple conceptual possibilities within a short period of time. However, this acceleration also reopens fundamental questions concerning originality, authorship, and creative responsibility. As AI systems increasingly participate in aesthetic decision-making, the designer's role shifts from a purely technical executor toward a figure who interprets, evaluates, and critically guides algorithmic outcomes (Cai & Jung, 2024). In this context, graphic design becomes a hybrid intellectual practice grounded in the interaction between human creativity and computational systems.

Figure 5. AI-generated visual composition produced using generative image systems such as DALL·E, Midjourney, and Adobe Firefly

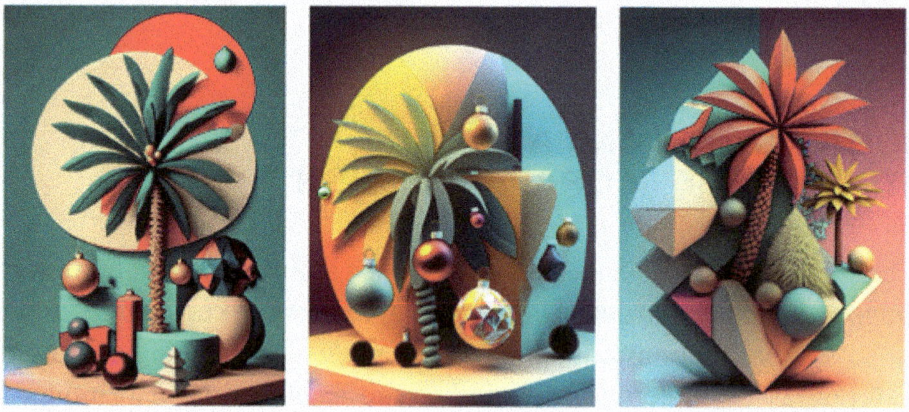

Digitalization has also transformed the pedagogical dimensions of graphic design. The increasing presence of generative design tools, text-to-image systems, and automated visual production platforms has redefined the competencies expected from designers. Contemporary design education emphasizes not only technical software proficiency but also visual literacy, critical interpretation, and conceptual thinking. Designers are increasingly required to function as visual strategists who organize meaning within complex technological environments. Consequently, the design process is no longer defined solely by the creation of a final visual product but also by stages such as conceptual research, contextual interpretation, and narrative construction. These transformations reposition graphic designers as interdisciplinary actors operating between technology, culture, and visual communication (Ametordzi & Olalere, 2024).

Artificial intelligence has also introduced an epistemological transformation in design processes. AI-supported systems structure creative production through modular operations such as data-driven planning, automated visual generation, and typographic organization. These systems make it possible to analyze and trace the design workflow in ways that were previously difficult to observe in traditional intuitive design practices. As a result, graphic design increasingly incorporates computational thinking into its creative structure. Rather than replacing human creativity, algorithmic systems introduce new forms of collaboration in which designers interpret and guide machine-generated possibilities (Zou et al., 2024).

The theoretical implications of this transformation can be understood within the broader history of media technologies. Media theorists have long argued that communication technologies reshape human perception and cultural production. Marshall McLuhan emphasized that each communication medium reorganizes the sensory and cognitive structures through which societies interpret reality. In the context of digital design, this perspective suggests that algorithmic systems not only facilitate visual production but also reshape how visual culture is perceived and experienced. Similarly, Vilém Flusser described contemporary visual culture as increasingly dominated by "technical images" produced through automated apparatuses rather than direct human gesture. From this perspective, AI-generated imagery can be interpreted as a continuation of the historical shift from manual visual production toward technologically mediated image systems.

The transformation of visual culture in digital environments has been further analyzed by Lev Manovich, who interprets contemporary media through concepts such as database logic, modularity, and algorithmic aesthetics. According to this perspective, digital images function as manipulable data structures rather than fixed visual objects. In graphic design, this shift is visible in generative design systems, adaptive interface structures, and data-driven visualizations. Visual communication increasingly operates within dynamic digital environments in which design elements are continuously modified, recombined, and personalized.

Despite these technological possibilities, the increasing presence of artificial intelligence also raises important ethical and cultural questions. Automated design systems often rely on large datasets composed of previously produced images. As a result, algorithmic production can reproduce dominant visual conventions and limit the diversity of aesthetic expression. Furthermore, the automation of design processes complicates questions related to authorship and intellectual ownership. As AI systems generate images through complex data correlations, the boundaries of creative responsibility become increasingly ambiguous (Meron, 2022).

The ethical dimension of artificial intelligence in design therefore extends beyond questions of efficiency or productivity. Designers must evaluate the cultural and social implications of algorithmic visual production, including issues related to representation, bias, and authorship. In this context, the role of the graphic designer expands beyond visual problem solving toward critical mediation between technological systems and cultural meaning. Designers increasingly function as curators of visual information who guide the interpretation of algorithmically generated content (Rodriguez, 2023).

Digital technologies have also transformed the material conditions of graphic design production. Since the widespread adoption of personal computers and desktop publishing systems in the late twentieth century, graphic design has shifted from specialized print studios to accessible digital environments. Software platforms and vector-based design tools allow designers to rapidly prototype ideas and experiment with multiple visual variations. This transformation has expanded participation in visual production while simultaneously increasing the complexity of visual communication environments (Lupton & Miller, 1996).

In digital media environments, graphic design is no longer confined to static printed surfaces. Instead, it operates within interactive systems that integrate motion, data visualization, and user interaction. Interfaces, mobile applications, and digital platforms transform visual communication into an experiential process shaped by user behavior and technological infrastructure. Consequently, contemporary graphic design must balance aesthetic composition with usability, information architecture, and cognitive accessibility.

Viewed within the broader historical trajectory of graphic design—from prehistoric visual communication to contemporary digital environments—artificial intelligence represents not merely a technological innovation but a transformation in how visual knowledge is produced and interpreted. Graphic design today operates within a complex network in which human creativity, algorithmic systems, and cultural meaning interact continuously. As digital technologies continue to evolve, the discipline increasingly functions as a field where aesthetic production, computational thinking, and ethical responsibility intersect.

CONCLUSION

Graphic design has historically functioned as one of the fundamental visual systems through which human societies organize knowledge, construct cultural memory, and communicate meaning. Rather than representing a purely aesthetic activity, design has evolved as a complex intellectual practice situated at the intersection of visual culture, technological infrastructures, and social communication. This study has approached graphic design not simply as a technical discipline but as a historical continuum that extends from the symbolic visual expressions of prehistoric societies to the algorithmic production environments of the contemporary digital age. Within this continuum, the development of visual communication reveals a gradual transformation in how images, symbols, and technological systems structure the production and transmission of knowledge.

The earliest stages of this transformation can be traced to the visual narratives found in prehistoric cave paintings such as those in Lascaux. These early visual inscriptions demonstrate that graphic expression initially functioned as a symbolic language through which communities organized collective experience and encoded cultural memory. With the emergence of writing systems, visual marks evolved into structured sign systems capable of preserving and transmitting knowledge across generations. The invention of writing therefore marked a crucial threshold in the history of graphic thinking, transforming visual representation into an organized system of symbolic communication.

The invention of the printing press introduced another decisive transformation by standardizing visual communication and enabling the large-scale dissemination of knowledge. Through the reproducibility of printed texts and images, graphic design began to operate within structured systems of typographic hierarchy, page composition, and visual order. These developments expanded access to information while simultaneously establishing the formal foundations of modern visual communication. Printing technologies reorganized the relationship between text, image, and knowledge, allowing graphic design to function as a systematic architecture through which information could be structured and circulated.

The institutionalization of graphic design during the modernist period further transformed the discipline into a rational and functional system of communication. Modernist design movements sought to develop universal visual languages capable of communicating efficiently within rapidly industrializing societies. However, the universalist claims of modernist visual order later became the subject of critique within postmodern design discourse. Postmodernism questioned the neutrality and universality of modernist design principles, emphasizing plurality, contextual interpretation, and cultural specificity in visual communication. Through these critiques, graphic design increasingly emerged as a field that not only produces visual forms but also reflects ideological structures and cultural narratives.

The emergence of digital technologies introduced a new phase in this historical trajectory by transforming both the production and distribution of visual communication. Digital environments replaced the fixed structures of print-based design with interactive systems, dynamic interfaces, and network-based communication models. In this context, graphic design began to operate within digital ecosystems where visual forms are constantly modified, circulated, and interpreted across global information networks. These technological transformations expanded the scope of design from static visual composition toward interactive and experience-oriented communication systems.

Artificial intelligence represents the most recent phase in this historical evolution of visual communication systems. AI-supported design tools have introduced new forms of visual production based on algorithmic generation, data-driven analysis, and computational creativity. While these systems increase the speed and diversity of visual production, they also raise important questions regarding originality, authorship, and ethical responsibility within design practice. As a result, the role of the graphic designer is undergoing a significant transformation. Rather than functioning solely as a producer of visual forms, the designer increasingly operates as a mediator who interprets algorithmic outputs, organizes visual information, and evaluates the cultural implications of technological systems.

From a broader perspective, the historical development of graphic design demonstrates that technological innovations rarely replace earlier visual systems entirely. Instead, each new technological stage reinterprets and reorganizes existing forms of visual communication. The symbolic imagery of prehistoric cave paintings, the structured sign systems of writing, the typographic order introduced by printing, and the rational visual frameworks of modern design all represent successive layers within the evolving architecture of visual knowledge. Artificial intelligence therefore should not be understood as a rupture in this historical trajectory but as a continuation of humanity's ongoing effort to structure meaning through visual systems.

Within contemporary digital culture, graphic design increasingly functions as an interdisciplinary mode of thinking that connects aesthetic production, technological infrastructures, and social meaning-making processes. The integration of artificial intelligence into design practice further expands this interdisciplinary dimension, requiring designers to engage not only with visual form but also with algorithmic logic, cultural interpretation, and ethical reflection. In this context, graphic design must be reconsidered not merely as a tool for visual representation but as a critical framework through which visual knowledge is produced, organized, and interpreted.

Consequently, the evolution of graphic design from the symbolic markings of Lascaux to the computational environments of artificial intelligence reflects a broader transformation in the epistemological foundations of visual communication. Throughout this historical process, design has continuously adapted to changing technological conditions while maintaining its role as a cultural system that structures meaning and organizes visual experience. In the age of artificial intelligence, this role becomes even more significant as designers navigate the complex relationship between human creativity and computational systems.

Ultimately, graphic design emerges not simply as a discipline concerned with visual form but as a cultural thinking practice that reflects humanity's evolving relationship with images, technology, and knowledge. Positioned at the intersection of aesthetic expression, technological innovation, and cultural interpretation, graphic design continues to shape how societies construct meaning, transmit information, and imagine the visual future.

REFERENCES

Adorno, T. W., & Horkheimer, M. (2002). *Dialectic of enlightenment*. Stanford University Press.

Albayrak, Z. (2016). *Yazının doğuşu ve ilk yazılı belgeler* [The emergence of writing and the first written documents]. İstanbul Üniversitesi Yayınları.

Ametordzi, S., & Olalere, F. E. (2024). The effect of digital technology on graphic design ideation output. *IDA: International Design and Art Journal*, *6*(1), 144–156.

Assmann, J. (2011). *Cultural memory and early civilization: Writing, remembrance, and political imagination*. Cambridge University Press. DOI: 10.1017/CBO9780511996306

Becer, E. (2015). *İletişim ve grafik tasarım* [Communication and graphic design]. Dost Kitabevi.

Blauvelt, A. (2011). *Graphic design: Now in production*. Walker Art Center.

Burke, P. (2001). *Eyewitnessing: The uses of images as historical evidence*. Cornell University Press.

Cai, L., & Jung, E. (2024). The impact of artificial intelligence on the graphic design job market: An analysis of the evolution and opportunities of the designer role. *Psychological Research*, *14*(8), 259–267.

Clottes, J. (2008). *Cave Art*. Phaidon Press.

Drucker, J. (2014). *Graphesis: Visual forms of knowledge production*. Harvard University Press.

Drucker, J., & McVarish, E. (2009). *Graphic design history: A critical guide*. Pearson Education.

Eskilson, S. J. (2012). *Graphic design: A new history*. Yale University Press.

Flusser, V. (2000). *Towards a Philosophy of Photography*. Reaktion Books.

Galloway, A. R. (2004). *Protocol: How control exists after decentralization*. MIT Press. DOI: 10.7551/mitpress/5658.001.0001

Geneste, J. M. (2017). *The Lascaux Cave Paintings: Meaning and Method*. Cahiers de l'Art Préhistorique.

Hall, S. (1980). Encoding/decoding. In Hall, S., Hobson, D., Lowe, A., & Willis, P. (Eds.), *Culture, media, language* (pp. 128–138). Routledge.

Ingold, T. (2007). *Lines: A brief history*. Routledge. DOI: 10.4324/9780203961155

Ivins, W. M. (1953). *Prints and visual communication*. Harvard University Press.

Jean, G., & Başer, S. (2008). *Yazının tarihi* [History of writing]. Dost Kitabevi.

Lupton, E., & Miller, J. A. (1996). *Design writing research: Writing on graphic design*. Phaidon.

Manovich, L. (2001). *The Language of New Media*. MIT Press.

Margolin, V. (2002). *The politics of the artificial: Essays on design and design studies*. University of Chicago Press. DOI: 10.7208/chicago/9780226518374.001.0001

McLuhan, M. (1964). *Understanding Media: The Extensions of Man*. McGraw-Hill.

Meggs, P. B., & Purvis, A. W. (2016). *Meggs' History of Graphic Design* (6th ed.). John Wiley & Sons.

Meron, Y. (2022). Graphic design and artificial intelligence: Interdisciplinary challenges for designers in the search for research collaboration. In Lockton, D., Lenzi, S., Hekkert, P., Oak, A., Sádaba, J., & Lloyd, P. (Eds.), *Proceedings of DRS2022 International Conference* (pp. 1–12). Design Research Society. DOI: 10.21606/drs.2022.157

Mirzoeff, N. (1999). *An Introduction to Visual Culture*. Routledge.

Moran, J. C. (1971). The development of the printing press. *Journal of the Royal Society of Arts*, *119*(5177), 281–293.

Mullen, L. (2008). Cave art and the origins of typography. *Visual Communication Quarterly*, *15*(1–2), 6–16. DOI: 10.1080/15551390801914546

Nomonov, B. (2022). Printing in Europe and the global spread of literacy. *European Studies Review, 34*(1), 88–102.

Poynor, R. (2003). *No more rules: Graphic design and postmodernism.* Yale University Press.

Rodriguez, C. (2023). AI in graphic design: Here to help or replace us? [Master's thesis, Liberty University]. Liberty University Institutional Repository.

Şan, E. (2024). Sanat felsefesinin hikayesi: Mağara resimlerinden dijital imajlara.

Schmandt-Besserat, D. (2014). *How writing came about.* University of Texas Press.

Siyanbola, A., Omolola, A., & Adeyemi, A. (2021). Visual communication in prehistoric societies. *International Journal of Anthropology, 13*(2), 45–58.

Uçar, E. (2004). *Görsel kültür ve iletişim* [Visual culture and communication]. İletişim Yayınları.

Zou, X., Zhang, W., & Zhao, N. (2024). From fragment to one piece: A survey on AI-driven graphic design. *Journal of LaTeX Class Files, 14*(8), 1–16.

ADDITIONAL READING

Bayazit, N. (2004). Investigating design: A review of forty years of design research. *Design Issues, 20*(1), 16–29. DOI: 10.1162/074793604772933739

Berry, D. M. (2011). *The philosophy of software: Code and mediation in the digital age.* Palgrave Macmillan. DOI: 10.1057/9780230306479

Bohm, D. (1996). *On creativity.* Routledge.

Bridle, J. (2018). *New dark age: Technology and the end of the future.* Verso.

Burdick, A., Drucker, J., Lunenfeld, P., Presner, T., & Schnapp, J. (2012). *Digital_humanities*. MIT Press. DOI: 10.7551/mitpress/9248.001.0001

Lister, M., Dovey, J., Giddings, S., Grant, I., & Kelly, K. (2009). *New media: A critical introduction* (2nd ed.). Routledge.

Lovink, G. (2011). *Networks without a cause: A critique of social media*. Polity Press.

Manzini, E. (2015). *Design, when everybody designs: An introduction to design for social innovation*. MIT Press. DOI: 10.7551/mitpress/9873.001.0001

Mitchell, W. J. (1995). *City of bits: Space, place, and the infobahn*. MIT Press. DOI: 10.7551/mitpress/1847.001.0001

Tribe, M., & Jana, R. (2009). *New media art*. Taschen.

KEY TERMS AND DEFINITIONS

Artificial Intelligence (AI): Intelligent systems capable of producing or assisting in visual creation, redefining authorship and design practice.

Design Thinking: A human-centered, creative approach to problem-solving within design, increasingly redefined by technological integration.

Digitalization: The transformation of design processes through digital technologies, reshaping tools, aesthetics, and modes of visual communication.

Graphic Design: The central creative discipline explored in the text, focusing on its evolution from prehistoric mark-making to AI-enhanced digital production.

Human–AI Interaction: The dynamic relationship between human designers and algorithmic agents in co-creating visual outcomes.

Lascaux: The symbolic and historical starting point of visual expression and semiotic design, representing the origins of graphic communication.

Posthuman Creativity: A theoretical lens on creative production beyond the human, involving hybrid processes between humans and machines.

Visual Epistemology: The concept of visual design as a mode of knowledge creation and intellectual inquiry.

Visual Semiotics: The study of how meaning is constructed through visual signs and symbols, essential in analyzing both historical and digital design.

Chapter 4
Digitalization in Art: Accessibility

Burcu Toğrul
http://orcid.org/0000-0003-1962-7543
Ağrı İbrahim Çeçen Üniversitesi, Turkey

Nurevşan Karaduman Başcı
http://orcid.org/0000-0002-6354-190X
Atatürk University, Turkey

ABSTRACT

This article explores the relationship between digitalization and accessibility in the art world. It highlights how digital technologies have transformed the creation, exhibition, and distribution of art, making it more globally accessible through online platforms. Digital tools like virtual reality and AI have expanded creative possibilities, while internet access allows people from diverse regions to engage with art. However, the digital divide still presents challenges to equal access. Overall, digitalization has made art more inclusive, innovative, and collaborative, reshaping how it is experienced and shared worldwide.

DOI: 10.4018/979-8-2600-0944-4.ch004

INTRODUCTION

Art is an original production field that reflects social values as a cultural form of expression and enables aesthetic and intellectual communication; at the same time, it produces meaning in a historical and sociological context by structuring the individual's emotions, thoughts, and imagination. In this context, art is not only an individual creation process but also plays an active role in the construction of collective memory and the shaping of cultural identity. Art is the form in which individuals and societies express their emotional, intellectual, and aesthetic experiences, holding an important place in the historical and cultural development of humanity. Art not only serves as a tool for aesthetic pleasure but also creates profound effects on a social, cultural, and individual level. The fact that art is accepted as a reflection of every stage of human history is an indication of its universal and timeless nature. Every work of art, while carrying traces of its own time and culture, also touches upon the universal themes of the human spirit.

The social function of art shows that it goes beyond merely expressing individual emotions. The common values, identities, and beliefs of societies are shaped and transmitted through art. Art ensures the transfer of a society's cultural memory and history from generation to generation through visual, auditory, or verbal means. In this sense, art is an important tool in the preservation of cultures and the strengthening of social belonging. At the same time, art also functions as a tool for social criticism; artists raise societal issues, injustices, and human rights violations in their works, paving the way for social change and transformation. In this sense, art continues its role in the historical process as the conscience of society and a tool for change.

Art is a fundamental cultural practice that feeds societal awareness and critical thinking, beyond merely developing individuals' aesthetic perceptions. By shedding light on the historical, political, and sociological processes of societies, it keeps the collective memory alive; it enhances empathy between individuals and creates a foundation for dialogue aimed at understanding differences. Art is a dynamic tool for both individual freedom of expression and social transformation.

The aesthetic value of art makes its place in human history even more meaningful. The aesthetic experience is not limited to visual or auditory perceptions; art carries intellectual and philosophical depth. Aesthetics includes the understanding of beauty, the human quest for meaning, and the efforts to explore the essence of life. Works of art offer the viewer different perspectives and enable them to develop their ability to question and think critically. Additionally, art theories allow for a more systematic examination of aesthetic thought and raise questions about the philosophical dimension of art. In addition to its aesthetic value, art's existence as a social language has the potential to create understanding and empathy between different cultures by affecting people on the same level.

Another topic is the economic value of art. Art, as an industry, is directly related to cultural production and consumption. The buying and selling of art works encompasses art markets, collecting, and the organization of artistic events. Art contributes to economic growth while also promoting local and global cultural tourism. The economic value of art is meaningful not only in material terms but also in terms of creating social capital and bringing communities together. Art-related events, festivals, and exhibitions create cultural revitalization and strengthen social bonds.

Art and Technology

Historically, art has existed as a reflection of social changes, cultural evolutions, and individual expression. However, in recent decades, a new and exciting era has begun, shaped not only by traditional forms of art but also by the technologies brought about by the digital age. This transformation has expanded the aesthetic values and creative boundaries of art, offering artists new forms of expression that were previously unimaginable. The impact of technology on art has radically transformed not only the tools of production and aesthetic perceptions but also the ways in which art is produced, shared, and experienced.

The concept of technology originates from the ancient Greek words "techne," meaning art or craft, and "logos," meaning the construction and continuation of the universe as a whole. Heidegger emphasizes that technology is a form of discovery and that every element that forms the potential for its emergence is dependent on humans; he highlights that humans have the power to manipulate technology, which is a tool (Eke & Yücel, 2023, p. 80).

First of all, digital art and computer-assisted production have gained significant ground in the art world. With the development of digital technologies and software, artists are now able to create works not only based on physical materials but also using digital tools such as software, graphic tablets, 3D modeling tools, and animation programs. These digital tools offer artists new creative freedoms and enable them to create aesthetic experiences beyond traditional art forms. For example, 3D printing technology allows artists to directly produce physical structures from digital environments in fields like sculpture and architecture, while disciplines such as video art and interactive media offer the opportunity for direct interaction with the audience.

The integration of technology into art has created a significant transformation not only in the production processes but also in the presentation and experience of artworks. New technologies such as virtual reality (VR) and augmented reality (AR) enable viewers to experience art in unprecedented ways. For example, through VR headsets, viewers can virtually walk through an art gallery and even interact with the works, discovering them from different angles. Similarly, with augmented reality (AR), viewers can see digital layers added to physical artworks, thus experiencing the work in an interactive and dynamic form. These technologies have created a new viewer experience in art galleries and museums, making the relationship between the artwork and the audience more participatory and dynamic.

The integration of technology into art has also deeply affected the relationship between the artist and the audience. Thanks to digital platforms, artists can quickly share their works on a global scale and reach a vast audience. For example, social media and art platforms such as Instagram and Behance offer artists the opportunity to exhibit, promote, and sell their works. These digital environments allow artists to create their communities independently of traditional gallery or museum systems. At the same time, digital artworks can be sold as unique and collectible pieces in the digital realm via NFT (Non-Fungible Token) technology, enabling artists to earn independent income and increasing the value of digital art.

The word "digital," derived from the Latin word "Digitus," meaning finger, is explained in the Turkish Language Institution and Oxford dictionaries as being numerical, or showing data electronically on a screen (Çakın, 2022, p. 46).

Digitalization in art refers to the medium and technique of the internet and technology. The first computer, ENIAC (Electronic Numerical Integrator and Computer), was invented by American scientists in 1946. Thus, it both shares and expands the conceptual infrastructure that defines contemporary art and integrates the data from social and mathematical sciences into the artistic process (Sağlamtimur, 2010, p. 218).

Although this form of art is very common today, its origins date back to the 1960s. In its early years, since it was incompatible with categories such as traditional painting, sculpture, drawing, and print, it was called Outsider Art. "For this reason, digital art has found itself in international institutions such as Ars Electronica, ISA, New York Digital Gallery, and ZKM, which are dedicated to promoting the potential features of this art and the new artistic style it offers, rather than traditional art, galleries, and exhibition halls. With the collective efforts of many scientists and artists, the American Art and Technology Experiments (EAT) organization was established in 1966 in New York. In 1968, two exhibitions were held: "Cybernetic Serendipity" curated by Jasia Reichardt at London's ICA and "The Machine as Seen at the End of the Mechanical Age" at the Museum of Modern Art (MoMA) in New York. These exhibitions represent a milestone in art history, marking the birth of Digital Art (Örs, 2022, pp. 3-4)."

Digitalization

The emergence of the internet has greatly changed the nature and scope of mass communication tools, known as traditional media (newspapers, radio, television). This new situation has been described by some experts as the "second media era" or the "second oral culture age." The distinctive feature of this new era, also referred to as the "digital media era," is the introduction of a series of surprising innovations in the creation and distribution of media content (Akgül, 2017, p. 204). Digitalization refers to a radical process that not only integrates technological tools into daily life but also transforms the ways individuals think, interact socially, and the logic of how institutions operate. In this context, digitalization should not be seen merely as a technological advancement but as a cultural rupture that reshapes the relationship between humans and their environment. Today, accessing information is no longer a privilege; it has become a necessity that shapes decisions rapidly, racing against time. As digital tools respond to this need, they position the individual as not just a consumer of information but even as a "data producer." The concept of digitalization has an important role in shaping the social fabric of our societies, alongside its connections with military, industrial, and entertainment complexes throughout history (Örs, 2022, p. 5).

Digitalization began with the process of converting analog data into digital form in parallel with the developments in information and communication technologies; over time, it has become a multi-dimensional paradigm that transforms societal structures and institutional operations, bringing not only technical changes but also socio-cultural, economic, and political reorganizations. As expressed in Castells' theory of "network societies," digitalization is preparing the ground for the construction of a new social order in the axis of the production, sharing, and management of information.

At the institutional level, digitalization is showing its effect across a wide spectrum, from governance practices to production processes, from human resources policies to customer relationship management. Technologies such as artificial intelligence, the Internet of Things, big data analytics, and cyber-physical systems, which are considered within the scope of Industry 4.0, enable businesses to maintain their competitive advantage sustainably. In this context, digitalization encourages the streamlining of organizational structures, the acceleration of decision-making processes, and the prominence of data-driven strategic planning.

However, when evaluating the process of digitalization in the context of critical theory, it should not be limited to a progressive discourse. Issues such as digital divide, algorithmic bias, data security breaches, and violations of digital privacy point to the potential of digitalization to produce inequality. Therefore, the processes of digital transformation need to be addressed from a multi-dimensional perspective, extending beyond the technological realm to include ethical, legal, and sociological aspects.

Indeed, digitalization should be viewed not only as a tool but also as a structural change process that reconstructs social power relations.

Moreover, the concepts that find their place in society through digital technology and the individuals living in that society have led to the emergence of social, cultural, and social definitions. Each new digital concept has become an intermediary that changes everyday practices and allows individuals to view the order they are in from a different perspective, with digitalization permeating from individuals to society, becoming the face of society that is seen from the outside. In fact, at the societal level, the distinct condition of a country's development today is equivalent to the society's relationship with technology. Countries that keep up with digitalization are considered developed or developing, while countries with limited access are seen as underdeveloped (Baloğlu, 2023, p. 1191).

Digitalization in Art

Artists no longer only use canvas, clay, or a notebook; they create works using tools like digital tablets, 3D modeling software, and artificial intelligence algorithms. For example, a painter can create digital paintings using applications like Procreate or Adobe Photoshop. Sculptors can turn their digital models into tangible objects using 3D printers. Composers can create orchestral compositions with digital sound libraries. In other words, production is both diversifying and accelerating.

Digitalization is also transforming how artworks are displayed and disseminated. Virtual museums (such as Google Arts & Culture) make artworks accessible to everyone from all over the world. Thanks to NFTs (Non-Fungible Tokens), artworks can be bought and sold in digital environments. With augmented reality (AR) and virtual reality (VR) applications, viewers can experience exhibitions without physically visiting them. This ensures that art becomes more inclusive, accessible, and global.

The foundations of digitalization in art go back to the mid-20th century when technological developments met artistic production. Especially from the 1960s, artists began using digital technologies in experimental areas like video art, computer-generated graphics, and electronic music. During this period, artists started to explore technology not only as a tool but also as an aesthetic element, and Nam June Paik's video art is one of the early examples of this transition. Therefore, digitalization should be regarded as part of the transition from the late period of modernism to postmodernism in art.

The first experiments in digital art began in the mid-1950s in the United States with industrial companies like Boeing and Bell Telephone Company and universities conducting computer studies; soon after, it spread to South America, Canada, Japan, and various European countries (Ak, 2013, p. 978). The first examples of digital art were created in 1950 by American artist Ben Laposky. By generating electronic images from waveforms, he created black-and-white optical effects, which are considered the beginning of the "Op-Art" movement. As a result of technological advancements, in 1968, the first "Computer Art Exhibition" was held in London, and thus, "Art Products" created in digital environments were recognized as "Works of Art" (Kızılaslan & İsmailoğlu, 2021, p. 108).

These digital tools not only provide speed and convenience but also radically change the artist's mode of expression. Art is no longer a singular work; it has become an ongoing process, an interaction. One of the greatest impacts of digitalization is seen in how art reaches the viewer. Speaking of virtual galleries and online exhibitions, especially after the pandemic, many museums and art galleries established digital exhibition infrastructures and began reaching audiences worldwide. Google Arts & Culture is a global example of this transformation. NFTs aim to solve the problem of authenticity and ownership of digital artworks. A digital artwork is made unique through blockchain technology and can be purchased. Beeple's digital collage, sold for $69 million, is one of the most striking examples in this field. Augmented Reality (AR) and Virtual Reality (VR) technologies are creating artistic experiences that take the viewer beyond physical space. For example, "The Night Cafe VR" application allows users to experience walking through Van Gogh's paintings.

This transformation not only makes art more democratic and accessible but also establishes a new relationship model between the viewer and the artwork. Digitalization in art is not just an instrumental convenience; it is a multi-layered process that redefines the ontology (what art is), epistemology (how it is understood), and aesthetics (how it is presented) of art. This transformation leads to the replacement of classical art paradigms with a more dynamic, participatory, and interdisciplinary structure. Art is no longer confined to the canvas or music sheet; it is created with data, algorithms, interaction, and even the viewer. The digitalization of art brings profound effects not only on the transformation of production tools but also on the presentation, circulation, and perception of art. The integration of digital technologies into art offers new opportunities and possibilities for both artists and viewers.

Figure 1.

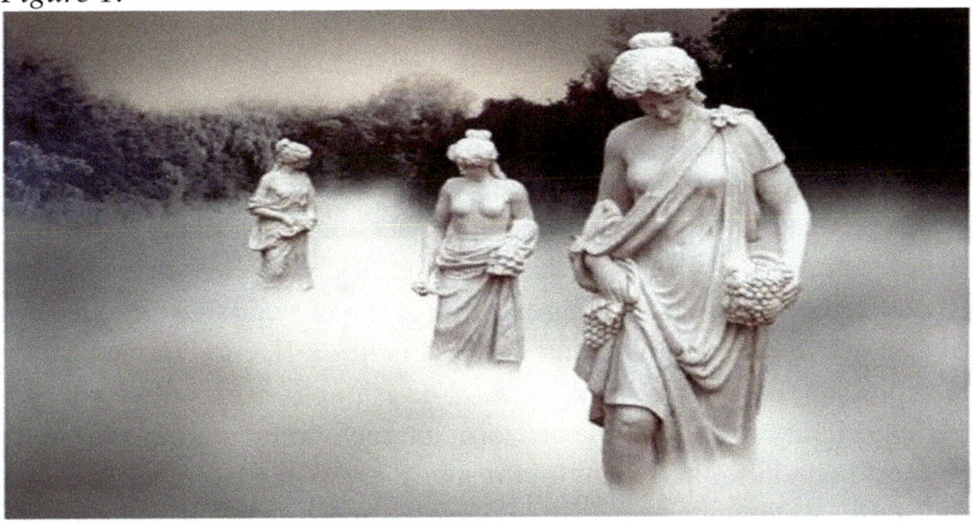

(Ak, 2013, p. 80)

SOME OF THE DIGITAL WORLD TECHNOLOGIES

1. VR (Virtual Reality)

Virtual reality (VR) allows technology to create a revolutionary transformation in the art world. It is defined as the merging of reality and imagination through constructs created by technology (Künüçen & Samur, 2021, p. 40). VR offers users an experience independent of reality in a completely digital environment, enabling them to experience art in an environment abstracted from the physical world. Artists have created a new form of expression and aesthetic understanding with VR technology, turning art into a personal experience where viewers can directly interact. Initially, virtual reality was a technique used in video games and films. Virtual reality headsets, visualization helmets, 3D screens, digital drawing pens, 3D sound speakers, data gloves, and position sensors are human-computer interfaces through which virtual sculptures are produced, combining art and technology (Solak, 2022, p. 372).

The place of VR technology in art is expanding the traditional understanding of art, taking it beyond just a visual perception level and involving the viewer inside a work of art. Traditional artworks offer a passive experience to the viewer, whereas VR art allows the viewer to actively participate and directly interact with the artwork, using visual, auditory, and sometimes tactile senses to experience the piece in a multi-dimensional way. This kind of experience enhances the viewer's perception of the artwork and makes the relationship with the work more personal. Especially in the field of interactive art, VR's impact has been significant. While in traditional artworks, the viewer's role is just to look at the piece, in VR art, viewers take an active role within the artwork. This is a reflection of new forms of expression used by modern artists. For example, artists offer viewers the opportunity to explore the artwork, interact with it, and transcend its physical boundaries in VR environments. Viewers can intervene in visual and auditory elements from different angles in the virtual world, altering the work or creating a new experience. This interactive experience turns art into a participatory experience and makes the viewer a part of the work. Another important area is the use of VR in art galleries and museums. Virtual reality allows the exhibition of artworks in different geographical locations and time periods through virtual tours and digital exhibitions in museums. Especially for individuals with physical limitations or art enthusiasts living in different geographies, VR enables access to art galleries and museums. VR is also used for the digital reconstruction and restoration of historical artworks. This provides viewers with the opportunity to see artworks that have been lost or damaged, especially in the preservation and restoration processes of artworks from the past. For artists, VR is a tool that transforms the creative process. It offers a platform where artists can showcase their creativity freely in a digital environment, stepping outside traditional artistic techniques.

Artists create virtual worlds in VR environments where viewers can enter and interact using digital 3D modeling and simulation technologies. This offers unlimited freedom to artists and provides them with an opportunity to transcend the boundaries of traditional art. Artists design their works not only in physical media but also in the digital world, adopting a form of creation that was previously impossible. Another important dimension of VR in art is the deeper sensory experience. Elements that are unseen in traditional artworks can be felt more impressively in VR environments in real-time.

2. AR (Augmented Reality)

Augmented reality (AR) continues to revolutionize art by merging digital technologies with the physical world. AR enriches the real world with digital elements, offering viewers a completely new experience. It changes the perception of existing reality by enhancing the virtual world created through the camera's captured images (Künüçen & Samur, 2021, p. 46). In the world of art, AR is a tool that allows viewers to see artworks physically present in a space while enriching this experience with digital elements. Thus, it provides artists with an opportunity to present their works in a more dynamic, interactive, and participatory way, while allowing viewers to approach art from a different perspective.

The most important innovation that AR brings to art is turning it into an interactive and participatory experience. While in traditional artworks, the viewer is a passive observer, with AR, viewers can interact directly with digital elements to experience art more deeply. For example, during a museum or gallery visit, when viewers look at an artwork with a smartphone or tablet, additional visuals, information, animations, or sounds can be presented to the viewer. These digital layers help viewers understand the piece more, explore its background, and better grasp the artist's intent. Thus, art becomes more than just an object, creating an interaction space between the viewer and the work.

The use of AR in art galleries and museums makes artworks more accessible to viewers and allows them to experience them in ways that would be impossible in traditional exhibitions. For example, thanks to AR technology, a digital version or interactive elements of a physical artwork can be created, and viewers can access these elements virtually, examining the piece in a more comprehensive way. An artwork displayed in a museum can be supplemented with animations showing the process of its creation or historical information through AR technology. This not only makes the artwork more meaningful but also increases the viewer's interest in art. For artists, AR technology offers a new form of expression in their creative processes. By combining digital elements from the virtual world with physical reality, AR allows artists to give their works a different dimension compared to traditional artworks. Especially in fields such as sculpture, painting, and installation art, AR provides artists with the freedom to enable their works to interact with the viewers. Artists can add different digital layers to their works, making them more layered and multi-dimensional. This allows for more innovative and unique creations, both aesthetically and artistically. The importance of AR in education and artistic experiences is also growing. Art students can use AR technologies to learn art in a more interactive way, experimenting with different art movements and techniques. For example, an art student can examine a famous painter's work live through AR technology, receiving digital cues and guidance on the artwork's creation process. In summary, AR technology is fundamentally transforming both the creation and the experience of art. Artists can use AR to add digital layers to their works, while viewers can approach art from different angles in an interactive way. The use of AR technology in art galleries and museums ensures that artworks are experienced by more people, making art more accessible. These developments transform art from a mere visual object into a dynamic and participatory experience that creates a deeper relationship with the viewer.

3. NFT Technologies

NFT (Non-Fungible Token) is a blockchain-based technology that validates the uniqueness and ownership of digital assets, which can be translated into Turkish as "değiştirilemez token." NFTs are tokens associated with a digital asset, each unique, and can be used to ensure ownership of a digital content like an artwork, music piece, video clip, game item, or other digital content. The most important feature of NFTs is that each token is unique and non-fungible; meaning every NFT has a specific identity number and represents an immutable record that verifies ownership in a digital environment. NFTs typically operate on blockchain technology, with platforms like Ethereum being commonly used infrastructures for the creation and trading of NFTs. Blockchain is a decentralized and secure digital ledger, where stored data can be used to verify and trade the ownership of digital assets. When an artwork, music piece, or in-game item is registered as an NFT, its identity information and the owner's details are stored on the blockchain, making ownership rights traceable for that asset. NFT technology has brought a significant revolution, especially in the field of digital art. In the traditional art world, the physical originality and ownership rights of artworks are usually monitored through art galleries and museums. However, since digital artworks are often copyable and reproducible, issues of originality and ownership arise. NFTs help digital artists solve this problem by providing a system that verifies the originality and ownership of their works in the digital environment. NFTs allow artists to trade their works in the digital space and guarantee collectors that these works are original and can only be owned by a specific person or group. When artists release their works as NFTs, the ownership, ownership history, and sales data are recorded on the blockchain with each transaction. This not only prevents the reproduction of artworks in digital environments but also ensures that the artist earns revenue with every sale (which can be in the form of royalties). NFTs offer several advantages for artists. First, they allow digital artworks to reach a wider audience. Artists can make NFTs available for sale on online platforms, allowing them to reach collectors and art enthusiasts worldwide. This reduces the dependency on physical galleries and facilitates the spread of art to a global market.

4. Artificial Intelligence

Artificial intelligence (AI) refers to the technologies and algorithms developed to replicate various aspects of human intelligence. This technology has the capacity to simulate the functions of the human brain, from complex data analysis and advanced learning mechanisms to visual and auditory perception, decision-making processes, language processing, and translation services (Gülpınar & Boyraz, 2024, p. 3). AI, at the intersection of art and technology, has led to significant transformations in many aspects of art production, evaluation, and exhibition in recent years. With capabilities such as data processing, pattern recognition, and algorithmic learning, AI is not only transforming creative processes in art but also opening new discussions about the meaning and forms of art. This technological development is reshaping the traditional understanding of art, expanding the boundaries of art production, questioning the identity of the artist, and transforming the relationship between the artwork and the viewer. Artificial intelligence can play a creative partner role in art production.

Through algorithms like Generative Adversarial Networks (GANs), AI can generate new and unique visual content by feeding on large datasets. These systems can mimic the forms of previous art movements or create entirely new aesthetic forms. For example, AI-generated paintings, photos, poems, or music compositions offer an "inhuman" form of art production, stepping outside the traditional creative process. Thus, AI becomes not only a technical tool for the artist but also a shaping part of artistic thought. Artists and curators use AI as both a production tool and a conceptual questioning object. Artworks created by AI often lead the viewer to think beyond aesthetic value, prompting reflection on concepts such as technology, intelligence, ethics, and creativity. In this context, AI art also feeds the critical aspect of contemporary art. Artists, due to the absence of consciousness and emotion in AI, are questioning whether this system can be considered a creative subject, how concepts like "originality" and "intention" in art should be redefined. Therefore, AI art is not only a technological experiment but also a field for philosophical inquiry. The integration of AI into exhibition practices is another aspect that transforms art. AI-supported algorithms can analyze viewers' behavior to provide personalized exhibition experiences, suggesting artworks based on the viewer's previous preferences or viewing time, creating a more interactive and individualized artistic journey. Additionally, in museums and digital platforms, AI can assist with content classification, curation suggestions, and artwork descriptions. Thus, AI becomes an active participant not only in the production of art but also in its distribution and presentation processes. However, the use of AI in art brings up ethical and aesthetic questions. Issues such as ownership, copyright, and artist identity of artworks created by AI are still not clearly defined. Who owns a piece created by an AI system? Is it the engineer who developed the software, the artist who used the algorithm, or can the artwork itself be considered a "creative subject"? These questions necessitate a reconsideration of the fundamental concepts related to the ontology of art. In conclusion, AI in art offers not only a tool but also a new form of narrative, creation, and inquiry. The use of AI in art enriches the interaction between human creativity and digital intelligence, going beyond automating the creative process. As AI takes on an even deeper role in art in the future, a radical transformation of aesthetic understandings, artist definitions, and viewer experiences is expected. This transformation opens new horizons in the relationship of art with both technology and humanity.

5. Vectorial Drawing

Vectorial drawing is the creation of graphics in a digital environment through mathematical expressions. In other words, it is a drawing based on formulas, points, and lines. In such drawings, images can be resized to any desired dimensions without experiencing pixelation issues when enlarged (Solak, 2022, p. 361). This type of drawing defines each shape not with fixed pixels but with values such as start and end points, direction, and ratio. In digital technology, vectorial drawing is a visualization method where graphics and visuals are defined through mathematical expressions instead of a pixel-based structure. In this method, drawings are created by defining basic geometric shapes like points, lines, curves, and polygons through mathematical formulas. The most important feature of vectorial graphics is that they are resolution-independent; therefore, they do not experience any quality loss when scaled to different sizes. This is because these graphics are based on continuously calculated coordinates rather than a fixed pixel structure. Additionally, vectorial drawings are indispensable in digital graphic design due to their generally low file sizes, object-based structures, ease of editing, and compatibility with various design applications. This method is widely used in areas such as logo design, typography, technical drawings, illustration, and infographics, and is carried out through software like Adobe Illustrator, CorelDRAW, and Inkscape. Vectorial drawings are saved in formats like .SVG, .AI, .EPS, and .PDF. Theoretically, this type of graphics is based on mathematical disciplines such as analytical geometry and linear algebra.

Digital illustrations created with programs like Adobe Illustrator, CorelDRAW, or Inkscape are entirely vector-based. In these types of drawings, since lines and shapes are mathematically defined, artists can easily alter color, size, or composition later. In logo designs, logos that exist at the intersection of art and graphic design are typically created as vector illustrations. For example, Nike's swoosh logo or the Apple logo can be used on any material and surface without distortion when enlarged because they are vector-based. Another example is geometric art (Vector Art), where minimalist or abstract digital artworks with flat surfaces, sharp lines, and abstract forms are created using vectorial drawing techniques. These types of works often utilize mathematical principles such as symmetry, repetition, and proportion. Looking at typography designs, special font designs, where art and text meet, are also drawn vectorially. Since the shape of each letter is defined by lines and curves, fonts remain clear at any size. Another example is infographics and data visualization art, where both aesthetic and informative graphics (icons, diagrams, shapes) are drawn vectorially, often used in scientific and cultural projects.

THE İMPORTANCE OF DIGITALIZATION İN ART

Digitalization in art is an important phenomenon that transforms various aspects, from the production of art to its presentation, from interaction with the audience to the economic value of art. The rapid adoption of digital technologies in the art world has increased the accessibility of art, introduced innovative methods to art production processes, and fundamentally changed the way audiences perceive art. The impact of digitalization on art is not limited to its physical exhibition in spaces; it also allows art to spread to the entire society, making art a more democratic and global phenomenon. The impact of digitalization on art is evident in various elements, from the techniques and tools used in production to the evaluation of works, from the expectations and aesthetic preferences of art consumers to the ways works are exhibited, and from ownership structures to intellectual property rights. Pigments have evolved into pixels, and pixels have evolved into processes. In the past, works produced to be exhibited behind closed doors for an elite group, with the allure of uniqueness, have been replaced by works displayed in virtual spaces where robots, AI-powered software, and even public-facing mechanisms produce the works in front of the crowd (Eke & Yücel, 2023, p. 79). One of the most significant contributions of digitalization in art is that it allows art to reach a broader audience. Traditional artworks are typically displayed in physical galleries and can only be seen by individuals who have access to these exhibitions. However, digitalization ensures that artworks are accessible over the internet. Through online galleries, virtual museums, and digital platforms, art can reach viewers worldwide, regardless of geographical limitations. Thus, art is no longer limited to spaces where it can only be exhibited physically, but can be experienced from anywhere and at any time on a global scale. Digitalization has also transformed the production process of art. Artists can now create their works using digital tools and software, moving beyond traditional methods. This not only allows artists to express their creativity in different ways, but also offers audiences more interactive and participatory experiences.

These interactive experiences deepen the viewer's connection with the art and transform them from passive observers to active participants in the creation process. Digitalization also creates significant opportunities in art education and training. The use of digital materials and online courses in various areas of art, from art history to production techniques, makes it possible to teach art to a broader audience. Digital art lessons, video tutorials, and interactive art programs offer individuals the opportunity to receive training whenever and wherever they want. Moreover, digital art platforms allow artists to create content that can also be used for educational and instructional purposes when presenting their works to audiences. Digital three-dimensional arts, such as sculpture, performance, video, and animation, are increasingly becoming hybridized, reaching multidimensional spatialities and volumetrics. Especially with the technologies of artificial intelligence and virtual reality, production is transforming into more collective consumption. This shows that the path for artists in the conventional post-digital age has been opened (Solak, 2022, p. 387). Digitalization in art creates great opportunities for both artists and art lovers, facilitating profound transformations in the production, sharing, and experiencing of art. Digitalization contributes to the globalization of art, increases its accessibility, enriches creative processes, and reshapes its economic value. In short, the current technological developments in the digital realm have expanded the number of new tools that artists wanting to produce within the context of digital art and contemporary art can incorporate into their creative practices (Wands, 2021, p. 215).

Digitalization of the Artwork

The digitalization of artworks has created a significant transformation in the production, presentation, and consumption processes of art. Digitalization has allowed artworks to transcend their existence as physical entities, making them accessible and interactive on digital platforms. This transformation provides numerous opportunities for both artists and audiences while expanding the social, cultural, and economic impact of art. Art, which evolves with changing technology, has contributed to the development of human production processes through various techniques (Ersöz & Askeroğlu, 2018, p. 410). First and foremost, digitalization of artworks significantly increases their accessibility. Traditional artworks are exhibited physically in galleries and museums and can only be seen by audiences who can access these exhibitions. However, when digital artworks are transferred to the internet, they overcome geographical and physical limitations and become accessible to people of all ages and backgrounds worldwide. For individuals who cannot visit art galleries or participate in such events due to financial reasons, digitalization greatly increases their access to art. For example, through online museums and virtual galleries, users can access and explore artworks and even discover the art of different cultures. This makes art a more democratic phenomenon, bringing it to a wider audience. The digitalization of artworks also transforms the production processes of art. Digital technologies offer artists great flexibility and innovative tools in their creative processes, allowing them to expand beyond the forms of expression previously limited by physical tools. Graphic design software, 3D modeling, video art, and animation techniques enable artists to express their artistic visions in new and dynamic forms. For example, digital paintings, animations, and interactive artworks allow viewers to actively engage with the piece and interact with it. This interactive structure turns the viewer from a passive observer into a part of the artwork. A digitized artwork is virtual, meaning it does not physically exist and is created by software. Therefore, digitalization creates a virtual representation of the physical art space, establishing the digital virtual space. Digitalization refers to the use of digital technologies and the integration of digital media into art (Vargün, 2023, p. 176). The digitalization of artworks also plays a critical role in preserving the historical value of art. Artworks stored in digital environments create an important cultural heritage for future generations. Digitalization reduces the risks of deterioration, damage, or loss over time by creating digital copies of traditional artworks. For example, old artworks can be digitally scanned and restored, making it possible to preserve historical works and study them in retrospect. Additionally, digital artworks form an important resource for documenting various phases and development processes of art. Digital art platforms provide a vast source of information for art education. Students can easily learn about the history of art, its techniques, and the works of artists through online platforms. Moreover, digital art software and tools offer artists the opportunity to learn new techniques and creative approaches. Online art lessons involve more people in learning art and facilitate education for individuals worldwide. Digitalization enhances the accessibility of art, contributes to its globalization, enriches creative freedom by expanding the artistic production process, reconfigures the economic value of art, and enables artists to secure their independence while preserving and transmitting art's historical and cultural heritage to the future. This transformation makes art more egalitarian and participatory, bringing it to a wider audience and strengthening its role in society.

Launched by the Google Cultural Institute in 2011, the project has digitized original paintings and objects by converting them into processable data (Ak, 2013, p. 176). In recent years, the changes created by digital technologies in the art field have reshaped not only the process of creation but also the way artworks are shared and viewed. Digital access makes it possible for art to reach a broader audience, increasing the global visibility of artworks. Museums and galleries can now exhibit their works on digital platforms, overcoming geographical limitations and reaching a global audience. Digital exhibitions and virtual galleries allow visitors to explore art without being confined to a physical space, enabling them to discover art from the comfort of their homes or other locations. This makes art more accessible, offering a universal experience that can be accessed from anywhere. The digitalization of art also creates an important societal transformation. Beyond traditional gallery spaces, artists can share their works globally through digital platforms and establish a direct connection with the audience. The greater reach of art has made it more accessible and provided artists with an independent space to exhibit and sell their works. These digital spaces offer artists an opportunity to present their works without relying on traditional art markets, while also enabling audiences to engage with art in a more interactive way. Social media and online galleries provide artists with the opportunity to promote their works and receive feedback, encouraging viewers to contribute to the works by commenting. Digital access has transformed the interaction between art and its audience, turning it into a more interactive experience. Augmented reality (AR) and virtual reality (VR) technologies allow viewers to not only look at artworks but also interact with them. Digital access supports the globalization of art and makes the relationship between art and its audience more dynamic, interactive, and participatory. This change allows more people to experience and interpret art, strengthening its social impact. In short, digital art is a form of contemporary art that uses digital environments and today's mass communication tools (Gülsoy, 2020, p. 221).

Digitalization in Art Examples

The process of digitalization in art is not limited to the use of technological tools in the production environment but also profoundly transforms the ontological status of the artwork, its mode of presentation, the relationship of consumption, and the interaction it establishes with the viewer. Beeple – Everydays: The First 5000 Days: This artwork is a digital collage created by digital artist Mike Winkelmann (Beeple), consisting of a combination of 5000 days of digital drawings. In 2021, it was sold for approximately 69.3 million dollars in NFT format at Christie's auction house. This situation shows the transfer of the paradigms of authenticity and ownership in art to the digital realm through blockchain technology. Here, digitalization emerges as a dynamic that redefines the immaterial form and economic circulation of the artwork. Walter Benjamin's concept of "technical reproducibility" can be used to explain how digital art is repositioned in the dilemma of authenticity (aura) and reproducibility in this artwork.

Figure 2. Mike Wilkenmann (Beeple), Everydays: The First 5000 Days

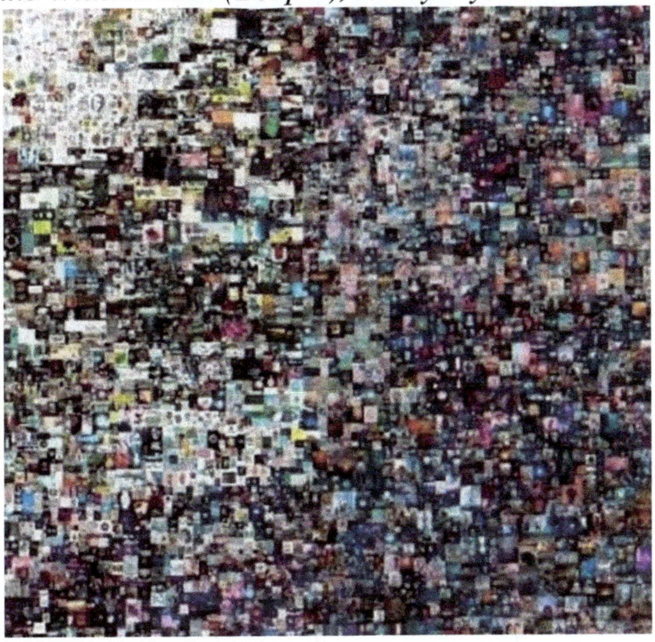

(Örs, 2022, p. 7)

Refik Anadol – Machine Hallucinations: Refik Anadol's works involve the transformation of large datasets into aesthetic outputs through artificial intelligence algorithms. Particularly in the installation titled Machine Hallucinations, "data dreams" derived from millions of visual data are transformed into abstract visual narratives. The artist's works bear traces of post-human aesthetics, algorithmic creativity, and digital consciousness in art.

Figure 3. Refik Anadol, Machine Hallucinations, Space,

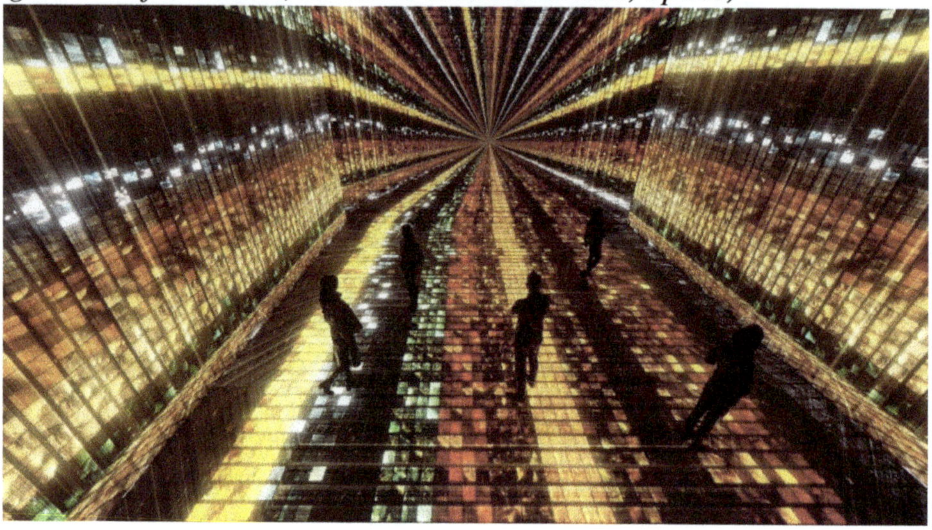

(https://kultur.istanbul/gorsel/2021/03/refik-anadol-Makine-Hatiralari-Uzay.jpg)

Google Arts and Culture - Virtual Museum Projects: Google's project provides free access to museums, art collections, and cultural heritage from around the world by transferring them into the digital realm. This development represents the transition of art from being tied to physical spaces to a new distribution model that is non-place and specific to the networked society. It also contributes to the more democratic circulation of cultural capital. The Night Cafe VR - Virtual Tour of Van Gogh's Paintings: By transferring Van Gogh's famous "Night Café" painting into a virtual reality environment, the viewer can almost physically enter the artwork. This application not only offers a visual but also a spatial and cognitive experience to the viewer; this example demonstrates the transformation of the viewer from a passive observer to an active experiencer and reveals the evolution of how art is consumed. (It can be viewed on the website https://store.steampowered.com). Digitalization in Art is not only a technical instrumentalization process but also a transformative one that deeply affects the production, distribution, and reception processes of art, restructuring it at cultural, epistemological, and economic levels. The works exemplified above show how art has evolved in the digital age, how it interacts with new technologies, and how it redefines its relationship with the viewer. This transformation generates new questions and possibilities in both art theory and art practice. In short, digitalization in art refers to the process of increasing accessibility, bringing art to a wider audience by enhancing accessibility in the production, presentation, and consumption processes of art. This process not only offers new forms of creation and expression for artists but also democratizes the opportunities for art lovers and communities to explore and experience art. With the digitalization of art, the works presented in digital environments become independent of physical spaces, and the accessibility of art becomes global, overcoming geographical, economic, physical, and cultural barriers. Digital platforms, online galleries, virtual museums, and augmented reality technologies play a major role in ensuring this accessibility. Digital art refers to artworks created using computers, software, and other digital technologies. This art form allows artists to produce works using digital tools rather than traditional media (painting, sculpture, photography, etc.). One of the most significant advantages of digital art is that the works can be accessed globally via the internet and digital platforms. Online galleries and virtual exhibitions make digital art accessible worldwide. Platforms such as Google Arts & Culture provide digitized artworks from the world's most prestigious museums and art collections. As a result, users can examine art pieces without leaving their homes, without time and space constraints.

Benefits Of Digitalization

Digitalization offers artists the opportunity to go beyond traditional techniques and develop more experimental and interdisciplinary forms of production. Thanks to digital tools, creative processes accelerate, reproducibility increases, and technical limitations are significantly reduced. For example, graphic design software, 3D modeling tools, or AI-powered art systems expand the artist's expressive possibilities, allowing them to create abstract and interactive forms that were previously impossible. This allows for the expansion of the aesthetic boundaries of art and the realization of creative potential.

Digital technologies have made it possible for artworks to be exhibited in digital environments, not limited by physical spaces, and reach millions of users simultaneously. Virtual museums, online exhibitions, and social media platforms bring art to a wider audience, increasing cultural participation. In this context, digitalization contributes to art evolving from an elitist structure to a more participatory and inclusive form. Moreover, digital works break down the barriers of geographical, economic, or physical limitations, making art globally accessible. Digitalization not only offers technical conveniences but also leads to a transformation in the ways art generates meaning. Digital technologies such as AI, data aesthetics, interactivity, and virtual reality offer artists new narrative techniques, turning the viewer from a passive observer into an active component of the artwork. This results in the reconfiguration of art not only as an aesthetic experience but also as a cognitive and emotional interaction. In this way, digitalization enhances the expressive power of art while enriching its epistemological dimension. Digitalization in art is not only a technical transformation process but also a multifaceted transformation area that includes ontological, epistemological, and sociological dimensions of art. The benefits, such as increased efficiency in production processes, democratization of access, and deepening meaning layers, show that digitalization is making art more inclusive, creative, and participatory. Therefore, digitalization should be considered an inevitable evolutionary necessity for art to sustain its existence in the contemporary world.

ACCESS FOR EVERYONE

Digitalization, while making art independent of physical barriers, enables it to reach larger audiences. Access to artworks and art experiences is no longer limited to physical museums; in the digital environment, art becomes accessible from anywhere, at any time. This democratizes art and provides equal access opportunities to everyone. For example, accessibility for low-income and disabled individuals is one of these opportunities. Being able to access digital artworks via the internet provides a significant advantage to individuals with economic or physical barriers to visiting museums, especially disabled individuals who cannot physically visit museums. In addition, low-income individuals or those living in remote areas can also access artworks through digital platforms. Another example is virtual museums and education. Virtual museums not only provide access to viewing art but also to art education and learning processes. Digitalized educational and teaching materials, such as online art courses, art history lessons, etc., can be made available to everyone, thus offering art not only to the art community but to a broader societal group, promoting an egalitarian approach in education. With digital art, the artwork itself can be created in the digital environment using technological means, as well as traditionally produced works can be exhibited through digital production methods, providing the opportunity to reach broader audiences (Ersöz & Askeroğlu, 2018, p. 412). Through these platforms, art can be discovered by previously hard-to-reach audiences. In online art communities, artists, art lovers, and critics can exchange ideas about art, participate in online exhibitions, and develop digital art products together. These platforms create a new space for creative collaborations and collective works for artists. In digitalization, art is democratically presented to previously hard-to-reach segments and geographical boundaries. Digitalization has increased accessibility to art in many ways, from the production of artworks to their presentation and the interaction with the audience. Furthermore, the opportunities provided by digital art are not just technical development but also represent an important transformation in cultural, social, and economic aspects. The future of digitalization points to a period in which art will become more interactive, participatory, and global. The societal access to art will not only be realized through digital platforms but also through the innovative experiences and opportunities these technologies provide. The importance of access to art ensures that art is experienced by not only a specific group but a wide audience. With the development of digitalization and technology, artworks can now transcend geographical borders and reach audiences worldwide. The accessibility of art increases people's interest in art and introduces them to different cultural perspectives. This strengthens the societal and cultural function of art while encouraging individuals to have different viewpoints. Access also greatly contributes to the preservation and conservation methods of artworks. Through digital archiving and online galleries, artworks can be stored without the risk of deterioration or damage over time and can be presented to a broad audience. This process plays an essential role in the preservation of historical artworks. Being able to access artworks digitally not only allows modern works but also transmits the cultural heritage of the past to the future. Additionally, digital access makes art a more interactive and participatory experience. Technologies such as augmented reality (AR) and virtual reality (VR) offer viewers the opportunity to engage more deeply with art. Through these technologies, viewers not only look at the artworks but also interact with them, creating a more personal and meaningful experience. Increased access not only brings art to a broader audience but also enhances viewers' attachment to art and contributes to the diversification of artistic production.

Access Issues

Despite the rapid advancement of technology and digitalization, there are still various challenges and obstacles. These challenges mainly arise from technological infrastructure shortcomings, economic barriers, cultural obstacles, and lack of digital literacy. These issues can hinder the widespread reach of art and deepen social inequalities. The primary obstacle is digital access and infrastructure issues. In many regions, especially rural areas and developing countries, internet access is insufficient. Inadequate infrastructure prevents individuals from benefiting from digital access to artworks. Furthermore, in areas with low internet speeds, attending online exhibitions or digital art galleries becomes difficult due to the loading of large file sizes and intermittent connections. This situation may limit the universal potential of digital art and hinder access for art lovers in low-income areas and developing regions. Economic barriers also represent a significant obstacle to art access. The production and presentation of digital art are often linked to specialized software, hardware, and technological infrastructure requirements. These types of equipment and software are not affordable for many artists and art lovers due to their high costs. Additionally, galleries and museums displaying artworks on digital platforms often charge for access, which restricts some groups' access to art. This situation prevents art from reaching a wider audience and makes art an area that only economically strong individuals or groups can access. Digital literacy deficiencies represent another important issue in accessing art. Digital art and online exhibitions often require a specific set of digital skills. This can lead to access problems when art lovers cannot effectively use technology. Especially older individuals, people with low education levels, and those newly entering the digital world may encounter difficulties accessing online art platforms. Digital literacy deficiencies may limit these individuals' participation in art and hinder achieving the goal of presenting art to a broader audience. Another issue is cultural and language barriers. Online art content is often presented in English, and art platforms with content in different languages are limited. Also, there may be a lack of knowledge or interest in digital art's understanding and value in some cultures. This is another factor preventing the global spread of digital art. Cultural differences and language barriers make it harder for art to become a universal experience. With the digitalization of artworks, issues related to authenticity and copyright also pose obstacles to access. Digital art can be easily copied and shared, increasing the risk of copyright violations for artists. Ensuring the protection and authenticity of artworks in digital environments is a major concern for both artists and art lovers. This situation poses an obstacle to the widespread reach of digital art to a broad audience

CONCLUSION

The digitalization of art has created a multifaceted evolution in the art world, fundamentally transforming the processes of artistic production, exhibition, and viewing. Digitalization has not only enabled artworks to reach wider audiences but has also reshaped the tools and methods used in the production of art. Digital platforms and virtual galleries have eliminated the geographical boundaries of art, allowing artworks to reach audiences independently of physical spaces. The exhibition of art in the digital environment now makes it possible for artworks, which once could only appeal to a specific elite group, to be presented at a level that is accessible to everyone. This process allows art to transform into a more democratic form and expands the audience base. With digitalization, the accessibility of artworks has not only overcome geographical barriers but has also made the artistic experience more participatory. Artworks can now be accessed via the internet, providing viewers with opportunities to gain in-depth knowledge about them and experience them interactively. As artists share their works on digital platforms, the societal and cultural functions of art are also taking on a different dimension. Artists, through digital media, can present their works to a global audience while also interacting directly with viewers. This situation allows artists to receive feedback about their works, paving the way for the creative process to become more dynamic and interactive.

Digital art has become a tool that strengthens the societal function of art by taking the relationship between the artist and the viewer to a deeper and more personal level. The new possibilities offered by technology are taking art beyond being just a visual experience. Digital technologies, such as virtual reality (VR) and augmented reality (AR), give viewers the opportunity not only to look at an artwork but also to enter it and interact with it. These types of interactive experiences allow art to be experienced in a depth that was previously impossible in traditional forms. These interactive and participatory experiences enable art to evolve from a static object into an experience where the viewer becomes an active part. At the same time, digital tools allow artists to explore their creative processes more freely. Digital media enable artists to create works across a broader spectrum of expression without being bound to traditional techniques. In this context, digital artworks push the boundaries of art both aesthetically and technically, diversifying the ways art is perceived. Another critical aspect of the digitalization of art is the preservation and archiving of artworks. Artworks stored in digital environments can be safely preserved without the risks of deterioration, damage, and loss encountered in physical spaces. Digital archiving plays an important role in the long-term preservation of artworks and their transmission to future generations. Additionally, digital artworks, through new technologies like blockchain, provide a more transparent and secure structure for issues such as authenticity and ownership. These digital security measures have made the trade and buying-selling processes of artworks more reliable. As a result, the value of digital artworks can be more clearly determined among collectors and audiences. In conclusion, the digitalization of art is a process that deepens the societal functions and cultural impacts of art, while also making artistic production and interaction with the audience more dynamic and interactive. Digital platforms allow artists to share their works on a global scale, while offering viewers the opportunity to experience art in a more participatory and liberated way. Digitalization has reshaped art not only as an aesthetic but also as a societal tool. This process transforms the ways art is created, shared, and preserved, while expanding its audience base. Digital art, by going beyond traditional concepts of art, is adapting to the dynamics of the contemporary world, becoming a universal language.

REFERENCES

Ak, H. (2013). *Dijital sanat.* XV. Akademik Bilişim Konferans Bildirileri (s. 978). Antalya: Akademik Bilişim 2013.

Akgül, M. (2017). *Dijitalleşme ve Din.* Marife -Dini Araştırmalar Dergisi, 17(2), 204.

Baloğlu, Ö. Ö. (2023). 6). *Teknolojik Bir Dönüşüm Olarak Dijitalleşme Kavramı ve Etkileri. Sosyal Bilimler Enstitüsü Dergisi, 13*(2), 1191.

Çakın, İ. (2022). *Dijital Sanat.* Çanakkale On Sekiz Mart Üniversitesi- Fen Edebiyat Fakültesi- Sanat Tarihi Anabilim Dalı-Lisans Bitirmr Projesi.

Eke, N. P., & Yücel, N. (2023). *Dijital Çağda Sanat ve Sanatçı: Ha: Ar Üzerine bir İnceleme.* Akademik Sanat(20), 79. DOI: 10.34189/asd.2023.20.006

Ersöz, S., & Askeroğlu, E. D. (2018). *Dijitalleşmenin Etkisinde Dönüşen Sanat ve Kuşaklar Üzerine Bir Çalışma.* İletişim Kuram ve Araştırma Dergisi(47).

Gülpınar, Ş., & Boyraz, B. (2024). *Sanatın Dijital Çağda Yeniden Tasarlanması: Yapay Zeka Perspektifinden Bir İnceleme.* Yıldız Sosyal Bilimler Enstitüsü Dergisi, 3.

Gülsoy, S. (2020). *Sanat ve Dijitalleşme.* Atatürk Üniversitesi Açık Öğretim Fakültesi.

Kızılaslan, N., & İsmailoğlu, D. K. (2021). *Teknolojinin ve Dijitalleşmenin Geleneksel Türk Sanatlarına Yansımaları.* Medeniyet Sanat- İMÜ Sanat Tasarım ve Mimarlık Fakültesi Dergisi, 7(1). DOI: 10.46641/medeniyet-sanat.930735

Künüçen, H. H., & Samur, S. (2021). *Dijital Çağın Gerçeklikleri: Sanal, Artırılmış, Karma ve Genişletilmiş Gerçeklikler Üzerine Bir Değerlendirme.* Yeni Medya Hakenli, uluslararası, e-Dergi(11), 40. doi:DOI: 10.34189/ymd.2021.11.003

Örs, M. (2022). *Dijital Sanatın Tarihi ve Güncel Sanat Eserlerine Yakından Bakış.* 1-2. İzmir, Türkiye.

Sağlamtimur, Z. (2010). *Dijital Sanat.* Anadolu Üniversitesi-Sosyal Bilimler dergisi, 218.

Solak, Ö. (2022, Aralık). *Dijital Sanatlar- Dijital Edebiyatlar.* Söylem Filoloji Dergisi(15), 387. doi:DOI: 10 29110/soylemdergi

Vargün, Ö. (2023). *Teknoloji ve Sanatın Dönüşümü: Dijital Sanat*. *Journal of Art, 6*(1), 176. DOI: 10.31566/arts.1968

WANDS, B. (2021). *Dijital Sanat sergi Küratörlüğünün 25 Yılı:1993-2018.* GSF Sanat Dergisi, 1-2.

Wands, B. (2021). *The Engagement of Digital Art With Contemporary Art.* Sanat ve İnsan, 215.

ADDITIONAL READING

Çelebi, F. (2023). *Dijital Dönüşüm ve Dijitalleşme.* Duvar Yayınları.

Gülpınar, Ş., & Boyraz, B. (2024). *Sanatın Dijital Çağda Yeniden Tanımlanması: Yapay Zekâ Perspektifinden Bir İnceleme.* Yıldız Sosyal Bilimler Enstitüsü Dergisi., DOI: 10.14744/ysbed.yildiz.edu.tr

Küçükosman, A., & Okkalı, İ. C. (2022). *Sanatta ve Müzelerde Dijital Dönüşüm.* Artuk Sanat ve Beşeri Bilimler Dergisi., DOI: 10.46372/arts.1198087

Özdoğan, N., & Yayan, G. H. (2024). *Görsel İletişim Tasarımında Dijital Sanat ve Örnekleri.* Kesit Akademi Dergisi., DOI: 10.29228/kesit.78072

Türkmenoğlu, H. (2014). *Teknoloji İle Sanat İlişkisi ve Bir Dijital Sanat Örneği Olarak Instagram.* Ulakbilge., DOI: 10.7816/ulakbilge-02-04-07

Türkyılmaz, S. (2024). *Dijital Dönüşüm: Tarihçesi, Tanımı ve İşletmeler Üzerindeki Etkisi.* DergiPark., DOI: 10.52122/nisantasisbd.1459265

Tüzün, M., & Abatay, D. (2022). *Dijital Sanatta Estetik Deneyim: Chris Milk.* Sosyal Bilimler Dergisi., DOI: 10.29228/SOBIDER.66460

Uğurlu, H. (2008). *Teknoloji Sanat İlişkisi: Günümüzde Teknolojik Sanatların Amacı*. Uşak Üniversitesi Sosyal Bilimler Dergisi.

KEY TERMS AND DEFINITIONS

Accessibility: It means being able to easily access, understand, and use digital content (such as websites, mobile applications, digital documents, etc.). This concept aims to ensure that digital services are equal and inclusive for everyone.

Art: Art is the effort to express human emotions, thoughts, and imagination in an aesthetic way. This expression can take various forms such as painting, music, literature, sculpture, and theater. Art is both a means of personal expression and a form of social communication.

Digital: Refers to electronic systems where information is processed using numerical data like 0s and 1s.

Digitalization: Digitalization is the process of converting information and processes from analog to digital format and managing them using digital technologies. This allows data to be processed, stored, and shared faster, easier, and more efficiently. Digitalization enables businesses and individuals to work more productively and brings innovations to many areas of life.

New Media Art: Art created with digital technologies such as video, AI, VR, and interactive installations. It integrates technological tools into the artistic process.

Technology: Technology is the application of scientific knowledge to meet human needs and solve problems. It includes the development of tools, machines, methods, and systems. Any technical invention or innovation that makes daily life easier is an example of technology.

Virtual Trip: A virtual trip is an activity that allows people to see and experience a place without physically going there, using digital technologies and the internet. It offers a realistic touring experience through tools like 360-degree videos, virtual reality (VR), and interactive maps. This way, people can explore different places without time or location limitations.

Chapter 5
Digital Art

Mustafa Bulat
http://orcid.org/0000-0002-2192-8508
Atatürk Üniversity, Turkey

Serap Bulat
Atatürk University, Turkey

ABSTRACT

In contemporary society, rapid advancements in information and communication technologies have significantly reshaped social structures and individual lifestyles. As access to information has become a key priority, digital technologies have transcended traditional boundaries of time and space, making knowledge globally available. The integration of computer technologies into everyday life has led to an information-driven transformation, influencing how people communicate, work, and learn.Digital technologies have not only revolutionized traditional art forms like painting, photography, and music but have also given rise to entirely new genres such as internet art, NFTs, and virtual reality. Digital art has developed its own theoretical and aesthetic foundations, challenging conventional ideas of the artist, artwork, and audience. Artists can now create, share, and preserve their works more efficiently using digital tools, reaching global audiences and redefining the artistic experience in the digital age.

DOI: 10.4018/979-8-2600-0944-4.ch005

INTRODUCTION

Art is as old as humankind itself. Art is a kind of creation; creation is an act unique to humans. By transforming nature, humans gain superiority over it, and the artwork becomes a transformation of nature (Bulat et al., 2014). As a being of reason and emotion, humankind has, from the beginning to the present, sustained its existence by bringing together daily life and art under one umbrella (Bulat, S., 1999). Artists, starting from natural forms, either transform or re-interpret nature while preserving its intrinsic essence, engaging in a kind of fictionalization process. In doing so, they have, in a sense, altered nature according to their own terms. In our era, artistic debates have intensified, and the social dimension of the artwork and the functionality of art have also begun to be questioned (Bulat-Bulat and Aydın, 2014).

The distinction between Modern Art and traditional works of art lies in the fact that the former reflects its most realistic and accurate aspects through freer, more enabling artistic values and harbors plastic richness within itself. Initially, there was a sense of astonishment toward modern artworks, which relied on perceptual tools such as color and style, and reflected the creator's personal life perspective and inner structure. Thereupon, reactions began to emerge against these presented attitudes (Bulat, M., 2007). The main dynamics that nourish works of art create a shared memory for each creative artist and establish a social and historical continuity (Şengünalp, C, 2019).

Science and technology, considered as a miracle of reason in human life, encompass the entire body of accumulated knowledge and practices used by humanity to change its surroundings. From ancient times to the present, as societies have continuously progressed, many past cultures have emerged; during this process, new inventions and ideas, along with significant technological advancements, have led to changes in the form, essence, and even aesthetic perceptions of artworks.

Technological developments have become an indispensable part of daily life and the social environment since the beginning of the 18th century. Many poets and philosophers have put forward ideas on the impact of advancing technology on social life, thereby contributing to the recognition of transformations in our universe brought about by technological developments. As one of these transformation fields, art has been influenced by technology in every phase—from the ideation process to the realm of creation, from exhibition spaces to varieties of experimental practices—and continues to be influenced. The act of exhibition without a physical gallery space, the idea that contemporary artworks embodying the concept of a museum can be presented in a virtual environment, has evolved into a digital medium in terms of accessibility. These phenomena make artworks accessible at all times and in all places, enabling the act of imagining and fictionalizing. To imagine the future of life without certainty is to see that when the relationship between art and technology is explored, a link is established between the past and the future. The development of form takes place through technology, and these advances progress with different understandings thanks to the relationships established between the past and the future. In this sense, disciplines such as painting, sculpture, and architecture, like ships navigating within life, participate in the vital adventure by recreating the universe within each obstacle they encounter along this adventurous journey, which contains its own unknowns.

Although these journeys into the unknown introduce complexity, the concept of "Cultural Memory," which the writer Kracauer refers to as "Existential Topography," constantly provides a source and a foundation for art audiences. The architectural discipline, which is part of these studies, represents an experimental flow by experiencing various intellectual channels (Boym, 2020). Through the continuous advancement of these interdisciplinary experimentations—such as literature, art, and philosophy—imaginative topographies are formed not as utopias but rather as examples for the future. In this sense, artworks do not merely copy nature; instead, they offer a depth in which the imagination can be advanced. All of our constructed imagination and accumulated knowledge create a non-existent time in addition to the existing temporal phenomena. Although it is considered functionless, aimless, and inadequate, the purpose of this formation is not to construct a future scenario but to establish an experimental connection. The interaction between technology and artwork has formed a foundation within the Russian Cosmic Art movement, which emerged in the early 20th century. According to Fedorov, who perceived humankind as the creative artist of the world we live in, the human being has laid the foundation for understanding the universe. This perspective is frequently encountered in contemporary space and science-fiction studies. Vladimir Tatlin's "Monument to the Third International" (1919–25), seen as aimless and functionless, enabled the convergence of technology and the discipline of art by presenting the power of image and experimentalism in an architectural context. With the rapid advancement of technological structures, materials and tools are continuously transformed; however, although the ideas behind them may change, these phenomena rely on specific foundations. In his monumental work "Monument to the Third International," Russian artist Vladimir Tatlin created a piece based on cultural accumulations from past periods, even though the materials changed. In the 21st century, similar phenomena are expressed through digital transfers. Even if the means and materials change in the fields of art and design, the bonds rooted in foundational infrastructure generally remain the same when dreams are constructed. In this sense, the conceptual approaches within the design and the artwork gain a new perspective. With the progression of technological developments and the innovation they bring, digital conceptual approaches emerge—particularly within social life—by establishing a new pathway, thereby opening up a new space for artworks. This phenomenon also creates functional possibilities such as increased creation and accessibility of digitalization in artworks. Contemporary artists have begun to create their works digitally, while algorithms have started to replace the role of the artist (Kayıhan, 2021:4). Through today's artworks, continual advancements are being made to understand and develop digital art. As technological developments progress, digital artworks diversify and evolve, resulting in contemporary digital art being produced in different environments of thought and exploration. Concepts such as algorithm, digital production, media, and artificial intelligence emerge from these phenomena and significantly broaden the conceptual framework. One such concept, "dataspace," is frequently utilized in the creation of digital artworks. Dataspace, by collecting data from a large number of objects, reproduces them and creates interconnections, thereby serving as a digital storage space. Beyond physical qualities such as color, style, and scale, it generates characteristics such as mapping, data memory, linkage, processing, and density, offering infinite combinatory possibilities (Imielinski and Goel, 1999). The recycling of data emerges from key points related to the referenced structure. Simultaneously, dataspaces are also used to solve existing problems by simplifying real data. Dataspace allows for machine learning, which is referred to as "Machine Learning." The concept of machine learning is a data component and continuously generates variance and growth (Atalay and Çekil, 2017). By using certain mathematical methods, such as algorithms, it presents these phenomena through classifications and predictions.

Therefore, it is able to evaluate the potential options that may arise. In digital creations, actions such as mapping data, making it efficient, enable the structuring of data, and the process of converting it into graphical form is also considered a significant advancement. Moving beyond the randomness and variability and subjectivity of the obtained data, it creates a new world by reaching very distant areas, including previously unknown or subsequently formed bodies of knowledge. This newly created world, described as a machine, presents an interaction that is functional, learnable due to learning, and experienced through digital means. Creators of digital artworks generally focus their work on dialogue (Atan, Uçan, and Bilsel, 2015). In today's life, with the increase in the use of social media, it has also significantly affected the visibility of digital artworks on social networks. The desire to produce new digital artworks simultaneously brings new perspectives to the forms of design creation. Therefore, revisiting previously created artworks and presenting new digital creations not only contributes to the perspective of new digital designs but also draws attention in social media fields due to communication networks. To explain this situation, we can give an example of the art approaches developed by Lev Manovich (2015) using algorithmic structures. With these approaches, color similarities in the works of many impressionist artists have been revisited by being presented in digital environments. The digitization of art, on the other hand, has brought about different discussions in terms of gaining a physical dimension. Author Hansen suggests that the immateriality of art has caused a different aesthetic understanding to emerge, and argues that digital artworks differ from other art practices not only because they are seen visually, but also because they are experienced (2004:22). Therefore, how the experiences of art perceivers in plastic art exhibitions are transformed by digital technologies is important. Through the "Art Project" created by the Google search engine, it has become possible to experience seventeen different art museums in digital environments with the work on "Digital Art" artworks. In this way, without making access to artworks in museums difficult, by bringing together art perceivers in an intangible virtual environment created in a digital virtual space, it provides great ease of access. During experimental examinations of digital technological art, it has been observed that by using a mobile "augmented reality" guide, art perceivers can tour exhibition spaces more freely in terms of process, and this duration has led to an increase in the viewer-space communication. This phenomenon is a result of the evolution of digital technology not only in art creation but also in terms of display and audience communication. Author A. Danto has revealed a new perspective by stating, "According to today's museum facilities, with an unlimited internet communication network, mankind has more interaction with the artwork" (1997/2014). Thus, digital artworks differ from other periods related to art by creating the concepts of "spacelessness and timelessness" provided by computer technological possibilities, and by eliminating the need for physical museum spaces. Author Danto argues that unlike the creative anxiety found in other art periods, in the field of digital art, there is more improvement, change, and communication with the audience, even without research (Yücel, 2012:26). With the great advancements in digital technologies, it has become possible for new working conditions to emerge. The development of new workspaces and the result of technological communications support fields such as "Media Art" (Avcı, Tuğal, 2018:261). The phenomenon of experiencing and creating the new provides rich support to the mindset of the creative artist. In this sense, the contribution of artistic creations on digital computer technologies has begun to gain importance. According to author Wands, "Artists of the future will never know a world without computers. Therefore, in their eyes, creating art with digital tools and environments will not be considered unusual at all" (Wands, 2006).

It seems quite difficult to definitively determine the specific actions, events, and phenomena that initiated the contribution of this technology in art. The contributions of technological phenomena to guiding artistic works are largely a structure of our contemporary age. Although it does not seem possible to set a limit to technological developments, it can be suggested that these first practical movements began in the fields of sculpture and architecture. Unless a limit is placed on the creative freedoms of artists, there is no benefit in opposing the fields they can or want to reach, and of course, technological developments (Bulat, S., 1999).

In today's era where technological progress is accelerating, the boundaries of art have expanded to an unprecedented degree; the communication between the artist and the viewer, the artwork and the space is evolving. In this sense, the intersection points of technology and art not only involve the processing of new tools but also emphasize the importance of reconsidering the philosophical, aesthetic, social, and socio-cultural functions of art.

Digital artworks are not only a technical innovation in the field of contemporary art but also a contemporary response to the fundamental problems of art's own nature. Questions such as "What is digital art?", "How is a digital artwork experienced?", or "Where do the boundaries of creativity begin and end in digital art?" are being continuously discussed in the context of digital sculpture. In this respect, the digital sculpture artwork should be seen not only as an aesthetic style but also as an expression of the ever-changing structure of technological contemporary culture, technological evolution, and technological contemporary art (Özselçuk, 2023).

Thanks to the collaborations emerging between technological research centers and artists, relationships with scientific disciplines from different fields have developed and accelerated. These collaborations between physicists, chemists, mathematicians, technicians, and creative artists have led to the emergence of artist-engineer and artist-chemist partnerships (Bulat, M., 2014).

With the adaptation and implementation of digital computer technologies into the art creation process, the integration of interactive media, "Augmented Reality" (AR), "Data Visualization", and "Artificial Intelligence" into artistic applications has rapidly increased. One of the most striking examples of this evolution is seen in the field of sculpture. The materiality that sculpture has historically possessed, its dialogue with form and space, has been revisited and presented through digital computer technologies. Through three-dimensional modeling software, algorithms, and digital fabrication techniques, a new aesthetic and plastic language of expression is also being constructed. This new plastic expression language not only transforms the creation styles of sculpture but also evolves its understanding, display conditions, and communication with the audience.

Processes related to the rapid evolution of technology have had significant effects on the modern human's worldview, lifestyle, and consciousness within their environment (Yağmur, Ö., 2018). Artistic practices naturally affect our worldview and adapt to new technological developments to create works of art.

Digital art is a term used in digital environments to describe artworks created through computer technologies. Digital art refers to a form of art creation with no clear boundaries, where computers, the internet, and other digital tools are considered by designer-artists as creative environments or mediums, describing an interdisciplinary situation. Although this discipline is generally referred to as digital art, it is also known by names such as "New Media Art," "Virtual Art," "Computer Art," and "Digital Media Arts" (Yücel, 2012). Digital art can also be defined as a new art form in which virtual objects created using digital computer technologies are constructed with aesthetic styles. The process of designing plastic forms on a digital screen using a new technical language mathematically formed by "0s and 1s," realized through graphical design programs or special software, and presented with artistic expressions and creations based on this existing infrastructure, is called digital art (Çizgen, 2007). With its characteristics of attraction, existence, and effectiveness, digital art leads the receiver to a different space—a non-real, virtual reality—and affects the entire thought structure, senses, and subconscious of the receiver (Arslan, 2018).

From the beginning of the 21st century, numerical programs that have begun to be employed in all fields of plastic arts, along with the output methods developed with these programs, have enabled the emergence of new possibilities in the field of sculpture as well (Bulat, M., Bulat, S., Aydın, A., 2014).

In 1834, Charles Babbage designed the "Analytical Engine," a manually operated mechanical device capable of performing automatic calculations, laying the foundation for many aspects of modern computers. In addition, notable advancements in the field of computing include the invention of Morse code and the telegraph, the emergence of the first keyboard initially designed for typewriters, and Alexander Graham Bell's groundbreaking invention of the telephone in 1876. Also, the invention of the Kodak camera and film roll by George Eastman in 1888 paved the way for George

Méliès to introduce the concept of animation through frame-by-frame shooting in 1895. These significant developments of the era demonstrate that it was a pioneering period where electronics, mechanics, and media came into existence (Wands, 2006).

Digital technological advancements have re-evaluated the traditional creation times of plastic arts, and beyond traditional and skill-based art approaches, they have successfully laid the foundation for philosophical and conceptual understandings. This period enabled art to develop more dynamic communications with space and time and led to the emergence of contemporary artistic expression styles (Coşkun, 2014). In this context, the relationship between plastic arts and digital technologies is addressed not merely as a change in tools, but as an energetic phenomenon that simultaneously affects the intellectual aspect of art in detail. In this sense, the ontological status of the artwork is directly connected to the creative act of the artist, and the social contribution of art becomes manifest in how personal creativity shapes itself in communication with the thought flows of cultural transmission. Author Gombrich (1992) also asserts that the artwork is an objective reality brought forth with the artist, highlighting the relationship between the personal creation process and the material representation of the artistic creation. The personal touches of the artist become one of the main elements that reveal the essence and style of the artwork, and this moment of creation is also considered in terms of cultural continuity and aesthetic evolution.

In connection with scientific developments, as the continuously emerging advancements and technological developments become a part of daily life, the concept that emerged in the early 1970s but began to exist as a new experimental research field with the advancement of internet technology at the beginning of the 1990s, is referred to in the new media literature with various names (Dilmen, 2007). These definitions not only attempt to overcome their own insufficiencies, but each also expresses the sociological, socio-cultural, political, and economic aspects of new media. Author Aytekin clarifies the matter with the following statement: "While some definitions related to new media (new communication environments) focus on a particular group of technologies, others agree that it should be explained as a process within the framework of traditional media" (2013). Within the scope of the study, new media is examined as both an era and as a cause and consequence of the transformation in the social structure and philosophical process that emerged from the beginning of the 21st century. In this context, its reflections on the field of art are addressed comparatively. Author Altunay defines this concept as: "All the contemporary digital communication tools and environments that emerged with the development of computer technologies, which allow for individual and mass communication needs to be realized instantly and in both directions, and enable individuals or institutions to stay online to manage different communication processes without any limitation of time or space" (2012). Author Özgül, while addressing the concept of new media, presents a comparative analysis with media from past periods, and through his studies in the fields of cinema and television, states that the technical advancements of our time aim to present a representation of reality, but even if they provide feedback to reality, they always produce a philosophically conditioned reality. Therefore, he argues, rather than having a reflective function, they are creative (2012). According to the author, the concept of new media "(...) creates a kind of simulation world in which even the reference to reality is disappearing" (Özgül, 2012). According to author Manovich, the existence of new media occurs with the transformation of the new reality created on television screens into data of digital computer technologies (2001). Manovich (2001:25) asserts that when graphics, shapes, sounds, colors, texts, moving images, and the spaces that encompass all these are transferred to the computer environment and each becomes a form of data (code), they transform into a reality independent of time and space, and thus, past media is replaced by new media understandings.

From the beginning of the 21st century, with the space- and time-independent characteristics of digital technologies, it is expressed that users and all people on a globalized planet who have access to these technologies can fragment, modify, direct, and integrate data created by these technologies into existing software to produce infinite new realities according to their own demands. In relation to the subject, author Altunay states: "It is a representational surface of a cultural form developed for a generation that can cut and copy everything and undo all operations when necessary" (Altunay, 2013). This experienced cultural form is not a narrative language of interaction advanced in a particular time within certain conditions, but an expression of the possibilities achieved through technological and scientific progress, which constantly makes leaps forward in accordance with the conditions of existence of life.

Investigating the new interactive state and the new mode of thinking of the 21st century—referred to as the mobilistic perspective—and its "slippery ground phenomenon" through digital technology-centered approaches and the "new screen concept," author Altunay clarifies the subject with the following statement: "While using the new screen concept, one must also accept the change and transformation of the corresponding technical possibilities. The concept of new can only exist until it becomes old" (2013). Comparing the concept of new media art with traditional media, and stating that at the core of this type of media lies the visual mode of perception in which the notion of perspective is found, author Rosen argues: "The principle of arranging the objects seen in perspective in reference to a fixed point enables the determination of the position of the subject, and a frame created with perspective presents a continuous and motionless whole, thereby producing the view of the completeness and homogeneity of existence" (Özgül, 2012).

These approaches constitute some of the most effective descriptions that succinctly elucidate the position of the individual situated before televisions. According to Özgül, who describes how older media receivers were brought into such a subject-object position, "Perspective, while simultaneously maintaining the viewer in a central position, dictates how and what they should see, imposing a single predetermined viewpoint" (2012). Çakır's articulation aligns with the notion that "as Nietzsche stated, media, which transforms the world into a 'tale,' erodes the sense of 'reality' while simultaneously diminishing human speech and thought capabilities with the infinite number of words and images it presents" (Akay, 1996). From the second half of the 20th century onward, the Pop Art movement, which emerged as a reaction against the consumer society structure, utilized everything to its own benefit, creating a causality of symbolization that also originated from these phenomena, as described in discussions of "New Media," "Fundamental Components," "The Changing Aesthetic Language of Art," and the "Journal of Communication Theory and Research." In the works created by Pop Art practitioners, figurative structures, by incorporating popular culture images into collage compositions, are centrally arranged within the formal design of the arrangement, while simultaneously becoming entities among the thousands of images surrounding them. However, design works created after the 1970s inverted the subject's state of being, erupting beyond the constrained surface of the two-dimensional structure and establishing a new state of being. In the 1990s, the internet and new media technologies moved the subject to a different position, while artistic works gained an interactive appearance, and computer-aided technologies pioneered a new, fluid reality. From this perspective, new media art and art itself expanded into various homogenous categories, including "Multimedia Art," "Digital Art," "Internet Art," "Interactive Art," and "New Media Art." These classification approaches have revealed and utilized different facets of media. When examining the reflections of contemporary humanity's computer-driven shaping perspectives on works of art, defining each of these desires and investigating the existing tendencies concerning the artwork and its creator are crucial for the scope of this study.

From this viewpoint, multimedia art (multimedia art) is prioritized as it positions itself between the traditional and the innovative, elucidating works created by employing the characteristics of both media types. Digital Art (Digital Art) exclusively reflects artworks created in a computer environment and rendered into visual reality via numerical codes. Kutup defines Internet Art (Net Art) as "any kind of art or cultural activity or event produced by accepting the Internet as the primary medium. At times, it is also an art concept that makes the medium it uses to perform this operation, namely the internet, an end in itself" (Kutup, 2010). Interactive Art (Interactive Art) encompasses artworks that utilize both traditional and new media, completed through communication between the artist and the receiver. New Media Art (New Media Art), resulting from technological advancements, can be explained as the general form of expression for these shaping perspectives. Consequently, rather than emphasizing these distinct art styles separately and demonstrating their individual visual existences, the primary verification of this study is the pervasive influence of "New Media Art" on a transforming aesthetic language of expression as a whole. The fundamental support for this determination is Manovich's view that the innovative methods created in the plastic arts in the 1920s transformed into computer interfaces and digital visuals in contemporary modernist communities. From this perspective, the present research compares how technology-driven advancement and transformation permeated the field of plastic arts throughout the twentieth century, in which direction it evolved, and which fundamental principles and visual inherent abilities it ultimately possessed, through the analyzed exemplary works. When Manovich's definitions of new media are examined, five fundamental principles emerge: "Numerical Representation," "Modularity," "Automation," "Variability," and "Transcoding" (Aytekin, 2013).

These systems describe the transformation of images into software on computer screens, their proliferation as countless screen images, their becoming mechanically independent of humanity for a period, and the plastic language of interaction between the individual and the computer environment. Manovich, in explaining these unique differences, interrogates the realities he put forth as the main principles of new media based on digital technologies, drawing from disciplines such as visual atomism, montage, typography, and photography in his works, during the periods of two major evolutions in the fields of plastic arts and cinema (E.Tokdil, 2018). In this context, the conducted investigations and research embody the characteristic of re-examination and aim for the materialization of the fundamental structures underlying digital art, in connection with the digital technologies created by contemporary communities.

Artists have historically held a privileged position within the social structure and played a definitive role in the communication between periods of art creation and social movements. Artistic creation practices, dependent on individual creativity, stand out as one of the essential elements distinguishing them from traditional and anonymous cultural formations. While the artwork, as an objective phenomenon, is shaped within specific aesthetic, technical, and intellectual frameworks, it is also formed in accordance with the individual initiatives and intellectual orientations of the artist, who is the subject of the creative process (Toptaş, R., 2022).

Artworks, beyond their aesthetic and intellectual value, have evolved into economic commodities, fostering the emergence of artistic circulation systems. This inherent interaction between creation and consumption establishes a critical framework for understanding art's position within free market conditions and the institutional structures that determine the value of an artwork. From this perspective, the connection between art and economy should be considered not merely as a period of material value generation, but simultaneously as a system that shapes cultural capital (Uğurlu, 2008).

The proliferation of digital plastic arts has gained momentum with the development of technology and the increased accessibility of personal computer technologies. From the 1980s and 1990s onward, while the creation and circulation systems of digital artworks shaped a concerning process, this period also led to a fundamental evolution in the ontology, status, and creation periods of art. Generally, with the existence of internet technologies and the development of technological digital imaging systems, artworks have been enabled to exist in digital environments, separate from physical representation. Consequently, the conceptual and aesthetic framework structure of digital artworks has been re-evaluated and restructured (Toptaş, 2022).

The initial infrastructures of the Digital Era began in 1946 with the invention of **ENIAC**, the first electronic digital identifier, at the University of Pennsylvania in America. In 1960, advancements in computer technology, spurred by American NASA space programs, led to significant developments among contemporary artists. During this period, artists Ken Knowlton and Leon Harmon created "Study in Perception," a pioneering artwork featuring compositions of a reclining nude figure. This creative and groundbreaking work was considered a seminal piece in the field of art created with computer technologies (Visual 1).

Figure 1. Ken Knowlton & Leon Harmon,"Uzanmış Çıplak Figür" & "Study in Perceptıon", Computer-Aided Digital Printing 1966.

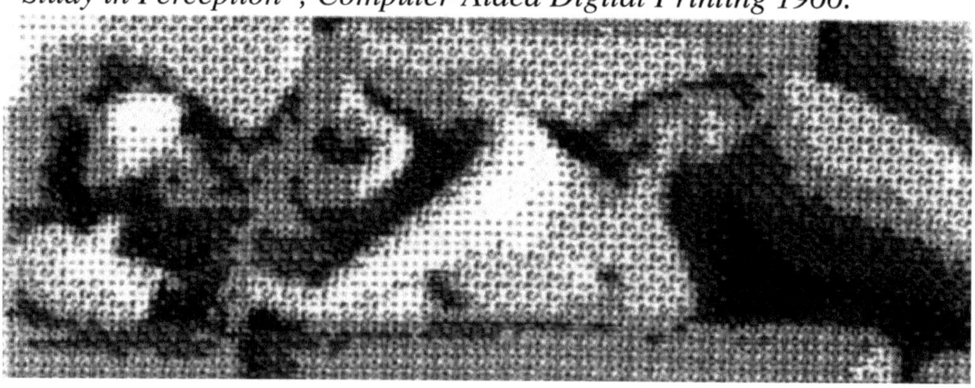

Technological societies have continually striven to adapt to the rapid, dynamic changes catalyzed by the Industrial Revolution, the Electronic Revolution, and the ongoing Digital Revolution. The advent of the rapid Electronic Revolution in our era propelled mass communication tools to new dimensions, extending their influence across the global sphere. Concurrently, in today's digital age, computer technologies have evolved into a new phase with the widespread use of the internet, acquiring a unique dynamism that surpasses traditional electronic mass media.

From 1960 onward, computer technologies began to be extensively utilized in the creation of artworks. The digital art endeavors of artists such as Charles Csuri, John Whitney, and Vera Molnar, who employed these computer technologies, continue to exert influence today, particularly through their examination of computer-designed creations via mathematical functions (Paul, 2003).

Figure 2. Charles Csuri, Hummingbird, Çemberde 22 Kuş, 1967.

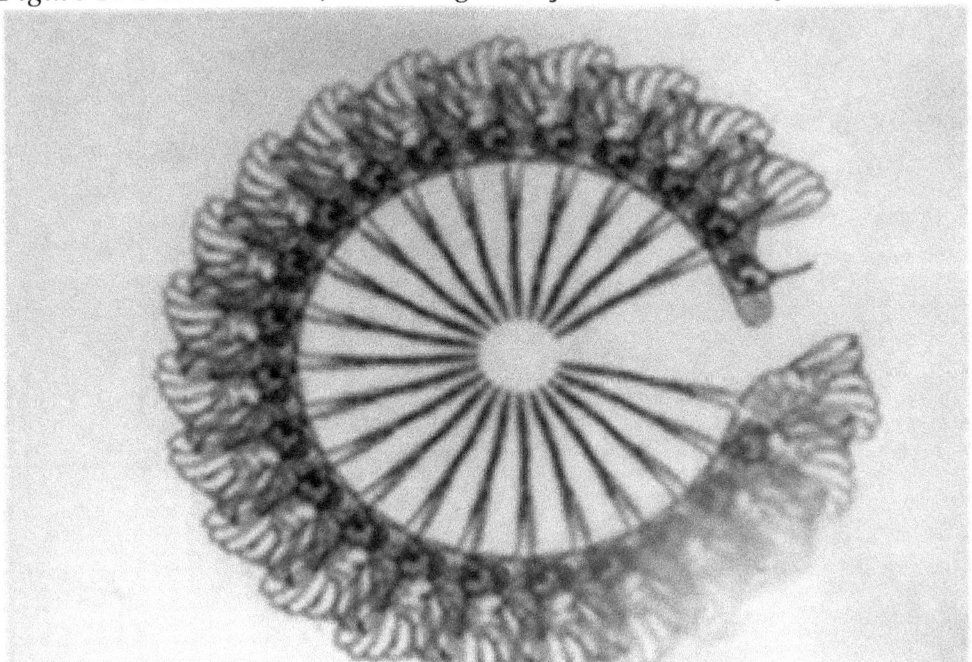

Digital Art is a virtual art form where artists create images of their ideas using computer technologies. The genesis of artist Ruane Miller's digital artwork titled "Blue Door" began with a photograph taken by the artist themselves. Subsequently, it was re-conceptualized and transformed through digital paint manipulations and compositional methods applied in a digital environment using Photoshop, a computer technology program (Rathus, 2013) (Visual 3).

Figure 3. Ruane Miller. Blue Door

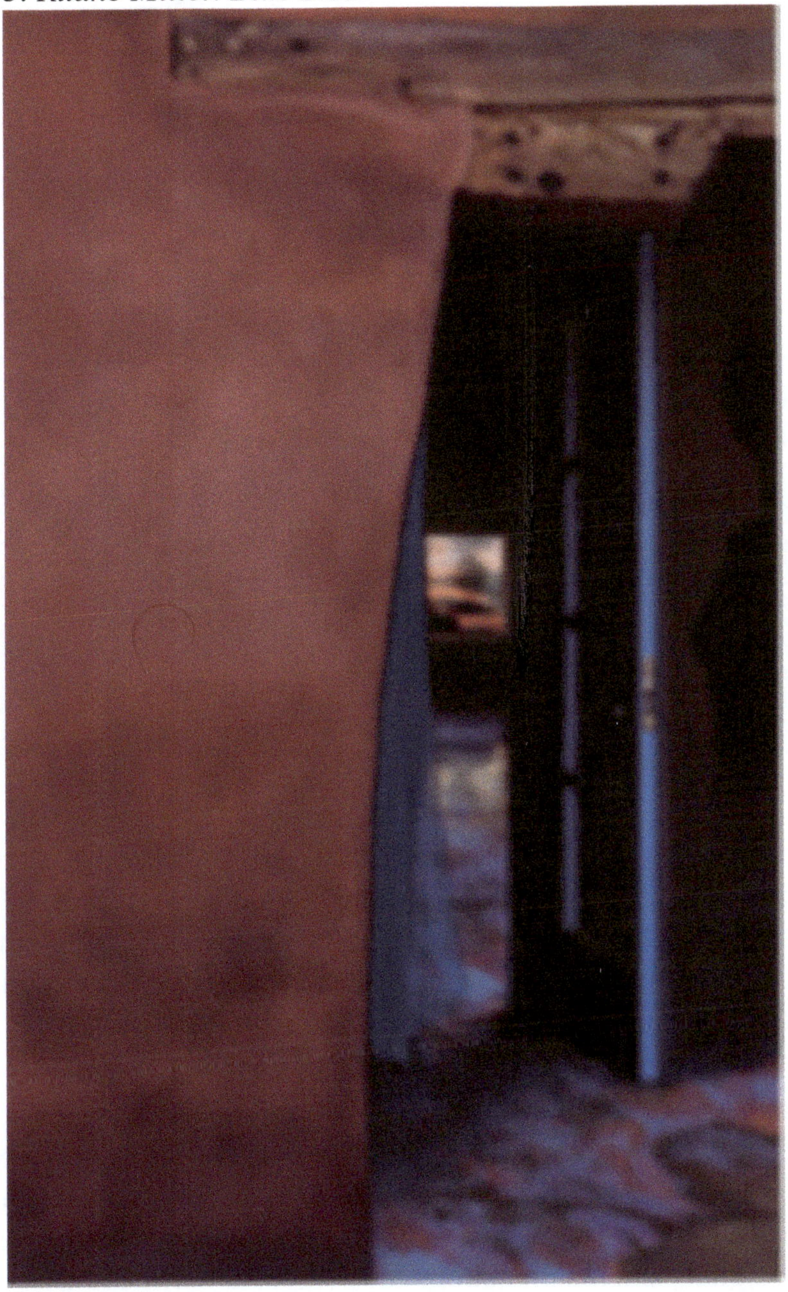

Some digital artists utilize graphical digital tablets for designing, painting, drawing, and sketching with computer technologies, while other artists produce hybrid paintings by applying digital elements to traditionally created artworks.

Figure 4. Viktor Koen, "Damsel no.6 ve damsel no. 15, damsels in armor serisinden", 2002.

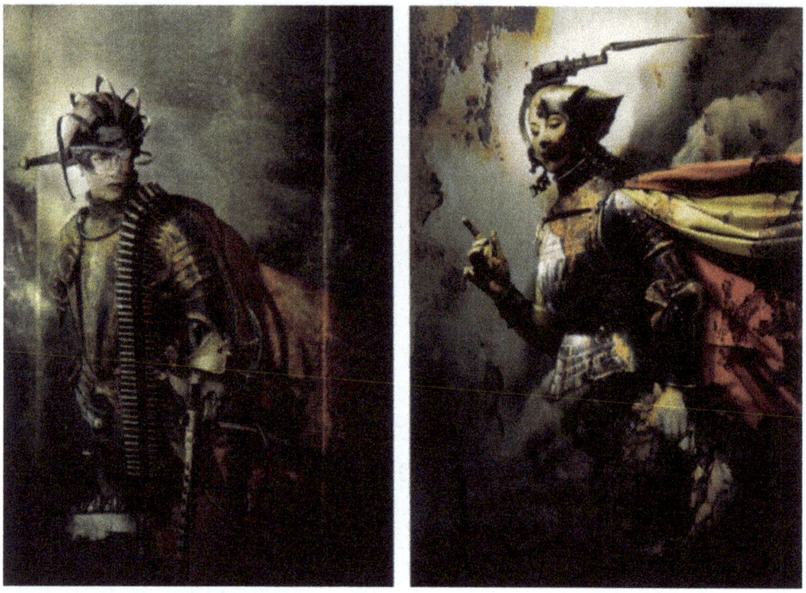

From 1960 onward, computer technologies began to be extensively utilized in the creation of artworks. The digital art endeavors of artists such as Charles Csuri, John Whitney, and Vera Molnar, who employed these computer technologies, continue to exert influence today, particularly through their examination of computer-designed creations via mathematical functions (Paul, 2003).

Digital Art is a virtual art form where artists create images of their ideas using computer technologies. The genesis of artist Ruane Miller's digital artwork titled "Blue Door" began with a photograph taken by the artist themselves. Subsequently, it was re-conceptualized and transformed through digital paint manipulations and compositional methods applied in a digital environment using Photoshop, a computer technology program (Rathus, 2013) (Visual 3).

Some digital artists utilize graphical digital tablets for designing, painting, drawing, and sketching with computer technologies, while other artists produce hybrid paintings by applying digital elements to traditionally created artworks.

When examining the works of digital artist Viktor Koen, we are compelled to mentally re-imagine the scenes we observe in his paintings. Although these works are produced through the most modern computer technology tools, their impact on receivers still evokes the sensation of works from past centuries. These digitally created artworks, by leveraging the aspects of technology that demand creativity and mastery, also reveal the destructive and brutal facets of war (Wands, 2006).

Art, defined as the sum of methods employed in the expression of an emotion, a design, or beauty, and the superior creativity that emerges at the end of such expression, has evolved and continuously progressed over a period of thousands of years to the present day. The history of art, which has witnessed many art movements, has entered a new era in the 21st-century information age with digital artworks, in alignment with the developmental characteristics and technology of the information society.

Computer technologies not only facilitate collage creation with found or scanned photographs, texts, sound, or digital video recordings, but also present possibilities for artistic utilization with images, motion-animations, and sounds that can only be created through computer technologies. For these reasons, it can be asserted that art is made possible through the use of computer technologies. With the advent of the World Wide Web (WWW), the widespread adoption of computer technologies and internet environments has opened up technological possibilities to all humanity, providing contemporary artists with new means of expression. Digital art, in a general sense, refers to art forms that come into existence through the creation of non-physical art objects, where computer technologies play significant roles in their production. In today's technological age, these digital technologies, which have a growing demand in relation to Graphic Arts, generally provide all designers with areas where they can express their imagination and talents throughout the entirety of plastic arts-related fields, including our design drawings, utopian projects, and even traditional painting, developed in line with information technology with advanced design programs.

Digital illustration, in turn, can be considered a digital output where prints are made onto canvas via software in computer environments. Computer technologies are the sole indispensable tool for creating digital artworks. Beyond these structures, creativity and imagination, a proficient use of computer programs, and knowledge of the hardware (Mac computer, Wacom tablet, 5D camera, flash units for lighting, and programs like Photoshop-Corel, etc.) necessary for digital art creation are essential. It becomes possible to design and create art using three-dimensional CNC printers. Other programs include Adobe Illustrator, Adobe Photoshop, Corel Painter, MyPaint, ArtRage, Autodesk Sketchbook, and Paint Tool Sai.

Digital artists such as Frieder Nake, Vera Molnár, and Harold Cohen are considered the first avant-gardists in the field of "Generative Art." These digital avant-garde artists created digital plastic images through written commands and mathematical functions, demonstrating that these creations were connected to specific aesthetic principles. Although sculpture itself was not directly part of this creation, it provided an intellectual background, laying the groundwork for the initial examples of digital sculpture. Simultaneously, digital artists like Nicholas Schöffer, with their understanding of kinetic and cybernetic art, produced three-dimensional digital artworks that were kinetic and responsive to their environment, spreading throughout the field. The initial emergence of digital art, and the desire to integrate artworks with technological infrastructures, formed the foundational steps that would enable the advancement of digital sculpture in subsequent centuries.

If we examine the historical process of art created with digital technologies, the Technical University in Stuttgart, Germany, a highly influential art school in photography and plastic arts, hosted the first computer technology art exhibitions at the Howard Wise Gallery in New York City, USA. Subsequently, in 1968, Europe's first computer technology art exhibition was held at the "Institute of Contemporary Arts (ICA)" in London, England, and this exhibition's legacy continued to expand and diversify vigorously.

Among artists who engage in digital production and design within computer technology environments using digital technologies are names like Alberto Seveso, Jared Nickorson, Pablo Alfieri, Pete Harrison, Chuck Anderson, Jerico Santander, Cristina Siquiera, Grzegorz Domaradzki, Jonathan Barr, and Mike Campau. In our country, among artists who perform digital production and design within computer technology environments using digital technologies, we can list names such as Özcan Onur, Başak Şenova, Emre Erkal, Erhan Muratoğlu, Ahmet Atan, Emre Turhal, Orhan Cem Çetin, Bahadır Uçan, Attila Ansen, and Refik Anadol.

One of the common misconceptions in the field of digital art is its confusion with digital photography. The extensive manipulation of photographs and the resultant departure of works from the definition of photography, due to the use of photography in digital art creations, lead to this confusion. However, the act of creating a digital artwork is an autonomous field of practice; while photography can be utilized, digital artworks can also be created without it.

The earliest examples of digital sculpture heralded not merely the development of a new technique, but simultaneously a lasting change in the nature of the artwork itself. For tens of thousands of years, sculpture was directly linked to physical materials, typically finding its expressive language through materials such as clay, plaster, ore, metal, stone, and wood. However, with the digital technologies that developed after the second half of the 20th century, individual artists creating art have transcended the boundaries of the physical universe, presenting new expressive forms shaped above virtual simulations, data sources, and algorithms. Recognizing these historical processes necessitates not only the advancement of digital technologies but also the clear manifestation of the intellectual, aesthetic, and political inclinations of creative artists.

The author has also used terms such as "Info-Sculpture," "Robo-Sculpture," "Tele-Sculpture," "Data-Sculpture," and "Computer Sculpture" to categorize areas within Digital Sculpture Art. These designations, on the one hand, signify the utilization of computer technologies at any stage of design and creation to ultimately produce a tangible sculpture; on the other hand, they also define the virtual, non-real sculpture that is modeled in 3D or scanned into a 3D environment and subsequently exhibited for art receivers in that non-real environment (Turhan, 2006).

The transformation experienced since the second half of the 20th century has led to radical changes in the expression of the traditional meaning of plastic arts, causing sculpture to transcend mere formal symbolization.

Creative digital artists, moving beyond traditional forms of expression, leveraged the possibilities offered by various art disciplines and developed interdisciplinary creation systems. During this period, the technical use and materials of contemporary sculpture were significantly enriched, and materials produced by industry, alongside new forms of expression such as "Kinetic Sculptures," "Ready-Made Objects," and "Installation Art," gained acceptance among artists of the era (Ballı, 2023).

With the ongoing process of digitalization, the transformations in digital sculpture art have been elevated to a more fundamental dimension, and computer-aided designs, along with digital tools such as "Algorithmic Modeling," "Augmented Reality," and "Three-Dimensional Printers," have been adapted for artistic use. These technological advancements have altered the relationship of sculpture to spatial and physical representation, offering artists new expressive possibilities through non-real backgrounds and data-driven creation schemes. The evolution of sculpture from its traditional structure to a digital idiom should be considered as a paradigm-driven differentiation that scrutinizes art's own ontology and boundaries.

Stylistic approaches in digital sculpture art correspond to the simplification and re-interpretation of existing entities or styles from the real universe within artworks. This presents receivers with aesthetic and expressive styles significantly different from traditional sculpture. Such approaches by artists and designers encompass the use of simplified and often abstracted forms rather than detailed expressions of entities or nature. Figurative works in digitally created sculpture can be produced very quickly using digital technologies such as computer-aided design (CAD) 3D programs or 3D modeling software. With the aid of these technological tools, artists and designers can modify, re-interpret, and reshape forms as desired when creating digital sculptures.

Although the terms "Digital Sculpting," "3D Modeling," or "3D Modellation" might appear to describe interconnected creation stages, these technological applications are fundamentally distinct production methods. The choice of method in the manufacturing process depends solely on the structure of the design/artistic creation and the necessity of its expressive power. 3D Sculpting/Digital Sculpting is an inherent method for digital sculpture creation and conceptualization. For these reasons, 3D Sculpting/Digital Sculpting is utilized by designer-artists who wish to create through mesh-based writing systems that support natural creation methods. Artists who employ these 3D Sculpting/Digital Sculpting software at an instrumental level and produce creations are referred to as digital sculptors. 3D modeling software also employs vectors, shapes, and lines to create 3D models. 3D modeling software is a type of model creation used by specialized designers in professional groups, such as industrial product designers who enable vectorial manufacturing from solid surfaces or geometric structures, architects designing architectural structures, and engineers. In this sense, this technological tool known as 3D modeling, being a form of software to be structured in technical designs, requires very few intuitive features. For example, a mechanical engineer would not use a digital sculpting-3D modeling software system to create a design. In this sense, although organic and solid surface modeling use similar digital-based software features, these designs encompass quite different techniques. In summary, the differences between organic and hard surface modeling are precisely what the designations emphasize. Organic modeling is generally not extensively used to create 3D models of living entities found in nature, such as humans and animals; solid surface modeling generally focuses on inorganic entities like buildings, furniture, and machinery. The most important reason why artists who can design with 3D modeling software used in three-dimensional artworks are called digital sculptors is their possession of an artistic intuition used in the creation of sculptural works, even if in a non-real design. These software programs used in sculpture enable the creation of a unique form from the outset, the processing of textures, and the transmission of the designer's method, individuality, and uniqueness through the sculptural work they create.

For these reasons, organic modeling technologies, which have not been used for 3D Modeling/Digital Sculpting, are more intuitive than traditional 3D modeling software. The reason is that manipulating a digital entity as if it belonged to a tangible reality is made possible by similar digital software. In response to the question "What is digital organic modeling?," it would be accurate to describe it as a general name given to software that creates closed geometric meshes through intricate nested calculations, enabling creation by shaping it like a real clay material that perfectly resembles the original. In the context of digital sculpture, examples of software that enable creation include programs such as "Blender," "Maya," "Zbrush," and "Sculptris." These programs, which encompass digital organic three-dimensional modeling technologies, operate with a Mesh-Based Geometry Algorithm. These programs are based on a mesh-based geometry, depending on an interconnected polygonal surface mesh where pushing and pulling are made possible. One of the advantages of this program is that the mesh can be organized at different levels of detail; while some sections with very fine details can contain small polygons, others can hold larger polygons. Through this mesh-based geometry algorithm, forms created using organic shaping systems can be stretched, pulled, and manipulated very rapidly. Thus, on a non-real clay material, intricate and detailed forms can be easily created by allowing real-time manipulations. High-resolution modeling software programs are simple software that can be easily used by a sculptor who can create art designs in our real world and is familiar with computer technology. With the support of this technology-oriented instrumentality of the contemporary three-dimensional sculpture discipline, countless figurative or non-figurative sculptures can be created in digital environments. In the original digital technological creations of our era, there are numerous digital sculptors who utilize these possibilities offered by technologies in the field of sculpture. Digital design artists can create many three-dimensional forms that cannot be genuinely realized in real life, with the support of three-dimensional modeling software. Artists who use these digital software in their designs are concerned with space, form-texture, and non-real material communication as subject matter and ideas, and even benefit from the figurative expressions that the plastic discipline of sculpture has long contributed to them. With the three-dimensional expression they create, they also make current judgments on the terms of space and mass within the virtual space of creation. In relation to the topic, the author states, "Sculpture, with its three-dimensional structure and traditional solid materials, possesses the characteristic of concretely meeting the concept of an object, and likewise, with its own tangible existence, it has had the characteristic of concretizing and questioning space" (Karacan, 2014).

Today's computer-aided digital software programs enable sculptors to move away from traditional production workshops and tend towards **sculptural conceptualization with digital technologies**, allowing for the re-evaluation of the artist's creative realization through new digital technological means. Three-dimensional applications such as "Digital Printing Technologies," "Algorithmic Modeling," and "Augmented Reality" encourage sculptors to create digital sculptures and to construct mechanisms of transformable, named data elements and parametric design approaches in their artistic creation stages. This change indicates that digitalization in contemporary sculptural artworks needs to be addressed not merely as a technical innovation, but simultaneously as a paradigm shift in an ontological and epistemological sense.

Figure 5. Jerico Santander, The Teapot

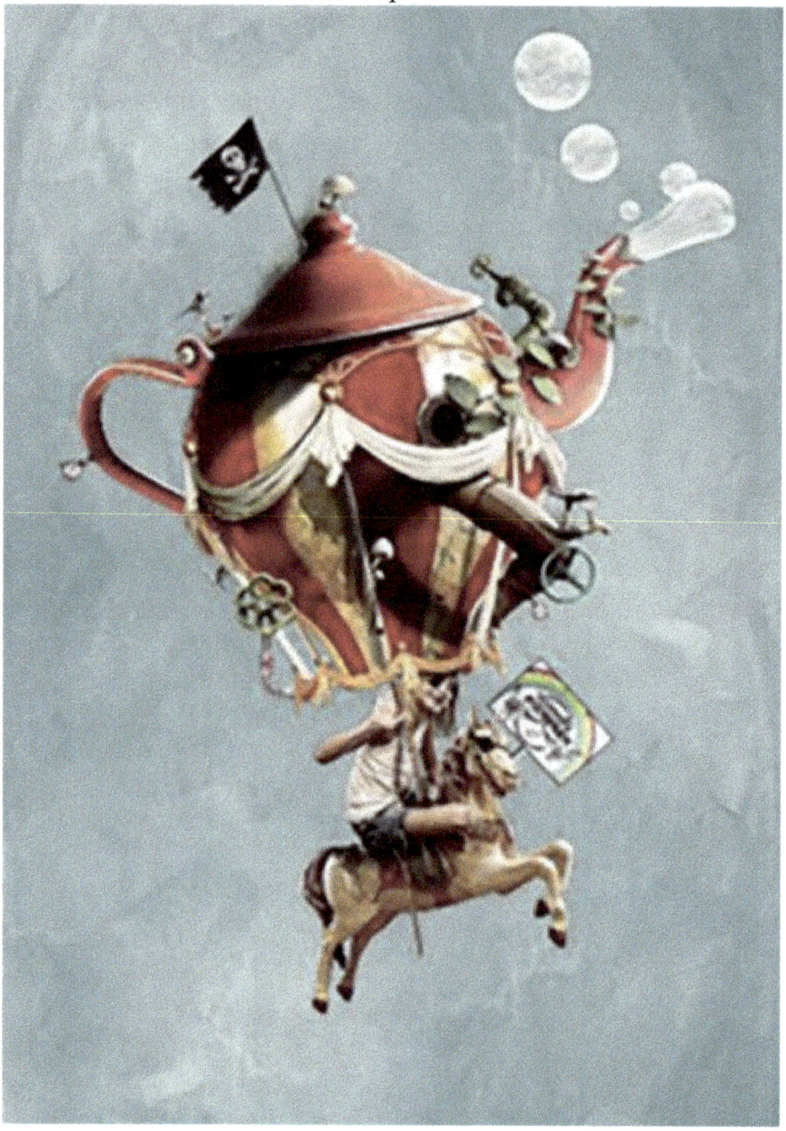

Digital Datamoshing or Glitch Art is one of the most widely recognized art forms implemented using contemporary digital computer technologies. Furthermore, the use of memes (phenomena disseminated as anonymous or famous images, sculptures, videos, words, or sentences, whose meanings are understood by broad communities) and GIFs is also observed in internet environments.

Digital Glitch Art, initially comprising visuals that emerged as a result of accidental technical malfunctions and problems, subsequently constitutes visual manipulations created by artists or designers through individual interpretations, thereby imparting aesthetic meaning. However, it is not always an artwork that originates from coincidence and accident. On the contrary, it is the ability of the accidental nature created by a structurally corrupted visual to give rise to diverse artistic conceptualizations.

Classifications of Digital Glitch Art applications include "Appropriated Glitch," "Accidental Glitch," "Coincidental Glitch," "Found Glitch," "Real Glitch," "Deliberate Glitch," "Planned Glitch," "Designed Glitch," and "Artificial Glitch." In the field of Digital Glitch Art, when creating works, we encounter two primary concepts in digital computer applications: The first is Datamoshing and Databending. Datamoshing refers to the process of creating new images or video visuals by modifying the compression and decompression algorithms used in compressed video images. The second, Databending and Circuitbending, refers to the act of altering the circuit that produces instant output, adhering to the original while using previously obtained data or different computer programs on that data.

Figure 6. Luziano Testi Paul, JPEGged Mona Lisa, (Glitch) 2003.

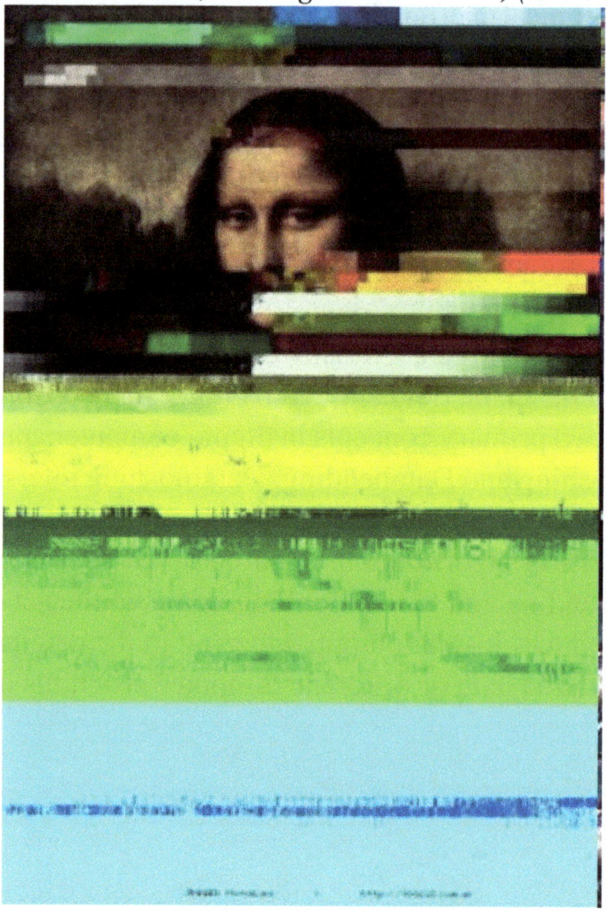

Within Algorithmic Art, an algorithm, in its simplest definition, is a grammatical structure comprising sequentially complementary and meticulously defined steps, phases, instructions, and codes for solving a problem or executing a task. Algorithmic art, conversely, is a generative art form created using a system of autonomous computer algorithms. In algorithmic art, the algorithm is created first; this structure then produces the artworks. These algorithmic structures can consist of expressions, functions, computer codes, or other forms of input in generative, computational, or mathematical formats. Designer-artists may opt for a deterministic algorithm or lean towards more random, experimental applications.

It is widely known that the earliest applications of algorithmic art date back to the years following the second half of the 20th century. However, these are not strictly considered digital art because the operations were executed or drawn by a plotter rather than a computer.

Figure 7. One of the most renowned works of **Algorithmic Art** *is Jack Ox's visualization of Kurt Schwitters' Ursonate (the musical notations of Kurt Schwitters' piece).*

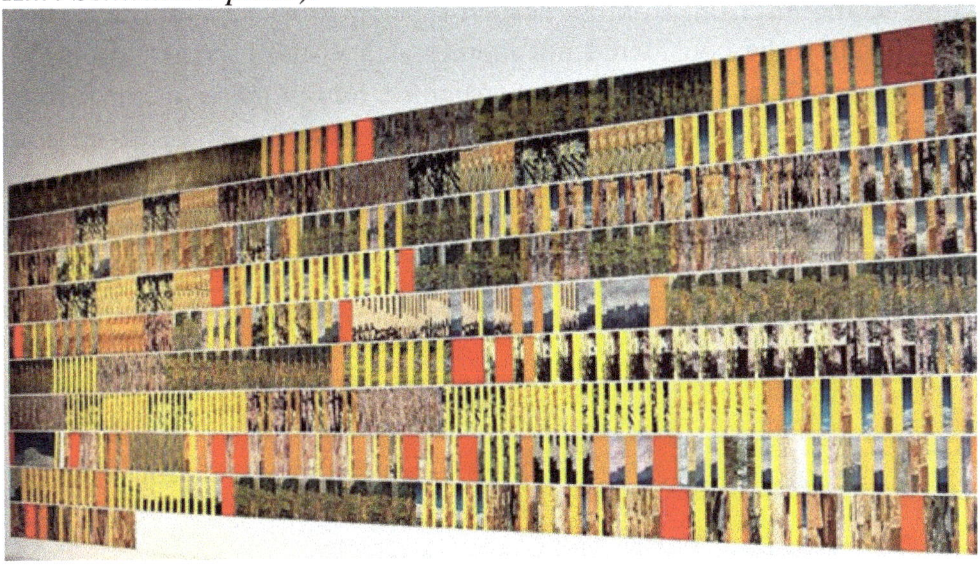

Fractal Art constitutes a sub-category of algorithmic art. In other words, a fractal is the name given to patterns structured with proportionally enlarged or reduced models of a form. The patterns within fractal structures in life are infinite and unique. These patterns encompass a sequence of all systems that, while differing in form, fundamentally bear the characteristics of a fractal structure. From past eras to the present, the fractal pattern structure has been a pervasive phenomenon, serving as an inspiration in many fields, utilized as a numerical expression, and acting as a source of inspiration for plastic artworks. The confluence of artwork and fractal geometry dates back to periods long before the present. Even in years when the conceptual expression of fractal structures was not yet formulated, various works were created through the visual manifestation of the “Golden Ratio” and the Fibonacci number sequence, or through different forms of fractal structures. From earlier periods, it is observed that these artistic approaches demonstrate a model of artistic understanding that progressed with the use of geometric structures. This phenomenon has been understood by many contemporary artists in our era and has manifested in highly diverse structural forms within the plastic arts. In this process, artists working in conjunction with systems such as “Parametric Design,” “Fractal Geometries,” and “Algorithmic Production” began to come to the forefront from an aesthetic perspective. “Digital Sculpture Art” began to be considered not merely as a visual representation, but simultaneously as a mathematical structure. Sculptors have constructed multi-layered narratives in their works by incorporating data derived from nature, social media communications, architectural forms, or historical accumulations.

Figure 8. Mıke Tyka, “Castles In The Sky With Diamonds”, (Fraktal Sanat) 2016

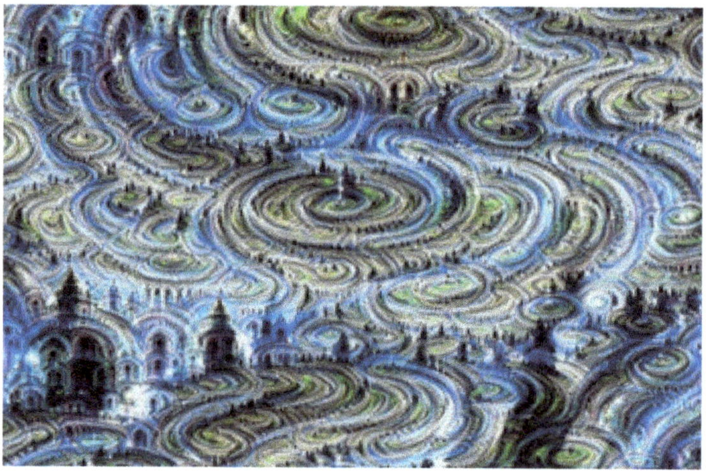

Digital artist Jared Nickorsan creates digital artworks at his company named JThree Concepts, which he founded as an art director and illustrator. Jared Nickorsan is among the artists who have stood out with his works reminiscent of animation frames since the beginning of the 21st century. Jared Nickorsan creates digital works with a rich expressive language. Artist Jared Nickorsan’s design named “Dead Astronauts” is one of his important works among those created with digital technologies. Artist Jared Nickorsan's works particularly narrate a perspective belonging to television culture, which was an important part of popular culture in the world in the 1970s.

There are certain stages and processes for ideas presented in digital computer environments to be transformed into serial products. These stages generally proceed as follows: Modeling and Design of an Idea and Concept: A structure or component designed in digital computer environments is generally created using 3D modeling software programs. Computer designers create very detailed three-dimensional core models of structures or components through computer-aided modeling tools. Preparation and Editing stages: After the three-dimensional modeling process, the design to be produced generally undergoes preliminary preparation and conceptualization stages. In these stages, deficiencies arising on the three-dimensional model are re-evaluated and adjusted, necessary improvements are made, and the system is made suitable for manufacturing. File Conversion and Preparation operations: The design to be produced is converted into a compatible file format to be used in the manufacturing stage. This operation is generally a file format that can be recognized by manufacturing machines, for example, the STL (Stereolithography) format. Selection of Production Machines: A suitable manufacturing machine is selected for the production of the design. This is selected based on the material, size, complexity, and other conditions of the design. For example, tools such as 3D printers, CNC machines, and laser cutting devices are used. Production stages: The manufacturing machine selected for the design is used to turn the three-dimensional design into a physical output. In this process, the machine can build the design in layers (3D printing), process the material (CNC machining), perform cutting (laser cutting), or apply different production methods. Finishing and Processing: The produced parts, if necessary, undergo finishing and processing stages. These stages may include operations such as smoothing the surface, applying paint or coating, and assembly.

The applications of contemporary art maintain the continuity of traditional art forms, preserving art's existing historical and cultural connection; however, simultaneously, with the contribution of developments in technology, they transform into new creation periods and expressive styles.

The digitalization era in art emerges as a factor that transforms the artist's existing creative practices from technical and intellectual aspects, and demonstrates paradigm shifts that fundamentally transform art's creation examples. In this sense, with the widespread adoption of digital computer-aided three-dimensional software programs, the more systematic treatment of digital technologies in art creations has been supported, preparing the ground for the emergence of new artistic expressive forms named "Digital Art" and "Digital Sculpture Art" (Kaya, 2023:3).

The "Digitalization Process" in art has introduced the use of technologies such as "Data Manipulation," "AI-Supported Systems," and "Augmented Reality," thereby creating possibilities for reshaping art's existing traditional creative forms, and has fundamentally transformed artists' creative practices. Artists shaping their artistic creations within systematic timeframes through computational algorithms and three-dimensional parametric modeling methods has created a radical paradigm shift in art's intellectual infrastructure (Al, B., 2019, S:78).

"New Media Art," an interdisciplinary art movement, treats the means produced by digital technologies as both expression and material. Moving beyond traditional media such as Painting, Sculpture, Graphics, or Photography, it establishes dynamic relationships with the receiver through communicative Installations, Network-Connected Projects, Virtual/Augmented Reality Applications, and Algorithmic Productions (Manovich, 2001). In this sense, artists define the forms and contents of their works programmatically by utilizing code, sensors, data, and network infrastructure.

Data visualization processes, in turn, are the period of transforming raw data sets into meaningful and visually comprehensible forms. Historically, this discipline, which developed in the fields of information design and statistics, has gained acceptance among contemporary plastic artists for aesthetic reasons and with the aim of gaining experience (Paul, 2016). Data visualization operations go beyond merely creating graphs, maps, or communicative diagrams, treating data itself as an artistic material and addressing all aesthetic, cultural, or social aspects of the data.

In conclusion, while "New Media Art" provides broad expressive spaces for data visualizations, in the field of data visualization, "New Media Art" adds a profound dimension to the richness of material and method. These contemporary and interdisciplinary interactions raise new problems and methods regarding how both artworks and information are created and perceived. The practices of new media digital artist Refik Anadol redefine the boundaries of digital aesthetics, presenting a concrete example of this interaction (Yüksel & Aşan Yüksel, 2024).

When we examine the history of art, one of the first artificial intelligence-related projects is Harold Cohen's Algorithmic painting program project named AARON (Cohen, 1973). Cohen taught AARON methods of line and form, enabling the machine to perform its own "Artwork" creation operations. These first steps in artificial intelligence proved that artificial intelligence could demonstrate a unique depth of creativity in art creation. In subsequent years, "Graphic Algorithms," "Artificial Life Simulations," and "Interactive Projects" created interdisciplinary "Collaborations" environments between artists and machines in the plastic arts by transforming the patterns and forms that receivers also learned (Boden, 2004; Colton, 2012). Artificial intelligence-related tools allowed artists to model their aesthetic demands at the code level, and at the same time, challenged their creative boundaries by confronting them with unexpected results.

At the core of the discussions at the intersection of artificial intelligence and art are questions such as; "To whom does creativity belong?", "How is aesthetic subjectivity defined?" and "How can a balance be established between machine production and human labor?". These questions have led to the acquisition of new perspectives and advancements in the fields of "Philosophy of Art" and "Cultural Studies." The contributions of artificial intelligence in Refik Anadol's digital art applications do not remain merely as an auxiliary, nor as a passive tool. In Refik Anadol's digital art works, the times woven with data create dynamic artistic experiences shaped together with the receiver. In this respect, Anadol assumes a pioneering role in deepening the interaction between art and technology by exhibiting the potential of artificial intelligence-supported art from both theoretical and practical perspectives (Yüksel & Aşan Yüksel, 2024). Today, "Generative Adversarial Networks" (GAN) and other deep learning techniques are being brought to the forefront with their abilities to create abstract and surreal images.

Today, artists are re-evaluating the material and intellectual existence of art through technologies such as "Artificial Intelligence," "Data Manipulation," and "Virtual Reality," and are scrutinizing the treatment of artworks within traditional aesthetic frameworks. AI-sourced artistic creation, by redefining the artist's existence, removes the art production process from being a human-sourced practice and transforms it into a collaborative creation model mediated by machines. In this sense, the communication between the artwork's creator and producer is re-examined; the search for how the artwork's inherent creative structure will be preserved within algorithmic processes is of increasing importance in contemporary art theory (Bulut, 2023;73).

As a result, digitally created sculpture art, by transcending classical art paradigms, necessitates a radical re-evaluation of art's inherent structure with changing art receiver profiles, aesthetic styles, and transformed creation periods. In a time when technology has rapidly advanced, where artificial intelligence has become a creating and learning system, and in our era, artworks are no longer fixed and absolute forms, but have been transformed into interactive, fluid, and continuously rewritable and recreatable structures. In this context, digital sculpture art is not only a part of contemporary artworks; it simultaneously represents the art of the future, cultural reflections of human-machine interactions, and harbingers of the forms that aesthetics will transform into in the near future. These transformations and changes are not only valid for the art fields but are also indicators that humanity is on the threshold of a new digital creation culture for its future.

REFERENCES

Arslan, C. (2018). *Dijital Yeniden Üretim Çağında Sanat Eseri: "Aura" Kavramının Dijital Sanat Bağlamında Yeniden Değerlendirilmesi.* Art-Sanat.

Bulat, M., (2007). Modern Heykelin Doğuşu, Atatürk Üniversitesi, Güzel Sanatlar Fakültesi Sanat Dergisi, Sayı, 11, S., 83-89.

Bulat, M. (2014). *Modern Sanatta Soyutlama.* Atatürk Üniversitesi Yayınları, Zafer Ofset.

Bulat, M., Bulat, S., & Aydın, B. (2014). Bilgisayar Ortamında Üç Boyutlu Tasarım ve Kopyalama, Akademik Sosyal Araştırmalar Dergisi, Yıl: 2, Sayı: 8. *Aralık, 2014*, 548–572.

Bulat, S., (2014).Teknoloji ve Modern Heykel Sanat, Atatürk Üniversitesi G.S.Fak.

Bulat, S., & Bulat, M. ve Aydın, B. (2014). Bauhause Tasarım Okulu. *Atatürk Üniversitesi Sosyal Bilimler Enstitüsü Dergisi.*, *18*(1), 105–120.

Bulat, S., Yağmur, Ö., & Aydın, B. (2014). Form ve Kompozisyon, Akademik Sosyal Araştırmalar Dergisi, Yıl: 2, Sayı: 6. *Eylül, 2014*, 478–488.

Bulat, s., (1999). Teknoloji ve Heykel Sanatı, Atatürk Üniversitesi, Güzel Sanatlar Fakültesi Sanat Dergisi, Sayı, 1, S. 133-140.

Bulut, Ş. (2023). Metaverse Ya Da Sanal Gerçeklik Kavramı Ve Sanatçı Refik Anadol'un Çalışmaları. *Cumhuriyet Üniversitesi Fen-Edebiyat Fakültesi Sosyal Bilimler Dergisi*, *47*(1), 69–76.

Çizgen, G. (2007). *Sanat Köprüsü Sırat Köprüsü.* Arkeoloji Sanat Yayınları.

Coşkun, R. (2014). Teknolojinin Olanakları ile Değişen Sanat Alanı. *Sanat Ve Tasarım Dergisi*, *6*(6), 76–89. DOI: 10.20488/austd.22705

Danto, A. C. (2010). *"Sanatın Sonundan Sonra", (Çev. Zeynep Demirsü).* Ayrıntı Yayınları.

Kaya, A. (2023). Çağdaş Sanat Formu Olarak Dijital Heykel, Dijital Heykelin Sağladığı Yeni Olanaklar. *Sanat ve İkonografi Dergisi*, (4), 2–9.

Özselçuk, S. (2023). A critical review on the use of artificial intelligence algorithms in the context of digital art: Refik Anadol's 'Machine Memoirs: Space' exhibition. *International Journal of Economic and Administrative Academic Research, 3*(1), 1–21. https://dergipark.org.tr/tr/download/article-file/4266984

Paul, C. (2003). *Digital art.* Thames & Hudson Ltd.

Rathus, L. F. (2013). Understanding art (10th Ed.). Usa: Wadsworth, Cengage Learning.

Şengünalp,C.,(2019). Çağdaş Sanatta İntihal ve Sermaye İlişkisi, Sosyal Araştırmalar Dergisi, 7, (88), S., 140-151.

Toptaş, R. (2022). *Türkiye'de Dijital Sanat.* Sanatçıları Ve Eserleri Hakkında Bir Araştırma, Sanat ve Tasarım Araştırmaları Dergisi.

Toptaş, R. (2022). Türkiye'de Dijital Sanat, Sanatçıları ve Eserleri Hakkında Bir Araştırma. *STAR Sanat Ve Tasarım Araştırmaları Dergisi, 3*(5), 170–186.

Turhan, Ö. (2006)." Bilgisayar teknolojilerinin Heykel Sanatına Sağladığı Yeni Olanaklar:

Uğurlu, H. (2008). Teknoloji Sanat İlişkisi: Günümüzde Teknolojik Sanatların Amacı. *Uşak Üniversitesi Sosyal Bilimler Dergisi, 1*(2), 247–262. DOI: 10.12780/UUSBD27

Wands, B. (2006). Art of the digital age. Londra: Thames and Hudson.

Yağmur, Ö.,(2018). Heykel Sinestik Düşünmek, Ordu Üniversitesi Sosyal Bilimler Araştırmalar Dergisi, 8, (3), S., 691-697.

Yücel, D. (2012). *Dijital Teknolojiler Ekseninde Değişen Sanat ve Kurumlar.* Genç Sanat.

Yüksel, İ., & Aşan Yüksel, O. (2024). Sanatta yapay zeka devrimi: Yaratıcılığın yeni boyutları. *Sanat & Tasarım Dergisi, 14*(2), 261–285. DOI: 10.20488/sanattasarim.1602572

ADDITIONAL READING

Akın, C. (2015). *Dijital Sanatlarda Etkileşimsellik: Türkiye'de Etkileşimsel Dijital Sanatların Konumu*. Doktora Tezi, Marmara Üniversitesi.

Alioğlu, N. (2013). *Yeni İletişim Teknolojileri Bağlamında Yeni Medya Sanatı: Kuramsal Bir Deneme. (Editör: Müge Demir). Yeni Medya Üzerine*. Literatürk Yayınları. Altınyıldız.

Anadol, R. (2020). *Yapay zekâ ve dijital sanat*. Sanat Yayınları.

Anadol, R. (n.d.). Machine hallucinations: Sphere. Refik Anadol Studio. https://refikanadol.com/works/machine-hallucinations-sphere/

Becer, E. (2019). *Sanatın değişen yüzü: Teknoloji ve estetik*. YKY.

Bingöl, H. (2019). *Heykel Sanatında Dijital Yaklaşımlar*. Yüksek Lisans Tezi, Atatürk Üniversitesi.

Çakmak, S. (2019). Dijital Sanatta Yaratıcı Bir Uygulama Olarak Airbrush Tekniği. İnönü Üniversitesi Sanat ve Tasarım Dergisi, 1(1), 56.

Can, E. (2019). *Seramik Üretim Sürecinde Üç Boyutlu Yazıcıların Kullanımı ve Sanatsal Öneriler*. Sanatta Yeterlilik Tezi, Anadolu Üniversitesi.

Erkek, B. (2020). Dijital sanatın ontolojisi: Yeni medya bağlamında sanatın dönüşümü. İletişim Kuram ve Araştırma Dergisi, 51, 25–46 https://dergipark.org.tr/tr/pub/ikad/issue/56462/763217

İba, Ş. M. (2022). Dijital Heykelde Yardımcı Teknolojiler, İdil Dergisi, 97 (2022 Eylül): s. 1287–1299. doi: DOI: 10.7816/idil-11-97-03

KEY TERMS AND DEFINITIONS

Art: The expression or application of human creative skill and imagination, typically in a visual form such as painting, drawing, or sculpture, producing works to be appreciated primarily for their beauty or emotional power.

Computer: An electronic device that processes data according to a set of instructions (called software), capable of performing a wide range of tasks such as calculations, communication, data storage, and multimedia operations.

Digital: Relating to or expressed in the form of digits (numbers), especially binary code used by computers and electronic devices to represent, store, and process information.

Digital Desing: The process of creating visual content, interfaces, or experiences using digital tools and software, often applied in graphic design, web design, user interface (UI) design, and multimedia.

New Media Art: Covers art forms produced and presented with digital technologies. Sculpture becomes interdisciplinary, merging with video, sound, software, and network technologies.

Post-Sculpture: It refers to contemporary approaches that go beyond the traditional understanding of sculpture. Digital tools, time-based media, and conceptual content shape this practice. Sculpture is no longer just a physical object; data, experience, and process.

Virtual Environment: A computer-generated, simulated space or world where users can interact with digital objects and other participants, often experienced through screens, VR headsets, or other devices.

Chapter 6
Desire to Be Liked and Exist in Mass Communication

Ece Nur Yalçınkaya
Fırat University, Turkey

Kainat Özpolat
http://orcid.org/0000-0003-1377-5262
Fırat University, Turkey

ABSTRACT

Since the beginning of life on earth, living beings have managed to communicate with each other in some way. The most notable of these creatures is humans. Humans, who have the ability to speak, have developed various communication skills in order to reach other people with whom they share a common life. Over time, verbal communication has developed and given way to communication methods. The internet and social media, which have developed along with the internet, have also made a great contribution to the communication adventure. Mass media, which have shown themselves in many areas of our lives, have not only strengthened the communication environment, but have also managed to play a leading role in many areas such as information exchange, entertainment or education. The most prominent of mass media are social media platforms. Social media platforms have also brought with them a number of problems.

DOI: 10.4018/979-8-2600-0944-4.ch006

INTRODUCTION

Since the beginning of life on earth, living beings have managed to communicate with each other in some way. The most remarkable among these creatures is human beings. Human beings, who have the ability to speak, have developed various communication skills in order to reach other people with whom they share a common life. Verbal communication has developed over time and has been replaced by the method of communication. A great progress has been made with the developing world in the communication network where various animals such as smoke and pigeons are used. With the invention of telegraph, radio, newspaper, television, telephone and most recently the internet, the communication process has become easier. The internet and social media, which developed with the internet, have also contributed greatly to the adventure of communication. The mass media, which has manifested itself in many parts of our lives, has not only strengthened the communication environment, but has also managed to play a leading role in many areas such as information exchange, entertainment or education. The most prominent of the mass media can be considered social media platforms. Social media platforms have also brought along a number of problems. These problems can be seen as problems that are becoming increasingly widespread in society, affecting the society and should not be ignored. In this study, problems on the desire to show off, to be liked and to exist in mass communication were investigated.

Mass communication, which is of great importance in our lives, has become an indispensable part of our age with its universality. Mass communication and mass communication tools, which are used by everyone from seven to seventy and which we need to use or have to be in considering today's conditions, continue to strengthen their place in our lives day by day. There is no doubt that mass communication, which is so intertwined with our lives, has brought about some changes. These changes can be individual or social and can be evaluated as positive or negative. In addition, people not only engage in various activities through mass media, but have also made some of these activities a routine. While it has become a routine for most people to pick up their phones or access social media as soon as they wake up, it can also instill different habits into daily life.

These habits can be quickly accepted by society and become indispensable. There is hardly a moment in the day when mass communication and mass media are not used. Every form of mass communication, especially social media, has become a large part of our lives and has become an unbreakable necessity.

People are able to exchange information, socialize, have fun and even trade through mass communication and mass media. The features such as convenience, freedom, unlimitedness, practicality, etc. that these actions contain can make mass communication somewhat indispensable. Mass communication and mass media, which are with us at every moment of life, continue to offer us all kinds of accessibility in accordance with the age we are in. In addition to these opportunities and benefits, some negative situations may also arise. Both experiencing and preventing these negative situations, which can be both personal and social, is entirely in one's own hands. If it is the dose that distinguishes medicine from poison, it is undoubtedly the way of use and dose that makes mass communication and mass media harmful or beneficial.

MASS COMMUNICATION AND MASS MEDIA

Mass communication and mass media are at the center of our lives. While a life without mass communication is unthinkable, it is an indisputable fact that mass communication and mass media make our lives easier. These two concepts, which have highly effective functions in various fields, are concepts that we frequently encounter and have become accustomed to hearing. The communication directed towards the masses, where the majority of the society is considered as the receiver, is called mass communication, and the tools that realize this communication are called mass media (Büyükbaykal, 2012, p.72). As can be understood from Büyükbaykal's definition, people are the receivers in the mass communication process. In addition, mass communication can become much more effective and easier with mass media. The first of the mass communication tools is the newspaper. The purpose of the newspaper, which appeals to those who can read and write, has been to provide the exchange of news between people. In 1450, the printing press was invented and printed communication, which came to life afterwards, was realized in Turkey in 1831 with the newspaper Takvim-i Vakayi. With the development of communication technologies in the following years, radio replaced the newspaper. The radio, which first appeared in the United States in 1906, met its audience in Turkey in 1951. Radio provided information flow not only to those who could read and write, but also to anyone who had a radio. In 1926, the golden age of radio came to an end with the arrival of television, which emerged in the UK and is both a visual and auditory communication tool. With television, people began to receive a wide range of information from where they were sitting, and over time they began to see different cultures and people. The internet, which developed in the 1970s, replaced television and became the most important mass communication tool of today (Erer, 2013, p.25).

The mass media, which constantly improves itself, has laid solid foundations in various parts of our lives with innovations and conveniences that are unlike its predecessors. We can say that not a day goes by without communication, and the number of days we do not come into contact with mass media can be counted on the fingers of one hand. At the same time, the mass media has developed people's horizons and perspectives, enabling them to think from a more universal perspective, creating both individual and social consciousness and facilitating the transition to modern society (Alav, 2001, p.83). This means that people have adopted mass media to a great extent and have mastered the use of mass media. Various mass media, which were popular in their time, can be considered as television, telephone or internet today.

Mass Media: Internet

The unabated development of technology is changing and improving our lives at the right rate. The Internet can be considered as an important part of rapidly developing technology. At the same time, it can be considered as the most widely used mass communication tool of today. Due to the age we live in, the internet is at the basis of almost every business and therefore this situation can increase the frequency of use of the internet. The internet, which means the network of networks, can also be considered as a system that connects millions of computers around the world (Geray as cited in Çakır & Topçu, 2005, p.75).

The internet, which is frequently used in many fields from health to education, can be considered as an indispensable mass communication tool for people. In today's conditions, the fact that many works and projects are realized through the internet may be among the factors that increase the indispensability of the internet. Since elements such as writing, sound and image are used in the same environment in universal communication on the internet, communication here is more effective than in traditional media. This means that the internet, by incorporating all the features of newspapers, radio or television, creates a more powerful and functional information flow (Çakır & Topçu, 2005, p.76). The fact that the Internet is more functional than other mass media increases its preferability. In addition, some innovations brought by the internet allow people to use the internet actively. Social media can be considered as one of the biggest innovations that the Internet has brought to our lives. Social media and personalized search engines create an intimate space where the outside world is eliminated. The person encounters only himself/herself and people who are similar to him/her. In other words, there are no negative factors to effect change. This "digital neighborhood" offers only the parts of the world that one "likes". In this way, while the internet turns into a private medium, it also evolves into an environment of comfort (Han, 2017, p.54). The internet and social media channels can be seen not only as an environment of novelty and comfort, but also as a powerful field of communication. In fact, social media environments can be used quite intensively in terms of communication and socialization today.

Social Media

There are two types of media known in communication research. These are known as traditional and new media. In traditional media, which existed until the emergence of new media, there is one-sided transmission. In new media, on the other hand, there is a communication and this feature of new media moves its users from the passive position of traditional media to an active position (Çapçıoğlu, 2019, p.662). People can be active in new media through social media platforms. Social media, which is at the center of our lives, is an innovation used by almost everyone. It can be said that it is generally used as a means of entertainment and socialization. Especially with the various platforms that have become widespread in recent years, the duration of use has also increased significantly. All platforms where content made by the person himself/herself is published or shared are called social media (cited in Öztürk, 2015, p.89). Platforms such as Facebook, X (formerly Twitter), Instagram, YouTube are defined as social media (Öztürk, 2015, p.288). We may encounter users who utilize all of these platforms or similar platforms. It may be correct to say that there are users who have accounts and are active in every medium. In fact, it is among the known facts that some people have more than one account. It can be said that there are few people who do not utilize or actively use social media platforms. It is also true that each medium has its own unique features and users may prefer these platforms just for these features. For example, a person who wants to watch long minute videos may visit YouTube, while someone who wants to watch shorter and instant videos, share photos or chat with other people through messaging may prefer applications such as Instagram or TikTok. Although these reasons for preference vary, it can be easily said that there are different features that distinguish the applications from each other. For this reason, it will undoubtedly be useful to explain, define and list the features of the most popular platforms that stand out and are most used by people.

Facebook

Facebook, which created today's social media channels, was founded on February 4, 2004 by Mark Zuckerberg, a Harvard university student, and his friends. In a very short period of time, it spread and became popular at a rate that even its founders could not have predicted. The Facebook platform, which used to enable communication between some universities in the US, has become a virtual-social space where people can share their accounts as they wish, find old or familiar friends, or make new friends by getting to know people they have never met before. In this way, Facebook has literally created social media, and all public and private institutions, including traditional media organizations, have taken the Facebook platform seriously and created their own Facebook pages. In fact, this situation has become almost mandatory (Aydın, 2014, p.134). When the Facebook platform first went online, it had 450 members. Later, 22,000 photo uploads were realized. In late 2004, the number of Facebook members reached 1 million. By 2005, the name "Facebook.com" was used under the naming rights and university students in Canada and the UK started to use the platform in late 2005. Later it was launched in Australia, Mexico, the United States, New Zealand and Ireland. In 2006, the system of inviting friends was introduced. Subsequently, every individual over the age of 13 and having an e-mail address had the right to become a member. The number of members reached 12 million in 2006. In 2008, German, Spanish and French languages were added to the application, marking another major innovation. Thanks to this innovation, the number of members reached 100 million. In 2009, an agreement was signed with CNN and the number of members increased to 150 million. The "Facebook username" was updated, making it simpler to register for the application. The Friends news application was purchased from Techcrunch and a unity was created. By the end of 2009, the number of members reached 350 million, and in 2010 this number reached 400 million, making it the application with the highest number of users (Öztürk, 2021, p.7).

Facebook can be considered as a medium that almost every individual actively uses and socializes, especially since it first became popular. Facebook can be defined as a major breakthrough for people both in terms of entertainment and socialization. This breakthrough has played a major role in laying the foundation for new and highly developed social media platforms. On the Facebook platform, users have gotten into the habit of directly uploading information about where they live, where and in which profession they work, where and how they study, where and how they have fun, their friends, what they are interested in during their free time, the activities they enjoy, movies, books and music, in short, a lot of information about themselves. As a result of such usage, the data owned by Facebook has become more personal data and Facebook has gained the feature of having personal data (Marr as cited in Suvay Eker, 2022, p.120). In this respect, Facebook may be the first area where people start to show something of themselves to other people and adopt and love this situation.

X(Twitter)

After Facebook, the second important development in the field of social media is the X (formerly Twitter) platform, which was launched in 2006. Founded in 2006 by Jack Dorsey, Noah Glass, Biz Stone and Evan Williams, X (Twitter) is an application that allows individuals to follow daily events and news in a comfortable way and reach large masses with hastags. Jack Dorsey's tweet "justsettingupmytwttr" is known as the first tweet (Ayan as cited in Öztürk, 2021, p.8). The X (Twitter) platform, which can be used both as a social network and a microblogging site, has entered the market from the point where Facebook was missing, in accordance with its mobile state. Before 3G technology and smartphones, it could take minutes to open or use Facebook on mobile devices, whereas the X platform is designed to be easily opened or read on an ordinary mobile device in accordance with mobile habits. With this mobile feature, X has made it easier to share content instantly, unlike Facebook (Irak and Yazıcıoğlu as cited in Aydın, 2014, p.134). Since its inception, the X platform has become one of the most popular social media platforms worldwide. X is a microblogging site and is more popular than other microblogging sites worldwide (Yıldırım & Ayan, 2024, p.115). To define microblogs, they are social media applications with a hybrid structure where functions such as instant chatting and status updates meet in a single medium (Toy, 2021. p.6).

X is a platform that has brought significant innovations in the history of social media. At the same time, this platform can be seen as a very effective and important tool for both politicians and news channels. The X application, which allows people to express their feelings, thoughts and events in words and sentences, has become a platform used by journalists, political party leaders, heads of state and government officials to inform the people who follow them, i.e. their followers. The reason for using the definition of "expressing in words" is to emphasize that X is different from other social media channels. This is because other social media channels generally progress and develop towards the production or consumption of elements such as photographs, videos and so on. In this respect, it is of course possible to share images on the X platform, but this platform emphasizes the power and ability of words. Another feature that makes

X different is its role in social events. The X platform is a very important space for the masses in terms of seeking rights, organizing and forming public opinion, and in this respect it is a very popular platform. In 2009, the X platform started to offer French, German, Italian and Spanish language support to its users. With this important development, the number of users of the X platform increased from 5 million to 71 million. Turkish language support was introduced in 2011. In November 2017, the number of characters in tweets increased from 140 to 280 characters. This led to the expansion of audiovisual content and thus the writing of longer messages (Kara as cited in Yıldırım&Ayan, 2024, p.129). With all these innovations, it can be said that the comfort environment of this platform has increased and accordingly the number of users has also increased.

Founded in 2006 to share messages limited to 140 characters, this platform is recognized as one of the most important networks in the market with 436 million active users according to the DataReportal Report of 2022 (Yıldırım&Ayan, 2024, p.128). At the same time, the X platform is a platform that officially emerged with Jack Dorsey's message “I'm just building my twtrr” on March 21, 2006, and the company first started operating under the name “Twtrr” and after a short period of time, the name of the company became “Twitter” (Kara as cited in Yıldırım&Ayan, 2024, p.128).

Twitter's Transformation Into X

The acquisition process of Elon Musk, who bought Twitter, took place in two stages. In early April 2022, Musk bought a 9.2 percent stake in Twitter for three billion dollars. At the same time, Musk is known as a user who actively used the platform during this process. After buying shares, Elon Musk also stated his plans for change on Twitter. In October 2022, Elon Musk bought all of Twitter, and as a result, Twitter changed hands for exactly $ 44 billion. Between May 2022, when Musk first bought the shares, and October 2022, when the acquisition was completed, some legal issues came to the fore. During this period, Musk conducted some research. These researches were on the subject of fake accounts and profiles. This can be considered as an indication that Elon Musk wants to turn Twitter into a more commercial medium. Because in general terms, there is no commercial income and profit from fake or unused accounts for social media platforms. In other words, real users determine or increase the value of a social media platform (Yıldırım&Ayan, 2024, p.130). On October 28, 2022, after Elon Musk acquired Twitter, he shared a message on Twitter, writing "the birds is freed". Although various comments were made on this message, which means "the bird is freed", Musk stated in his statement that he aims to create an environment where people can discuss/ communicate in a healthy way without resorting to violence, and that his goal in the acquisition process is to help humanity. The first change Elon Musk made after purchasing Twitter was to change the logo and name of the platform. After this change, Twitter became known as "X" and started to carry out its activities as X. In addition, Musk established the X platform under its parent company, X Holdings Corp, and at this point, he actually went to a new company structuring. With the establishment of this new company, new policies, practices and discourses came to the agenda, while these changes caused the platform to lose value. In fact, according to 2024 data, the value of X dropped to 14 billion dollars (Yıldırım&Ayan, 2024, p.130-131). According to asset management company Fidelity, the platform lost 71 percent of its value after Elon Musk acquired the company (Kalelioğlu as cited in Yıldırım&Ayan, 2024, p.131). The main reason for the depreciation of X may be Elon Musk and his policies. In addition, the European Union declared that X is the social media platform that harbors the most disinformation and hate speech worldwide and sent a warning letter and report to Elon Musk. Musk's indifference and failure to take any position on the issue caused X to lose both its users and advertisers. After this process, the platform tried some ways to prevent or reduce the loss of value. These included charging fees for approved accounts, premium membership, changes to the interface and logo design, monetization, and the creation of a marketplace where usernames could be bought and sold. However, this is a clear indication that the platform is becoming more commercialized. It can be said that there are quite large and significant differences in terms of policies between the early days of Twitter and its current position (Yıldırım&Ayan, 2024, pp. 131-132).

It can be said that the biggest change in the platform after Elon Musk's purchase of Twitter was the logo and name. The new logo of the platform is an "X" positioned in white on a black background. This logo also serves as a badge symbolizing the company's employees. Twitter's old logo, the bluebird, or Larry the Bird, has been a symbol of the platform's identity since its inception. It has also become an iconic symbol of the social media world, as the platform's old logo symbolized the innovative and creative spirit of the medium, the ability of users to communicate quickly and interactively, and the ability of people around the world to interact. The implemented logo and name change was negatively received by many people using the platform and caused reactions (Arısoy as cited in Yıldırım&Ayan, 2024, pp.132-133). In addition, the color blue generally evokes more positive and warm feelings in individuals, while the bird logo evokes freedom. However, both the new logo and the name evoke a more despotic connotation due to both the color and the sharp lines. At the same time, the use of the X as a badge expresses uniformization. In addition to all this, Twitter used to give blue ticks to accounts with high followers and verified accounts without any charge. These accounts usually included prominent public figures such as politicians, journalists or artists. It can be said here that these people have the potential to influence society and that even a single line they write can be very important. While this is how blue tick is used on Twitter, X has changed its blue tick policy. In X, the blue tick badge is now available for a monthly subscription fee. With this innovation, the X platform has removed the blue tick from the accounts of famous names such as Pope Francis, Donald Trump, Beyonce, who do not pay a monthly fee and are world-renowned. In this process, many non-profit organizations, including public service organizations, lost their blue tickers and became unverifiable accounts (Yıldırım&Ayan, 2024, p.133).

As is well known, the need for news is higher than usual in extraordinary situations such as social events, disasters, crisis moments, natural disasters or war. Thanks to one of the most important features of new media, instant news delivery, people in the society can access the information they want or need much more easily and easily. In such cases, the information conveyed to people by reliable sources is important. Because the internet and new media environments are the environments where disinformation is most frequently encountered. Therefore, this policy implemented by the X platform regarding verified accounts can be considered as a very damaging policy in the name of public interest. Elon Musk's introduction of a subscription system for verified accounts on the X platform can be seen as a capitalist perspective (Yıldırım&Ayan, 2024, pp.133-134). There is another decision taken by Elon Musk and X management about the blue tick issue, and this decision has caused the reaction of users. This decision is about fake accounts or so-called bot accounts getting a blue tick. Bot accounts are accounts that are created through software or programs and can share posts as if they were a real social media user, but are not real accounts and can interact with other users when necessary. As in other social media channels, there are many fake or bot accounts on the X platform. These accounts not only create artificial agendas, but can also mislead users and spread disinformation. Elon Musk stated that this is not against the terms of service and that there is no problem with these accounts receiving a blue tick as long as they do not imitate a person (Ulusan as cited in Yıldırım&Ayan, 2024, p.134). Elon Musk's attitudes and discourses on this issue show that the change of ownership in new media is not only a purchase or trade, but also a direct change in policies. This policy shows us that the X practice is shaped and changed entirely on profit. For both the X management and Musk, it does not matter whether disinformation is spread in practice or whether individuals are exposed to and engaged in false agendas. The only thing that matters to them here is financial gain (Yıldırım&Ayan, 2024, p.134). Based on all this information, it can be said that Elon Musk has made big and radical changes to the X platform. Throwing aside old habits, Musk has managed to make all users feel that the platform has changed hands by making innovations and differences both on the inside and outside of the application. At the same time, Elon Musk, who did not back down from his decision despite receiving negative feedback from users, also managed to introduce Twitter as X to the whole world.

Instagram

Instagram application, where visual elements are at the forefront, is among the most popular and widely used social interaction channels of our age. Instagram, which is a combination of the words "instant" meaning "instant" and 'telegram' meaning "telegram" in English, was launched by Kevin Systom and Krieger in 2010 (Türkmenoğlu as cited in Kardaş, 2025, pp.50-51). Launched in October 2010, the popularity of the Instagram platform increased and Mark Zuckerberg, the founder of Facebook, purchased the entire Instagram platform. Thus, with the merger of Facebook and Instagram social platforms, the use of social networking platforms has become significantly widespread. In 2013, the Vine application, which is popular for video sharing, was added to the Instagram application, which was mostly focused on photo sharing. With this breakthrough, the number of Instagram users increased day by day, making its reputation known to the masses and becoming more widespread (Türkmenoğlu as cited in Kardaş, 2025, p.51).

At the same time, smartphones brought by the developing technology have also contributed to the widespread use of the Instagram application. People who use the Instagram platform can share the video and photo content they have produced or taken with other users in the form of stories (insta-story) or live broadcasts on the profiles they have created. In addition, Instagram is a platform that includes tools such as "explore", which offers customized areas according to the profile used or viewed and its content/movements, and the personal message (DM) feature that allows communication with friends, as well as content sharing, and "Reels" sections where video content shot between 15-30 seconds can be shared, just like in the Vine application, and consists of these algorithms (as cited in Kardaş, 2025, p.51). Instagram application is one of the most prominent platforms among businesses with commercial purposes and is used for interaction. At the same time, the Instagram platform is a platform where visual elements and visuality are used most frequently among social networks. It plays an important role in combining the strategies developed in marketing with visual elements and delivering them to users and the targeted customer base in a wide framework without any language barriers. Businesses and organizations aiming for commercial profit have the opportunity to convey the information of all the products and services they offer in detail, in the form of photos or videos, in an audible way. In addition, buyers have the opportunity to ask questions about the product or service if they wish, or to make various evaluations and opinions about the product after the use of the preferred product (Kardaş, 2025, pp.51-52). In this respect, Instagram can be considered as one of today's most widely used social media platforms for both socializing and shopping or trade, and almost everyone has an account. In addition, the Instagram platform was conceived and designed as a photo-sharing application from the very beginning. This main feature of the platform has never changed, but nowadays, users also have various possibilities and opportunities such as sharing videos or live broadcasts with this platform. The Instagram platform offers its users a wide range of enhancement tools to edit or improve the images they want to share. These enhancement tools are known as functions such as filtering, cropping or rotating. At the same time, the Instagram application also gives users the opportunity to like or comment on any shared content (Kıyan & Dikmen, 2019, p.129).

In addition, Instagram users can share the photos, videos or articles they add to the stories section with their followers for 24 hours. Although these posts disappear after 24 hours, users can view and re-share their stories from the archive section at any time. Thanks to this archive feature, users can remember their memories by looking at the stories they have shared in the past (Sağlam, 2024, p.47). In this respect, it can be said that Instagram's archive section serves as a digital diary that is open to the environment. One of the features of the Instagram platform is the "blue tick" badge. With the latest update, Instagram users can access the blue tick badge in two ways. The first way is free of charge, but users must meet the criteria offered by Instagram. The blue tick badge is usually awarded to well-known people, celebrities, big brands, public figures or influencers in specific industries. The verification process involves accounts that Instagram selects based on specific criteria, usually aimed at verifying the authenticity and influence of the account. The second way is to officially purchase the blue tick badge for a certain fee. Instagram is known to give the blue tick badge to users who do not meet the aforementioned criteria in exchange for paying a set fee each month. This badge of approval is used to increase the credibility of accounts among users, to neutralize fake accounts by blocking them, and to clarify the true identity of content creators. In short, the blue tick badge can be defined as a security measure that increases the level of credibility on social media platforms and aims to provide a safer experience (Sağlam, 2024, p.47).

YouTube

The YouTube platform was launched in 2005 by 3 former PayPal employees, Chad Hurley, Steve Chen and Jawed Karim, based in the US. The application was acquired by Google 1.5 years after it was founded. The YouTube platform allows users to watch and upload videos. There is an age limit for accessing and watching some videos. People over 18 years of age can access such videos. Negative videos are removed from the YouTube platform. The person who uploaded the first video to this platform is known as Javid Karim. Day by day, the number of people using the application has increased and it has become an actively used platform. This application allows people to open a channel and upload videos to the platform. Users earn income by increasing the number of views through this platform. Thanks to the various videos uploaded, many people can get information about the country they will visit or the products they will buy and take advantage of this. People who actively use this application are called Youtubers. YouTube is a platform that includes titles such as music, documentaries, etc. and is widely used today (Ayan as cited in Öztürk, 2021, pp.8-9).

YouTube is named after the phrase "Broadcast Yourself" in English. YouTube, which is an application where video content related to personal experiential, instructional and many other areas can be shot and shared, allows its users to both watch and share these videos, and to interact with them by liking and expressing their opinions as they wish. In this respect, YouTube is increasing its number of users day by day. At the same time, YouTube consists of a set of services that aim to remove barriers to sharing online videos with other people. It was established with the aim and desire to provide a simple interface where users can upload, publish and watch videos as they wish, without the need for advanced technical knowledge (Burgess and Green as cited in Kardaş, 2025, p.53). Acquired in 2006 by Google, the YouTube platform was a platform known to be no different from the video sharing sites published or used before these years, but with Google's support, it has rapidly developed and grown to become the most popular and most preferred application in the field of video sharing (Burgess and Green as cited in Kardaş, 2025, p.53). Underlining this development process, Morreale states that YouTube has managed to become one of the top 10 most visited websites worldwide after its acquisition by Google (Morreale as cited in Kardaş, 2025, p.53).

The YouTube platform, as it is known, is an application that allows users to watch or share video content via the internet. Thanks to its mobile applications, users can access videos wherever and whenever they want. The YouTube platform includes videos in various fields such as education, games, music, sports, movies, travel, fashion, etc. Users can upload videos for free through their accounts and share the videos they upload with other users who want to watch them. At the same time, users can comment on the videos they watch and put a like or dislike icon. They can also save videos to their playlists. The YouTube platform also has a social network structure where users can subscribe to other channels or create personalized video lists. In addition to these features, YouTube users can also benefit from live streaming. YouTube Live allows not only individual users but also professional television companies to broadcast through their accounts (İlhan as cited in Sağlam, 2024, p.50). One of the advantages of YouTube Live is that it offers access to a large audience. As one of the world's largest and most important video platforms, YouTube allows live broadcasts to reach millions of people. For professional television companies, the use of YouTube Live allows them to reach their target audience in a convenient way, while at the same time generating potential advertising revenue. In addition, thanks to the analysis tools offered by the YouTube platform, the performance of broadcasts can be tracked and audience feedback can be evaluated. With new features such as "shorts", YouTube offers users short and alternative video options in terms of both content and viewing. In addition, the YouTube application can be considered as an important platform for advertisers in terms of revenue generation. The success of the YouTube platform is based on the fact that it fulfills users' needs to produce and consume content in various fields. The fact that YouTube offers a wide range of content, from educational and instructional videos to entertainment, music videos and news, makes the platform accessible to all segments of society. At the same time, YouTube's "user-friendly interface" and algorithms allow users to spend more quality and more time on the platform by recommending videos that are of interest to them or that may attract their attention. Analyzing and evaluating the user-based demographics, content preferences and interaction patterns of the YouTube platform greatly contributes to the advancement of digital marketing strategies and social media policies. The YouTube application's large and diverse audience provides content creators and brands with various opportunities to reach their target audiences. Especially for content creators and advertisers, this data is important in strategic planning and content production processes, while the fact that the YouTube platform reaches 33.4 billion visits per month reveals the platform's strong stance, solid position and the magnitude of its impact in the digital media world. (Sağlam, 2024, p.50-51).

TikTok

ByteDance, a software company based in China, has launched TikTok, a video sharing application that is one of the most widely used applications today. The TikTok platform offers its users a variety of filters, animations, stickers and various editing options to add visual richness to their content. In addition to these features, users can also benefit from various content suggestions tailored to their interests (Lu and Lu as cited in Kardaş, 2025, p.53). Today, the TikTok platform has nearly 300 million active users in China alone, while this number exceeds 800 million worldwide (Shao, Wang and Hao as cited in Kardaş, 2025, p.53). The TikTok application is a mixture of Vine and Snapchat applications, combining some features of Musical.ly, which ByteDance acquired in 2017 (Salinas as cited in Kardaş, 2025, pp.53-54). People who download the TikTok application can watch videos on the application without having an account or opening an account. However, for activities such as creating content, sharing, commenting on watched videos, chatting and interacting with other users, they need to open an account on TikTok, just like other social media networks. After opening an account, users can access content in various fields such as music, entertainment, animals, art, humor, science, education, sports, travel, food and drink and popular culture according to their interests. While this option is entirely up to the users, TikTok also has a “discover” section that is shaped according to users' likes and interests, just like Instagram. In the TikTok application, a “For You Page” is designed, and content is randomly presented in a flow according to users' tastes, likes or interests (Kardaş, 2025, p.54).

The TikTok application, which has gained great popularity in recent times, attracts great interest especially among young people as a social media platform where users can interact by sharing short videos (Diken as cited in Sağlam, 2024, p.52). By adopting platforms that advocate freedom of creative expression, Generation Z can see the TikTok platform not only as a means of entertainment but also as a place of social belonging (Sağlam, 2024, p.52). The TikTok application is referred to as a global platform for video sharing and is known to be a leading application among short video applications today. People who use this application can enrich their content by shaping it as they wish with various effects, music and other editing tools before publishing their videos on TikTok. In addition to this, there are also innovations such as increasing the attractiveness of the video by adding appropriate music to the video to be shared, making it more attractive and obtaining videos with high viewing pleasure. Since the TikTok platform is an application that focuses on short and instant sharing, videos are usually limited to 60 seconds. In addition, combining multiple videos together allows for the creation of longer movies. At the same time, improvised excerpts from people's daily lives are frequently seen in the stream of this platform. The video content may need to be improvised, but the equipment or tools used in the shooting of the videos do not have to be professional. In short, users can edit the videos they create with short shots made from their smartphones, but they do not have to exhibit these videos professionally and can present sections from their daily lives (Zeng, Abidin and Schafer as cited in Kardaş, 2025, p.54). In addition, the TikTok platform is recognized as a technology platform that aims to deliver the appropriate content to the right consumers and to accurately reveal the product-target consumer matching. This application uses a content recommendation system based on algorithms and artificial intelligence. This system identifies the interests of users and offers various opportunities according to this analysis. This system is a system created entirely with artificial intelligence algorithms. This powerful and effective algorithm not only increases the effectiveness of the use of artificial intelligence in TikTok, but is also important for the future development and progress of the platform (Xu, Yan, Zhang as cited in Kardaş, 2025, p.55).

SOCIAL ETHICAL PROBLEMS CREATED BY SOCIAL MEDIA

With the widespread use of social media and the increase in the duration of its use, various problems have emerged in society. In order to address the social ethical problems caused by social media, it would be useful to first look at the concept of "ethics". Ethics is a very old concept and has been defined by many thinkers. If we look at the dictionary meaning in order to reach the most accurate definition; ethics is defined as a set of behaviors that should be practiced or avoided by the parties between various professions (Turkish Language Association Presidency Ethics Guide, 2015). When people in social media environments do not behave in accordance with the definition of ethics, social ethical problems may arise. It is a fact that most people think and feel that they exist by the way they express themselves in social environments. The individual, who needs other people to express himself/herself, also recognizes himself/herself, knows his/her place and reveals his/her identity through feedback from other people in the society. This process is called socialization. The individual can be characterized as the sum of the characteristics of his/her own essence, together with the characteristics revealed by all external factors that have undergone changes by leaving his/her own self aside (Taylor, 2015, p.1218).

It can be said that people have a tangible stance and life in social media environments. Situations such as people who think that they are socializing through social media, not being able to determine their boundaries while sharing in digital environments, sharing their personal information, sharing their current location, and tagging the people they are with, if any, pave the way for security problems. It is also known that people's deleted information is not deleted even if it appears deleted on the platforms, it is stored in memory, and even many platforms such as Facebook sell users' information (Öztürk, 2015, p.308). Such situations are quite common problems today. Although being careful when using social media platforms prevents many possible bad situations, the development and change of these environments with the development of technology brings new problems. The transformation of people into introverted or asocial individuals without realizing it may be one of these problems. Thanks to social media, it has become easy to communicate with a distant relative. Although social media has provided such an opportunity, this situation can sometimes cause us to be unable to establish a healthy communication with the people around us. Thanks to technology, instead of coming together on special occasions (such as holidays, birthdays), people can handle the celebration with a single message by simplifying the current situation (Çapçıoğlu, 2019, p.666). Such situations can inevitably isolate people from society and individualize them. Therefore, more introverted, more asocial individuals may emerge. Many people who are disconnected from the real world may encounter various problems in their social lives. As a result of the misuse of social media, some people's family ties are damaged, kinship relations are gradually forgotten and individuals who lose their emotional richness emerge. People whose social lives are getting worse and worse may see social media as a branch to hold on to when they face loneliness. In such cases, the process can be difficult for both the individual and society. In addition, people who encounter criminal elements can come to the point of arrest with the emptiness they fall into, and they can turn into people who are deprived of their freedom and doomed to an unhappy life (Çalışkan & Mencik, 2015. p.274). Such situations can lead to tangible weakness in society and raise social ethical problems. People become lonelier, and the lonelier they become, the more attached they become to social media, and this attachment can reach dangerous levels. For example, when a person who is lonely and feeling bad about himself/herself comes across depressive, pessimistic or stimulating posts (speed videos of motorcycles or cars, smoking or drinking videos, etc.), it can create a ground where he/she can harm himself/herself in various ways. Therefore, it can be said that social media endangers both individuals and moral values.

As the rate of use of social media has increased, the rate of users sharing their private lives and developments in their private lives has also increased. Users can easily share private information such as where they live, their hobbies, daily activities, family, workplace or travel memories. This situation exceeds the boundaries of privacy and brings about the intervention of other people in the private sphere (Soydan, 2023, p.205). In addition to all these, social degeneration is also taking place. People may be influenced by what they see and watch on social media and may want to make a personal change or even try to change or emulate themselves and their lives. In case of a conflict between the identity revealed in virtual media and the identity in real life, the person may face negative and bad situations such as isolation, alienation or role confusion (Aldemir, 2019, p.67). Social media platforms, which have entered our lives and brought the social environment with them, can also be considered as an area that has caused both personal and social problems. While these problems can be encountered in various ways, it may be a useful method for users to use both technology and social media channels carefully.

THE DESIRE TO SHOW OFF, BE LIKED AND EXIST IN MASS COMMUNICATION

The impact of mass communication and mass media on society is undeniably known. Social media, one of the most popular and widespread mass media of recent times, has become indispensable in our lives. Especially platforms such as Instagram, Facebook and TikTok are among the platforms where users are very active and visible. Social media environments, which individuals frequently use for entertainment, socializing and even expressing their thoughts and opinions, have become indispensable today.

In the current age, social media platforms seem to offer an unlimited space for new lifestyles and habits, but this is not the case. The real picture is that individuals who think they are becoming more and more liberated are actually becoming more lonely and unhappy, and the increase in the communities consisting of these individuals (Çapçıoğlu, 2019, p.666). These channels, which are not limited to sharing photos and videos, but also live broadcasts or chat channels, can be considered the most popular channels where digital socialization takes place. Social media environments, which satisfy people's desire to socialize in a very professional way, can stimulate this desire of users with various innovations. The fact that people can add text, music or emoji to their profiles according to the mood they are in and that this action receives feedback from their followers or target audience can be considered as part of the socialization process. However, it should not be forgotten that this socialization also brings along some problems. It is obvious that people are influenced in many areas from beauty perception to lifestyle and create changes in their lives due to this influence.

Posts on social media can receive likes and comments in a short time. While getting too many likes affects human psychology positively, negative comments can cause psychological distress. In addition, the desire to be liked or the psychology of being liked has become the disease of our age. This can be seen especially on Instagram. Some people may share posts in virtual environments by drawing a portrait far from their real life and self and display a profile that is far from themselves. This makes people feel as if they belong to a group that they do not actually belong to (Of&Kılıçaslan, 2020, p.3767). In addition to the desire to belong to a group, the desire to be in the public eye, to be liked, to exist or to show off can also influence many people. A popular product, movie, song, dance, dance, food or even chocolate can trigger these desires. For example, the most popular chocolate of recent times, Dubai chocolate, has become a trend, attracting people's attention and admiration to a great extent. People have shared this chocolate either by buying it or making it at home, showing that they are present on social media and that they follow the agenda and popularity. While those who were really curious about that chocolate were content with eating it, those who shared the video or photo of the chocolate satisfied their desire to exist by saying "I am here too". People's participation in the popular phenomenon of the period may be an indication that they are not separated from the existing herd.

Again, if we evaluate it in this context, there is also the ostentation dimension of such posts. The phenomenon of ostentation is defined as transforming one's possessions into an image or presenting oneself (Yıldırım, 2021, p.128). With social media, it can be very simple for people to show off their lives or any situation in their lives. Users can not only share information about their lives, but also show off their lives. A product or gift received, a place visited, or even a cup of coffee can be used as a means of showing off on social media. When people show off their possessions or activities to other people, they do not even realize that they are actually giving themselves psychological satisfaction. The gender reveal parties of couples preparing to have a baby can be seen as one of the clearest examples of the desire to show off. Gender reveal parties, which have become more of a tradition than a trend in recent years, are just one of the things people love to show and share. These parties, which can transform from a small celebration to a big invitation, can further consolidate their place in society with the influence of social media. The meals eaten, the tables set, the coffees drunk in popular places, the books read or pretended to be read, vacations, even the airplane taken on the way from one place to another can fall into this category. In addition, sharing the food eaten can be one of the most prominent Instagram posts. Many people take a photo of the food before eating and share it with their followers. For this, the best light and the best angle are chosen and an aesthetic look is tried to be captured. More than a quarter of Instagram users worldwide share photos of the food they eat or the table they sit at. This is called "Foodstagramming" (Of&Kılıçaslan, 2020, p.3770).

Another important issue in social media is the desire to be liked. Just as it is important for some people to be approved or accepted by society, it can be just as important to be liked in social media environments. At the same time, situations such as ostentation, presentation of the self, and the phenomenon of consumption can manifest and shape themselves in social media environments. In addition to communicating or interacting on social media platforms, people also fulfill their desire to be liked and their need to show off (Yıldırım, 2021, p.127). In addition, people may expect to be liked with photos or videos that people usually pretend to be happy and share up to their private lives. They even pay attention to who likes the images they share. This expectation may be based on the psychology of gaining people's appreciation. If the desired or expected likes are not received, emotional changes such as demoralization and mental breakdown may occur. In a way, people seek their happiness in the number of likes. These mood changes are sometimes caused by an existing personality disorder, but sometimes they are caused by a personality disorder created by social media (Of&Kılıçaslan, 2020, p.3768). While the number of likes of a shared photo or post is important for the person sharing it, various ways can be used to increase this number. Applying effects or photoshop to the photos, adding popular music to the post and increasing the attractiveness of the post can be among the most common methods used. While the number of likes below the expected number is perceived as a failure, it is also common for posts to be removed simply because the number of likes is low.

The social network, as a performance arena, can direct individuals to share posts due to its structure and functioning. The individual can be rewarded with the title of "micro-fame" according to his/her performance in the network. At the same time, the need to exhibit oneself on social networking channels can lead to situations such as the desire to be approved and liked by the society, to think that one is not ordinary and like everyone else, that one's thoughts and life are worth considering or following. The person satisfies himself/herself with the number of likes, the number of followers and the interaction rate, experiences a satisfaction with these data and may feel addicted to all these (Aldemir, 2019, p.66). In addition, while the user measures the quality of the post he/she shares not by his/her own thoughts and ideas, but by the number of likes or the number of likes, he/she may often not realize that this situation actually has a psychological dimension. Leaving their own thoughts aside, they may shape themselves around the thoughts of others on social media channels. They may even undergo various aesthetic operations to achieve the current perception of beauty or social status and buy status when necessary. It does all this to win the favor of other people using the medium. At the same time, the number of likes on a tweet/post can show how many people that post brings together in a common thought. The support or opposition to an idea or an event can also arise from the number of likes. All these factors are common in social media channels. Especially applications such as Instagram and TikTok can put people in a state of competition and users may not feel this state of competition. It may not be a wrong statement to say that people turn the wheel of platforms that can put people into various patterns and direct them in line with these patterns with their own hands. For this reason, it may be the best choice to live without putting these platforms at the center of our lives, without sharing every moment, every situation, and without revealing every feeling on these platforms.

THE IMPACT OF SOCIAL MEDIA ON HUMAN PSYCHOLOGY AND EMOTIONS

People may be psychologically influenced by the events/situations they experience in their daily lives or throughout their lives and may face various consequences of these influences. Social media platforms can also be considered as a structure that has influenced most people today and has managed to affect them psychologically. Social media platforms have become an area where people who cannot express their feelings openly in their daily lives or who want to attract attention, so to speak, who like to be in the spotlight, can make posts reflecting their emotional states. People who may have difficulty in expressing themselves in their daily lives think that they can express themselves freely at any time, in any way they want, thanks to social media channels (Kıran, Küçükbostancı & Emre, 2020, p.436).

Social media channels can be considered as a tool that affects people in every aspect. The most prominent of these aspects may be psychology and emotions. Psychology and emotions can appear as elements that are very important for both the individual and society. Because individual health means community health. It can be predicted that an individual who is mentally and psychologically tired, worn out and in a bad condition will not be able to show or express himself in a healthy way in society. The transfer of needs such as communication, self-expression and entertainment, which were met in social life before the internet and social media became so widespread, to the virtual environment can trigger the demand and addiction to social media. This situation may cause individuals to live in isolation by breaking away from social life and cause some mental problems (Çömlekçi&Başol, 2019, p.174). It can be said that mass media and social media channels can sometimes (perhaps mostly) negatively affect human psychology. Although mass media sometimes provide psychological satisfaction in some cases, they can turn into a factor that gradually consumes or even prevents the individual's socialization or other psychological needs (Babacan, 2016, p.16).

Apart from activities such as communicating and sharing on social media networks, it has been stated that spending two hours or more than two hours a day on these networks has negative psychological effects (Sampasa-Kanyiga & Lewis as cited in Büyükçorak & Dinç, 2020, p.31). Of course, using mass media can be seen as the norm of today, but as a result of excessive use, negative feelings and thoughts may arise in the person. Various negative feelings and thoughts such as comparing oneself or one's life with others, feeling inadequate and incomplete in various aspects, and feeling that one is late for life can affect the individual. It is also possible to state that the rate of use and the way it is used has turned into a kind of addiction due to the fact that social media technology has strong sociological, psychological and sociopsychological issues (Babacan, 2016, p.18). Immersing oneself in social media environments for hours and spending time on social media by taking hours out of one's daily life can be seen as a situation that people now consider normal. It can also be said that this situation has become a routine. It is an indisputable fact that a person spends a certain part of the day on social media. While a day without social media is unthinkable, it can be said that this situation is an indicator of addiction. Just as gaming addiction, shopping addiction, alcohol or drug addiction are considered as psychological problems, social media addiction is also considered as a psychological problem. Social media addiction can be defined as a person's intensive use of any social network and losing control over its use (Kıran, Küçükbostancı & Emre, 2020, p.436). Social media addiction can be considered a serious issue that can reach very dangerous dimensions. This addiction can also cause irreversible problems. It can negatively affect the person in many ways, from physical disorders (posture disorder, eye disorders, headaches, etc.) to mental disorders (anxiety, feeling of inadequacy, pessimistic thinking, etc.). In addition, attention disorder is one of the most widespread problems in society. The proliferation of short videos and "scrolling culture" can leave individuals with attention disorders and intolerance. Being affected by negative news on the agenda and becoming anxious can also be considered as one of the problems that arise in social media channels. While the main reason for this situation may sometimes be the sharing of uncensored images on social media channels, sometimes it may be due to the fact that the news is a completely annoying, painful or frustrating news. However, this does not change the fact that there are people who are negatively affected by uncensored or negative posts. The rapidly changing agenda can also be considered as one of the factors that increase the rate of use of social media channels and the time spent on these channels. While the rapid change in the agenda arouses curiosity in people, this sense of curiosity may cause people to frequently log on to social media environments. This behavior, which has become a habit, can become the "norm". At the same time, unpleasant emotional states or conditions such as pessimism and irritability that occur in people who actively use social media when they cannot access social media due to reasons such as illness, vacation or travel can be called "withdrawal symptoms", while the state of feeling much better than necessary or the opposite, numbness, can be defined as "mood change" (Çömlekçi & Başol, 2019, p.176). People whose sense of backwardness is triggered may feel deprived and inadequate. The person may think that other people are more adapted to the flow of life, happy and active compared to him/her, and these thoughts may cause him/her to feel bad. Therefore, these emotional states can bring with them a bad psychology and mood. In other words, people can become depressed and have a depressed mood due to the intensive use of social media channels or social media addiction.

Virtual Depression

Depression is generally a chronic and disabling condition. It can also be defined as a momentary state of mind, illness or syndrome. Depression as a mental state can occur in a person's life for no particular reason or after daily problems. Depression as a syndrome, on the other hand, encompasses all mental, physical and social problems and complaints that are based on sadness. At the same time, depression ranks fourth in the emergency category according to the World Health Organization (Öztürk, 2021, p.1). In short, depression can be defined as a state of depression that occurs with various symptoms such as lack of self-confidence, pessimistic thinking, feeling worthless, feeling hopeless, feeling guilty about events, sleep and eating disorders, physical pain and apathy towards life (Budak as cited in Öztürk, 2021, p.14). People may feel bad in the face of difficulties or negative situations they face in their daily lives and may face mood disorders such as depression. In addition to these situations, another factor that negatively affects the person and leads to depression may be virtual environments. Social media environments, where people think or feel that they can meet their psychological or emotional needs, have become an indispensable part of daily life in many areas such as socializing, being accepted as leisure time entertainment and being evaluated in this context, communicating with the opposite sex or establishing a relationship. In this respect, the desire to meet many of one's psychological, emotional and intellectual needs on social media channels, although it causes addiction, is also seen to pave the way for the formation of a new identity. These identities, which are often of a virtual nature and cannot find a correspondence in real life, reflect the complex situations that the person cannot reach in real life, wants to be but cannot be (Babacan, 2016, p.17). Therefore, these complex situations may cause a psychological and spiritual breakdown in the individual. The "virtual life and virtual identity" that the individual wants to reach but cannot achieve may cause the individual to build a different world within himself/herself and disconnect from the real world. Individuals break away from life and relationships and attempt to build a new identity and socialize in the virtual world. These efforts not only distract individuals from socializing in real life, but also reveal negative emotions such as hatred, anger and hatred, and allow them to develop the practice of using these emotions (Babacan as cited in Cerrah, 2016, p.1400).

People who make depressive or pessimistic posts on their social media accounts and whose depression can be observed according to their posts are more likely to need psychological support with a diagnosis of clinical depression than other individuals (Çayırlı as cited in Balcı & Baloğlu, 2018, p.218). Liking or sharing sad and pessimistic posts (videos, photos, music, etc.) may be a sign of actual depression. At the same time, given the extent to which online social networks are involved in the routine lives of individuals, ignoring the clinical and social impact of this situation can cause great harm. The results show that the way individuals use online social networks and the meanings they use during interaction can be a critical determinant of depression or vice versa (Baker & Algorta as cited in Balcı & Baloğlu, 2018, p.228). It can be said that social media channels affect some people negatively, although not all people. Social media environments, which have a very strong impact, can create negative perceptions and make people feel bad about themselves. In addition, the algorithmic structure brought about by developing technology can be skillfully used to influence people on social media. For example, by calculating the time users spend watching videos, determining which videos are watched more, or determining which videos users spend more time on, videos, photos and music targeting the current mood or interest of the user can be presented to the user, so to speak, and the user can be put into the stream. This can cause a person in a bad mood to become depressed by fueling their negative thoughts. Considering all these effects, it can be said that people can fall into a virtual depression through social media platforms and it can be emphasized that the virtual form of depression should not be underestimated.

If we briefly summarize the negative effects of social media on human psychology and emotions; psychological disorders such as attention disorder, addiction, depression, narcissistic personality disorder, schizophrenia can be given as examples. According to a study conducted by US psychology professor Rowland Miller, social networking sites such as Facebook and X (formerly Twitter) have various effects on human character and mood. According to Miller, sharing the details of one's life on social media platforms such as Facebook and X, which are shared by the whole world, destroys people's sense of shame. There are also many scientific claims ranging from deepening people's sense of jealousy and turning them into monsters to narcissism. Negative results have also been found in similar studies conducted on Facebook. These negative results can be listed as the emergence of sleep and anxiety problems, depression and stomach pains in children who spend more time on Facebook than other children, higher rates of alcohol use in people who use Facebook more than other people, low academic performance of students who frequently check their accounts on the social platform, and the emergence of psychological disorders, asocial behavior or aggressive attitudes in adolescents who spend more time on Facebook than necessary (Cerrah, 2016, p.1409). It can be easily said that unconscious or addictive excessive use of social media can lead to mental and psychological breakdown, and even if it does not have such a big effect, it can cause a person to feel depressed and depressed. It is important to use social media platforms without losing logic and willpower. The fact that users use social media platforms within certain limits and in a conscious manner can be considered as a very useful behavioral model, not only for their own health but also for the health of society.

CONCLUSION

While the elements that distinguish human beings from other living beings can be defined as reason and will, human beings' use of technology unwillingly and mindlessly can take its place among today's problems. While mass communication and mass media are at the center of the lives of most people in society, it may be important how and for what purpose individuals use these platforms created by technology. Social media channels, which have influenced people from their lifestyles to their characters, continue to be widely used by people, and it can be said that this continuity will continue in the near future. It is an indisputable fact that using mass media carefully both now and in the near future will benefit both the individual and society. In addition, it should not be forgotten that situations may arise in which we not only need to act carefully but also need to protect ourselves. Therefore, taking care to use the technology at our disposal in the most efficient and correct way for ourselves and our society can be a medicine for the present and a hope for the future. It should also be remembered that every innovation brought by technology can evolve into a technological weapon with the way people use it. Social media platforms, which can be among the biggest innovations of technology, can be used in various ways, both as a means of socialization and communication and as a source of information. At the same time, social media platforms can be used actively by almost everyone. Social media platforms, where people can be positioned as users or producers, can be considered as the channels where socialization is the most intense. Social media platforms, which host different lives, different cultures and even different worlds, can also play an important role in the information process. However, it would be unreasonable to say that that is seen, said or written on social media is true and real. As fake news has increased, fake people such as have started to emerge and this situation has reached the level of fraud.

It can be said that some of the problems and deterioration in society stem from these platforms. One of the first things that may be noticed is that people try to resemble other people they see on social media and try to be like them. This kind of use may inevitably lead to social degeneration. Both individualization and universalization of the person may appear as one of the common situations. A person who experiences loss of self-confidence or regression in social skills due to social media may become increasingly lonely. At the same time, they may want to be like the people they see on those platforms. With such situations, asocial individuals may increase, personality disorders or self-identity problems may occur, and even life risks may arise. In other words, on social media platforms, man can man's wolf, and as people compete with each other in competition, it can be their self-esteem and self-respect that is lost. It can also lead to moral degeneration of society, as there are all kinds of videos on social media platforms. Or it can lead to damage within the family, as too much sharing of personal life can lead to a lack of privacy. Comparing ourselves, our lives, even our work or our family, with what other people on the platform have, and starting to question after comparing, can be the biggest basis of the blows that social media platforms inflict on a person. Of course it is necessary to use social media platforms. Because the age we are in and the rapid change in the agenda may lead us to hug our smartphones. However, stepping into every innovation brought by the age, keeping up with every trend and coming to the point of mixing real life with virtual life can lead one to dead ends. Therefore, using every medium without getting carried away and keeping our willpower in our hands will create a healthier mind, a healthier body and a healthier society.

REFERENCES

Alav, O. (2001). *Mass Communication and Local Media*. Faculty Bookstore Publications.

Aldemir, A. (2019). The Intensity of Transparency and Lack of Aura in Social Media. [AKİL]. *Akdeniz University Journal of Communication Faculty*, (32), 54–70.

Aydın, B. (2014). Transformation of the Understanding of Privacy in Social Media Platforms. *Istanbul Arel University Journal of Communication Studies*, *3*(5), 131–146.

Babacan, M. E. (2016). Social media usage areas and the relationship between addiction. *Addicta : the Turkish Journal on Addictions*, *3*, 7–28. DOI: 10.15805/addicta.2016.3.0017

Balcı, Ş., & Baloğlu, E. (2018). Relationship Between Social Media Addiction and Depression: "A Field Research on University Youth". *Galatasaray University Journal of Communication*, (29), 209–234. DOI: 10.16878/gsuilet.500860

Büyükbaykal, C. (2012). Mass Media and Social Life. *Journal of Family Communication*, *21*, 71–75.

Büyükçorak, M., & Dinç, M. (2020). Psychological Effects of Excessive Use of Social Media and Social Media Usage Characteristics of Turkish Youth. *Psychological Research*, *1*(1), 30–33.

Çakır, H., & Topçu, H. (2005). Internet as a Communication Language. *Social Sciences Institute Journal*, *19*, 71–96.

Çalışkan, M., & Mencik, Y. (2015). The New Face of the Changing World: Social Media. Academic View Journal, 50, 254-277. Access address: http://www.akademikbakis.org

Çapçıoğlu, İ. (2019). Social Media, 'New Human Type' and Ethical Problems. *1st Congress of Human and Social Sciences Research.*

Cerrah, L. (2016). Social Media and Some Institutional Interactions and Critical Approach to Social Media / Some Institutional Social Media and Interactions and Critical Approach to Social Media. *Atatürk University Social Sciences Institute Journal, 20*(4), 1393–1414.

Çömlekçi, M. F., & Başol, O. (2019). Examining the Relationship Between Social Media Usage Purposes of Young People and Social Media Addiction. *Manisa Celal Bayar University Journal of Social Sciences, 17*(4), 173–188. DOI: 10.18026/cbayarsos.525652

Erer, S. (2013). Mass Media and Medical Ethics. *Düzce University Health Sciences Institute Journal, 3*, 24–28.

Han, B. C. (2017). *Transparency Society*. Metis Publications.

Horzum Taylor, I. (2015). Facebook and the being liked motive. *International Journal of Social Sciences and Education Research, 1*(4), 1216–1227. DOI: 10.24289/ijsser.279131

Kardaş, M. (2025). Conspicuous Consumption and Social Appearance Anxiety: A Study on Instagram Women and Female Users (Published master's thesis). Çanakkale Onsekiz Mart University Graduate Education Institute, Çanakkale.

Kıran, S., Küçükbostancı, H., & Emre, İ. E. (2020). Investigation of the Effects of Social Media Usage on Individuals. *Journal of Information Technology, 13*(4), 435–441. DOI: 10.17671/gazibtd.693331

Kiyan, Z. & Dikmen, E. Ş. (2019). "The Role of Social Media in Advertising: A Research on Instagram". İlef Journal, 6(1), 121-146. Doi: https://doi.org/DOI: 10.24955/ilef.554036

Ozturk, Ş. (2015). Ethical Issues in Social Media. *Selcuk Communication, 9*(1), 287–311. DOI: 10.18094/si.57598

Ozturk, Y. (2021). The relationship between active social media use and depression and self-esteem: a foundation university student sample (Published master's thesis). Istanbul Gelisim University Graduate Education Institute, Istanbul.

Sağlam, N. (2024). TikTok Usage Habits of Generation Z in the Context of Uses and Gratifications Theory (Published master's thesis). Uşak University Graduate Education Institute, Uşak.

Soydan, B. (2023). New Media and Social Media: Ethical Problems and Solution Approaches. *New Media Electronic Journal*, *7*(3), 198–215. DOI: 10.17932/IAU.EJNM.25480200.2023/ejnm_v7i3002

Suvay Eker, H. (2022). How Social Networks Benefit from Big Data: Facebook and Twitter. *Journal of International Management*, *5*(1), 118–130. DOI: 10.33721/by.983553

Turkish Language Association Presidency Ethics Guide. (2015) Access address https://tdk.gov.tr/wp-content/uploads/2016/11/TDK-Etik-Rehberi .pdf

Yıldırım, O., & Ayan, V. M. (2024). *From Twitter to X: Evaluation of the Change in Ownership Structure in Social Media on the X Platform*. İlef Journal., DOI: 10.24955/ilef.1432738

Yıldırım, S. (2021). The Phenomenon of Showing Off in Social Media and the Consumption of the Sacred. *Iğdır University Journal of Social Sciences*, *28*, 125–143.

KEY TERMS AND DEFINITIONS

Communication: The exchange of feelings, thoughts, information, and news between individuals; the mutual transfer of feelings, thoughts, information, and news from person to person in any form and by any means imaginable.

Mass Communication: Mass communication is the process of conveying information to a wide audience. This process plays an extremely important role in modern societies. This type of communication is used to keep society informed about current events, provide access to information, and expose people to different ideas.

Mass Media: All forms of media, including radio, television, magazines, and newspapers. **Internet**: The Internet is an electronic communication network that connects computer systems to each other.

Virtual Environment: The virtual environment refers to a space created through information technology that resembles the real world but is not physical. This environment allows users to engage in social interaction, share information, and carry out educational activities through random and varied connections.

Social Media: Social media is an interactive communication platform where users search, use, and produce content on the internet. With the advent of Web 2.0, social media has evolved from a one-way content sharing platform to a two-way content exchange platform.

Showmanship: Deceptive, artificial behavior intended to impress others, make oneself appear attractive to others, or simply boast.

Chapter 7
Early Examples of Glitch Art in the Works of Vera Molnár

Melis Sucuoğlu Doğan
http://orcid.org/0000-0001-6183-2941
Ardahan University, Turkey

ABSTRACT

Vera Molnár, who discovered computer art at an early stage in the 1960s and was one of the first female artists to work in this field, utilized algorithms and produced digital artworks. She developed a method called the "Molnárt System," which introduced a 1% degree of irregularity into her compositions. This method enabled her to incorporate deliberate distortions into her works, overlapping with the principles of Glitch art. This study will analyze how Molnár's digital works produced in the 1960s and 1970s intersect with Glitch art. Her works will be examined using visual analysis and literature review methods. The findings indicate that Molnár's works, created through deliberate distortion and randomness, can be regarded as early examples of Glitch art. In conclusion, it is observed that Molnár's works expand the boundaries between computer art and traditional painting, developing a new aesthetic approach. Furthermore, her art allows for a reevaluation within the context of Glitch art, thereby more clearly revealing her position within digital art.

DOI: 10.4018/979-8-2600-0944-4.ch007

INTRODUCTION

Throughout the centuries, art has not only been an expression of aesthetic pursuit but also the most powerful means of communication reflecting the culture, values, beliefs, and imagination of societies. In the Middle Ages, iconography served as a representational language; in the Renaissance period, a humanist perspective emerged; and in modernism, abstract forms of expression shaped art both as a way of thinking and a representational tool. Each era and movement changed the function, form, and meaning of art; social events and the position of artists within these events have guided the definition of new social, political, and cultural dynamics of art. Especially after the Industrial Revolution, societies rapidly entered a process of modernization, and as a result, artists began to question traditional understandings of art. During this period, art moved beyond being a tool of individual expression and adopted new forms of representation by embracing political, social, and technological transformations. In this context, Wands (2006) states that the foundations of the computer revolution were also laid in the 19th century, a period marked by intense scientific progress. Charles Babbage, in 1834, designed the Analytical Engine, a mechanical computing machine considered a precursor of modern computers. Noting that inventions such as the telegraph, Morse code, keyboard for typewriters, telephone, Kodak camera, and film reel emerged in the same century, Wands emphasizes that these developments were harbingers of the mechanical and electronic media age (Wands, 2006, p. 20). Especially in the second half of the 19th century, as mechanization gained momentum and social structures changed, the aesthetic understanding in art also shifted, transforming the ways in which art was produced. In this context, in England, the 'Arts and Crafts' movement emerged as a response to mechanization and mass production. The artworks exhibited at the First London World Exhibition in 1851 raised concerns about the disappearance of handcraftsmanship, and this movement subsequently spread from England to North America, Europe, and Japan (Avcı Tuğal, 2018, p. 17).

By the 20th century, avant-garde movements emerged in art, and it began to be perceived not merely as a representational tool but also as an important component in societal transformation. During this period, many artistic movements emerged in search of ways to reflect the development of technology and its impact on society. Artists of this period did not produce their works solely with aesthetic concerns; rather, they adopted an approach that criticized the system, questioned and followed technological developments, and embraced new forms of expression through various production tools. Especially in the second half of the 20th century, when digital technologies began to come to the forefront, this era reflected a period in which artists began to incorporate them into their artistic production practices. Computers have now started to come to the forefront as tools in creative processes. In art, terms such as randomness, repetition, system malfunctions, and errors have begun to be used, and in this context, artists working with algorithms have started to emerge. While these artists aimed to establish systematic structures in their works, they also benefited from intentional distortions to question new aesthetic experiences. In this context, the research examines the artistic practice of Vera Molnár by associating the intentional distortions she applies within the orderly structures produced with algorithms with Glitch aesthetics, and aims to analyze what kind of rupture and randomness strategy she developed in the visual narration of her works. Within the scope of the study, it is investigated how the aesthetic understanding and algorithmic structures that Molnár developed through the Molnárt System, starting from her early digital drawings, can be conceptually related to today's Glitch aesthetics. The random deviations placed within the systematic structures by the artist will be discussed in comparison with the perception of "error" in the digital age, and thus Molnár's position in the development of contemporary digital art will be re-evaluated.

ALGORITHMS AND THE MOLNÁRT SYSTEM IN VERA MOLNAR'S WORKS

At the beginning of the 20th century, with the advent of Cubism, the appearance of material on the surface as an object represents one of the most significant breaking points in the history of painting. With this new approach, the artwork ceased to be merely a visual representation and began to embody an intellectual and conceptual structure as well. During this period, when significant debates emerged in art, Cubist collages were also recorded in history as an important milestone. These works, which are considered precursors to today's digital collages, represent a significant transformation of the artwork in the later stages of the 20th century. In this period, art did not only undergo a transformation in terms of material, form, and content. At the same time, due to the influence of technological developments, new forms of artistic expression began to emerge.

One of the first movements that tried to demonstrate the connection with technology was Futurism. In the Futurist Manifesto published by Filippo Tommaso Marinetti in 1909, it was argued that traditional values should be replaced and transcended by the embrace and glorification of new technologies. The artist's passion for speed and machines soon spread to many areas of art and was reflected in the works of artists (Farthing, 2024, p. 396). The Dada movement, which followed the same period, sometimes criticized technology and at other times integrated it into art. While artists adopted a critical approach towards the mass destruction caused by industrialization and technological advances, they also used technology both as a critical and aesthetic symbol. "Many Dada portraits are hybrid representations, combining machine and human. Dadaists held contradictory views on the role of technology in the industrialized modern society. They embraced the liberating aspect of technology. But unlike the Futurists, they did not glorify the machine; on the contrary, they opposed mechanization and rationalization" (Altınyıldız Artun, 2016).

The Constructivism movement, which emerged in Russia and emphasized that art should serve social benefit, was inspired by industrial production methods and produced works that developed abstract and geometric forms. "The three-dimensional sculptural objects produced during this period generally exhibited geometric simplicity, reduced to fundamental formal elements and, as much as the technology of the time allowed, were made with industrial materials" (Antmen, 2009, p. 104). In the same period, similar to the Constructivists, the Bauhaus school adopted an approach that prioritized social utility. Artists such as Kandinsky, Klee, and Schlemmer tried to construct a workshop-school concept based on both functionality and aesthetics, one that abolished the traditional distinction between art and craft and prioritized individual self-discovery. Farthing (2024), notes that in its early years, Bauhaus moved away from the traditional understanding of craftsmanship, and one of the best examples reflecting this is the exhibition held at the school titled 'Art and Technology: A New Unity'.

In the 1920s, the first examples of Kinetic Art began to emerge. These works, which used light sources and created a sense of movement, were nourished by the mechanical and technological developments of the time and changed the structure of art. Art began to evolve into a structure that established a connection with the viewer. The kinetic sculptures produced by László Moholy-Nagy between 1921 and 1930 represent the first examples of Lumino-Kinetic art (Avcı Tuğal, 2018, p. 38).

From the mid-20th century onwards, it is observed that technological developments in art began to accelerate. With this development, both the means of production changed and the artistic structure began to transform. Thanks to this new technology, artists did not remain bound to traditional methods in their production processes and tried to integrate innovations into their artistic representations using computer art. Within the framework of the possibilities offered by computer systems, artists came to the forefront with a new aesthetic understanding that developed around concepts such as randomness, order, deviation, and repetition. With the development of computer technologies, the concept of digital art began to emerge and gain popularity, especially after World War II. Technological systems developed for the war were adapted to different fields; in this process, the ENIAC computer developed in 1946 at the University of Pennsylvania was considered the beginning of the digital age. During this period, people began to use the mathematical processing power of computers for aesthetic purposes. One of the first names to use technology in artistic production was Ben Laposky. In the early 1950s, Laposky created electronic images from waveforms using an oscilloscope device and photographed these images to create aesthetically complex compositions that could not be drawn by hand (Wands, 2006, p. 24). During this process, the art object created a new field of experience in communication with the viewer. Another breakthrough appeared in the 1960s with the Fluxus movement. Nam June Paik began using television technology as an artistic material, establishing an important bridge between art and media and becoming a pioneer of video art.

Paik was one of the first artists to use a portable video camera in 1965. In 1969, he created a significant representation in electronic image production by combining and manipulating images with the 'Paik–Abe video synthesizer' developed together with Japanese engineer Shuya Abe. Using television as a new media tool, Paik laid the foundations of digital art by creating video works and installations such as Global Groove, TV Buddha, and TV Garden (Smithsonian American Art Museum, n.d.).

Figure 1. Nam June Paik, TV Garden 1974-7, Germany

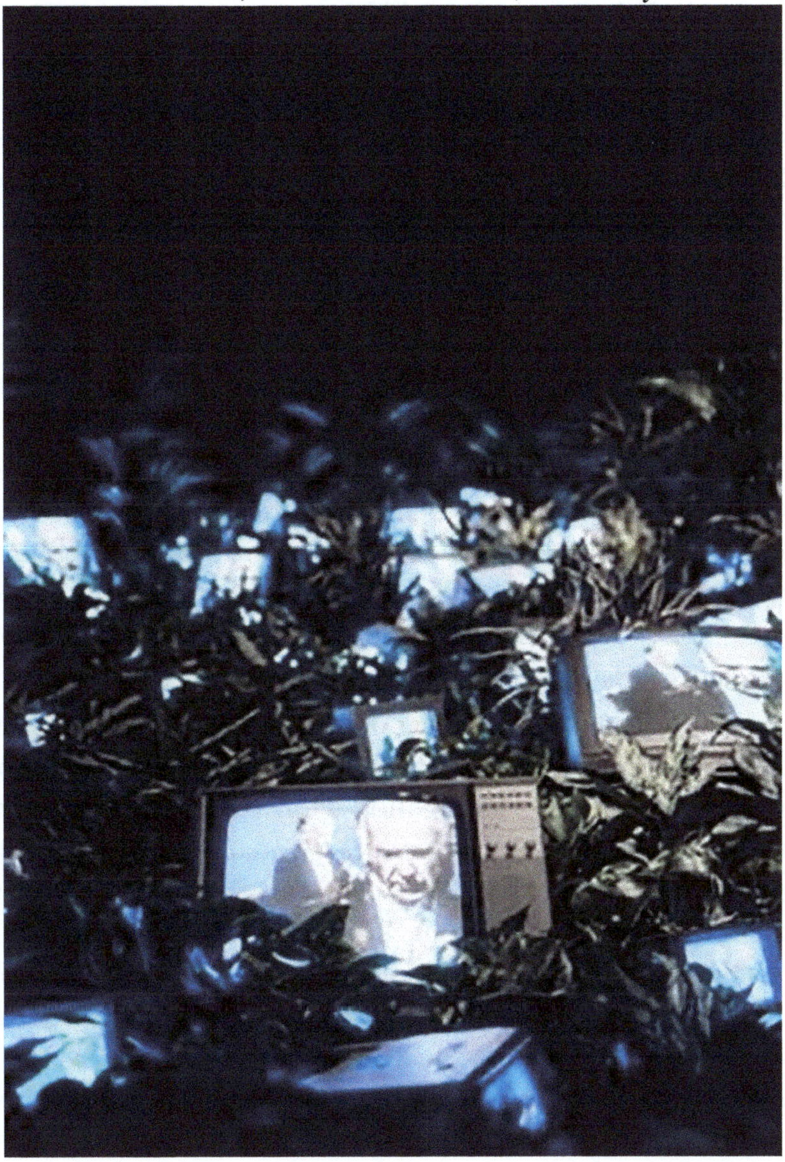

https://www.tate.org.uk/whats-on/tate-modern/nam-june-paik/exhibition-guide

"The artist, through his video installations, distorted signals, mixed images, and approached televisions as sculptural objects. In his work titled 'TV Garden', he created moving images on numerous televisions among flowers, producing a kind of spiral chaos" (Godfrey, 2024, p. 42). It was reported by Micheal Noll that the artist visited Bell Laboratories in 1966 to learn how digital computers could be used to create art and animation (Avcı Tuğal, 2018, p. 60). During the 1960s, groundbreaking computer art exhibitions were organized in some galleries in Germany. In 1966, Billy Klüver, in collaboration with artists and engineers such as Andy Warhol, Robert Rauschenberg, Robert Whitman, and John Cage, founded the organization Experiments in Art and Technology (EAT) to promote collaboration between the arts and engineering. Two years later, with the Cybernetic Serendipity exhibition held at the Institute of Contemporary Arts in London, the British Computer Arts Society was established. These developments marked important steps for the institutionalization of digital art and the growth of interdisciplinary collaborations (Wands, 2006, p. 24). With these advancements in the 1960s, terms like Computer Art and Algorithmic Art began to find a place in the field of art. Works produced with computers between 1960 and 1990 are considered the first examples of Computer Art. Artworks created using algorithms, which form the basis of computer systems, are recognized as Algorithmic Art between the 1960s and 1970s .

Computer-generated art is seen as directly related to the rapid advancement of computer technologies during the Cold War period. During this time, the United States and the Soviet Union intensively developed computer-based systems to consolidate their military and technical superiority. The opportunities provided by these technological advances paved the way for new experiences not only in engineering and defense fields but also in artistic production processes. Especially between 1963 and 1965, computer art production was largely conducted by military institutions or large-scale research laboratories. In this context, institutions such as Westernhouse Electric Corporation, Bettis Atomic Power Laboratory, California Computer Products, Inc., and Calcomp Plotter come to the fore. Military support played a role not only in the development of computer technologies but also in the financing of exhibitions dedicated to computer art. Indeed, in 1968, the United States Air Force partially funded Cybernetic Serendipity, the first international exhibition of computer art (Taylor, 2014, p. 29). "During this period, artists established various research groups in an effort to create a pioneering art movement. For example, in France, Groupe de Recherche d'Art Visuel (GRAV) was formed, with Vera Molnár—one of the leading names in computer art—as one of its founders. In Germany, the Stuttgart School was formed around Max Bense, one of the founders of the concept of Information Aesthetics. In former Yugoslavia, in Zagreb, science-based artists initiated the New Tendency movement" (Daudrich, 2016, p. 37). Among these efforts were the Institute of Artificial Art in the Netherlands and the algorithmic art exhibition organized by Marshall Bern at Xerox PARC. This exhibition featured various artists who focused on generative algorithms in their works (Wilson, 2002, p. 314). One of the pioneering elements that played a significant role in the global recognition of computer art was the journal Computers and Automation. Starting in 1965, it became the first platform to treat computer art as an independent category by featuring the works of artists and technologists from various countries. Technology experts from Canada, Germany, London, Italy, and Japan published their works in this journal. By 1970, artists from France, the Netherlands, and Sweden also began to appear in this platform. The journal organized competitions to promote international participation and increased engagement by publishing the contact information of the contributors. At the same time, it became the first medium in history where computer art was sold (Taylor, 2014, p. 30).

However, despite all these developments, the majority of the fine arts community initially approached this field with considerable skepticism due to the scientific and technical origins of computer-generated art. For this reason, such productions were classified more as a technical field, separate from traditional art history. Pioneers of computer art such as Herbert W. Franke, A. Michael Noll, and Frieder Nake did not make efforts to position their works within the canon of 20th-century art history. Furthermore, when these pioneering artists wrote about their works, they often focused solely on the technical aspects of the production process (Taylor, 2014, p. 10).

"These artists found the idea of a logical sequence embedded in the machine intellectually compelling and considered the notion of externalizing the image-making process as a proper challenge and opportunity for art. In his work Computer Graphics-Computer Art, Herbert W. Franke listed several mathematical operations that he believed could form the basis of computer graphics: symmetrization, transformations, mathematical functions, moiré patterns, permutation, interpolation and

extrapolation, matrix calculations, and random numbers" (Wilson, 2002, p. 314).

Faced with the broad domain of digital art, many computer artists have sought to redefine the central role of the computer within art. Over time, as seen with postmodern artists, these practitioners abandoned the term "Computer Artist" and instead began to adopt definitions such as "Proceduralists," "Transmitters," and eventually "Algorists" (Taylor, 2014, p. 24). Artists who have identified themselves as Algorists include figures such as Charles Csuri, Helaman Ferguson, Jean-Pierre Hébert, Manfred Mohr, Ken Musgrave, and Roman Verostko. Many of these artists have been producing work in this field for decades (Wilson, 2002, p. 313).

"An algorithm, in its simplest definition, is a set of steps, stages, instructions, codes, or grammar, defined in detail and sequentially structured to solve a problem or carry out a task" (Artun, 2021). Algorithms form the foundational components of computer programs. They are used to define the logical operations to be executed by the processor. Computer algorithms can instruct the computer to generate visual outputs. Pioneers of computer art, such as Herbert W. Franke, Kenneth Knowlton, and Charles Csuri, took significant steps in exploring algorithms within their artistic practices (Wilson, 2002, p. 313). Algorithmic art is defined as "visual art generated on the basis of algorithms that completely determine the process of image creation. This type of art is closely related to contemporary computer technology, particularly to computer programming. Another key influence on algorithmic art is the mathematical structure that underlies the algorithms used in image production" (Ceric, 2008). Manfred Mohr, an artist based in Paris, developed programs for a mainframe computer system that generated abstract drawings using a digital plotter. The commands he wrote included elements of randomness, which allowed for variations in the geometric forms; thus, his compositions emerged as a process shaped in conjunction with the artificial intelligence of the machine (Fortenberry, Melick, 2015, p. 122).

Algorithmic artists have typically opted for general programming languages developed for drawing basic graphic elements (lines, circles, rectangles, etc.) instead of using specialized graphic software. These artists shaped their aesthetic ideas through the structure of these codes. Although this method requires control, it offers the artist greater freedom of expression and flexibility. Algorists have begun to create their own software using programming languages. The visual outcomes they produce are not modified through any image processing software (e.g., Photoshop); rather, they can only be altered by rearranging the program itself-that is, the algorithm (Ceric, 2008).

In this context, Vera Molnár, one of the pioneers of algorithmic art, turned toward computer-assisted production in the 1960s, creating abstract geometric compositions through simple algorithms. Molnár's artistic practice began in the late 1940s. She challenged the boundaries of traditional painting and focused her work on the problems of structure and order, especially through geometric abstraction. These geometric compositions, typically created by hand, laid the groundwork for her later computer-assisted works.

After World War II, Molnár moved first to Rome and then to Paris with her husband, where they settled. This period marked a kind of rebirth for the artist. While Art Informel painters depicted the devastation of war in their works, Molnár produced cold, emotionally detached works, close to abstraction, drawn with ruler and compass. Although she claimed that the circles, squares, and triangles in her work were apolitical, it can be argued that she was striving to re-establish a sense of control in a chaotic world marked by the horrors of war (Valyi-Nagy, 2024).

When examining Molnár's early works, one observes an approach that questions the boundaries of abstract art not only in terms of composition, but also through color and material. Influenced by leading figures of the time such as Malevich and Mondrian, she focused on simple forms and repetitive motifs in her works. In deliberate opposition to Mondrian's rigid views-particularly his insistence that abstraction should employ only primary colors like red, yellow, and blue-Molnár placed a golden rectangle on a neon orange monochromatic surface in her 1964 piece Icône, consciously rejecting such aesthetic dogmas (Lepercq, 2024).

Figure 2. Vera Molnár, Icon, oil on canvas, 73 x 73 cm, 1964

https://hyperallergic.com/941179/vera-molnar-fascination-with-the-glitches-in-the-matrix-centre-pompidou/

The artist's work demonstrates a systematic methodology in which geometric forms are arranged through algorithms. It is possible to note a strong resemblance to basic design principles. Her mode of expression relies on fundamental elements such as dots and lines. In her practice, the concepts of order, disruption, and repetition emerge as a coherent system (Bayraktar, 2024, p. 41). One exemplary work believed to form the foundation of her algorithmic pieces is M comme Malevitch, which was drawn by hand. This pencil-on-paper drawing derives its title from Kazimir Malevich; the letter "M" in the title simultaneously refers to Malevich, Mondrian, and Molnár herself. The artist deliberately makes reference to key figures of Modern Art. The repeated "M" characters within the composition generate a visual recurrence, structured within a simple and rule-based system.

Figure 3. Vera Molnár, M comme Malevitch Pencil on paper, 42.5 x 42.5 cm, 1967

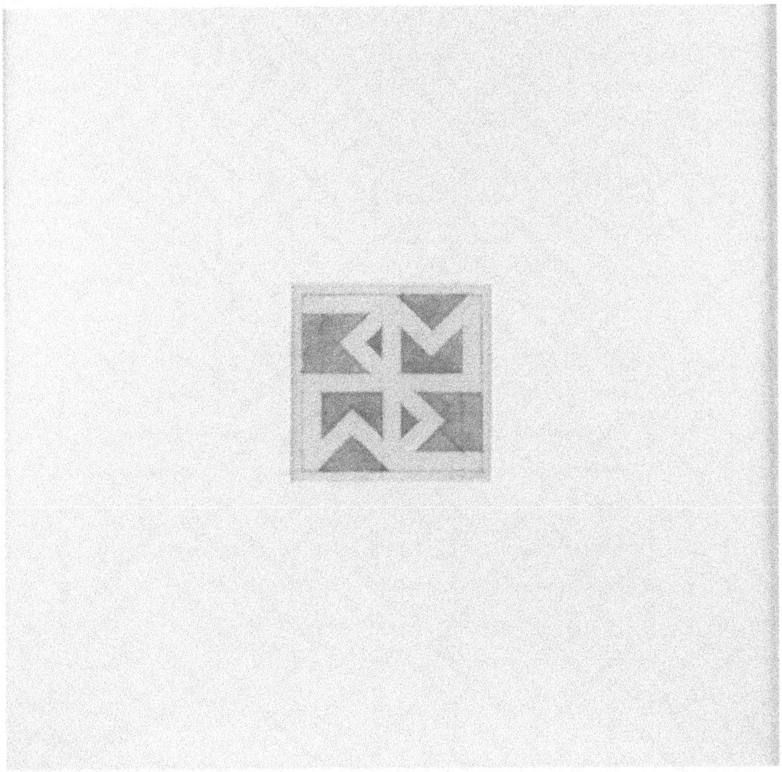

https://ropac.net/artists/231-vera-molnar/works/12818-vera-molnar-m-comme-malevitch-1967/

Molnár's 1966 work 4 éléments distribués au hasard (Four Elements Distributed at Random) is a significant example in which she explores the relationship between formal order and randomness. In this piece, the artist arranged short adhesive film strips in horizontal, vertical, or slightly inclined positions-tilted either to the left or right-creating a dynamic visual composition in which the elements are sometimes isolated, sometimes connected, and never identically repeated. This work reflects Molnár's deep interest in systematic structures, while also revealing an aesthetic approach that consciously avoids formal repetition (Lepercq, 2024).

Figure 4. Vera Molnar, Quatre éléments distribués au hasard, 1959.

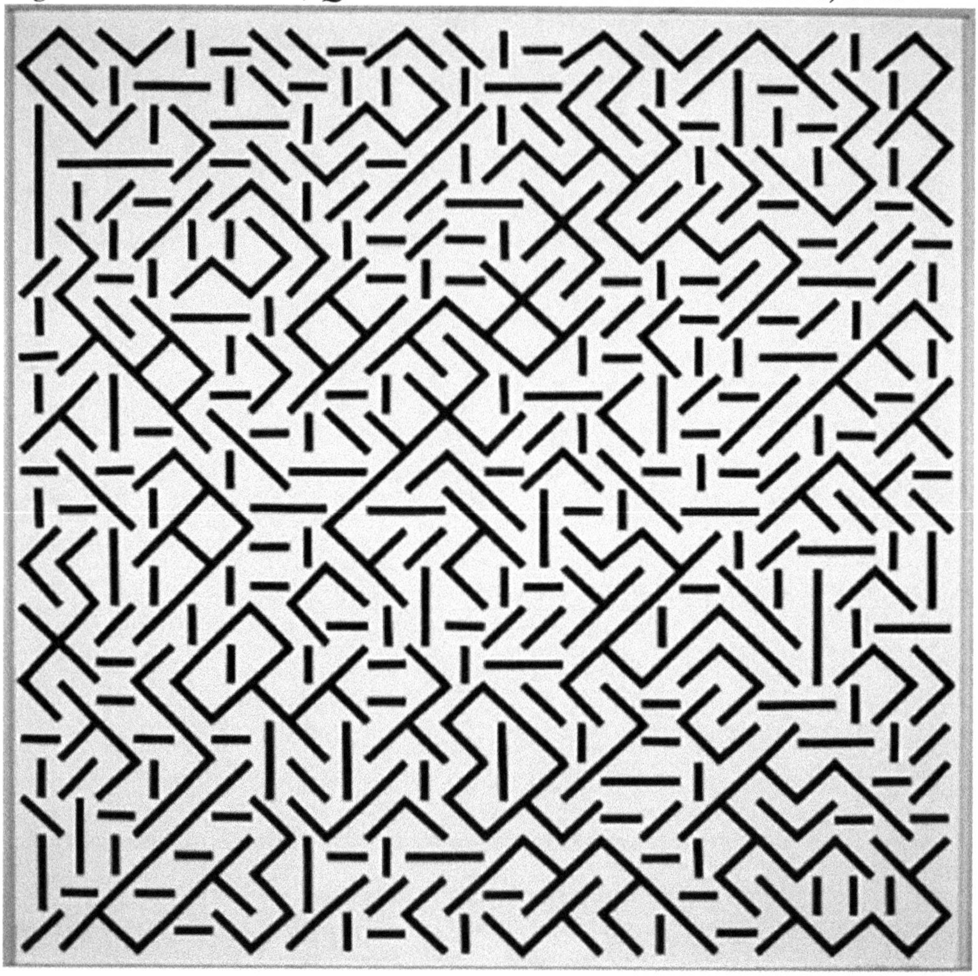

https://www.artsy.net/article/artsy-editorial-vera-molnar-mother-computer-art-pioneered-future-abstraction

In the 1960s, Molnár developed a method she referred to as machine imaginaire ("imaginary machine"). Through this approach, she aimed to function like a machine herself, producing formal repetitions based on specific rules and constraints. One of the most significant works from this period is the series À la Recherche de Paul Klee (In Search of Paul Klee), created between 1969 and 1970. Inspired by Klee's 1927 piece composed of colored striped squares, Molnár filled a grid of 81 squares with parallel and diagonal lines, generating a perception of color on the surface through dense line usage. The resulting composition is characterized by optical complexity and dynamism. In 1968, Molnár's imaginary machine became an actual machine (Lepercq, 2024). At the Sorbonne University, she gained access to a computer for the first time in a research laboratory and taught herself Fortran, one of the pioneering programming languages of the time. With this technical knowledge, she was able to input numerous algorithmic variations into the computer, directing commands based on the binary system (0 and 1) to a device called a plotter-a drawing machine equipped with a moving pen (Galerie Thaddaeus Ropac, n.d.).

In an article in which she reflects on her artistic process, Molnár explains that her algorithmic art practice, unlike that of her contemporaries, did not rely on a strict set of predefined rules. While other artists used grammars that defined how parameters should be changed in algorithmic art, Molnár shaped these rules during the creative process itself. As she drew with the help of a plotter, she altered parameters such as scale, shape, and line thickness, producing a new drawing distinct from the previous one. This control allowed her to evaluate whether she was approaching the visual result she desired. As she neared the intended aesthetic outcome, the interventions she made to the drawings became more subtle. However, she emphasizes that her actual method diverged further. Since waiting for each drawing to be plotted after changing parameters could take hours, she visualized them on a CRT screen. She termed this technique a "dialogue-based method." She selected a few of the screen images and then recorded them via plotter (Molnar, 1975, p. 187). "One of the series from this period, Molnaroglyphes (1977–78), investigates the deformation of a grid composed of squares. In the first version of the series, the squares are aligned regularly, but in subsequent drawings, they begin to move and overlap resembling cells in a petri dish" (Lepercq, 2024). The artist introduces systematic disruptions into her works by employing random functions, deliberately adding imperfections, manipulating geometric shapes, and engaging with interactions between the human and the machine. Lastly, these disruptions are repeated through iterative processes that also involve subjective judgment (Bayraktar, 2024, p. 42).

The Molnárt System, developed in 1973, which introduces small, deliberate deviations into algorithms, occupies a significant place in the history of algorithmic art as a pioneering approach to exploring the relationship between randomness and order. This approach proposes a new system that demonstrates the possibility of integrating mathematical order and controlled chance. In this system, Molnár added 1% irregularity to computer algorithms, producing works that brought randomness and control together on the same plane. In these pieces, order ceases to be merely an aesthetic concern, and small distortions are applied intentionally to enhance perceptual strength. Lines within the grid structure are often deliberately displaced, their angles or orientations altered. Molnár's systematic distortion approach shows parallels with Glitch art, which gained prominence much later in digital art. Although glitches may seem like accidental errors, like Molnár's 1% deviations, they have often been intentionally used by many artists.

TRACES OF GLITCH ART IN VERA MOLNAR'S WORKS

Glitches and Glitch Art are part of a media tradition that emerged in the 19th century and demonstrate that questions which initially appear clear and definitive in art and aesthetic perception actually belong to a temporary, problematic, or contradictory order (Betancourt, 2023). The term glitch is now widely used. However, its meaning often varies depending on context, and in many cases, it is used ambiguously. "At its core, a glitch is a form of accident not unlike those encountered repeatedly throughout history. However, the specific contexts that make such accidents possible have only existed for the past sixty years. This makes the glitch a relatively modern phenomenon" (Schultz-Figuero, 2011, p. 4). When examined etymologically, the term glitch most likely derives from the Yiddish word "glitsh," meaning slip or error. It comes from the German verb "glitschen" (to slip), which is connected to its older form "gliten," and further rooted in the Old High German verb "glitan" (to slide). Although the term seems to enjoy widespread contemporary usage, its first appearance in English literature dates back to 1962 in the writings of John Glenn. Glenn noted that astronauts used the term during the space program to describe issues they encountered. In its strictest sense, glitch was used to denote a sudden surge or fluctuation in electric current. Over time, however, the meaning expanded to include unexpected operational problems in everyday contexts. In this regard, astronauts played a key role in the popularization of the term (Houghton Mifflin Harcourt, 1992).

Moradi (2004), who conducted the first academic research on the topic, categorizes glitch art into two main types: "Pure Glitch" and "The Glitch-alike." He defines "pure glitch artists" as those who collect and display glitch images that occur without any software or programmatic intervention. Artists who consciously produce glitches for artistic purposes are referred to as "glitch-alike artists." In general, other artists do not consider pure glitch examples as genuine artistic production because such works typically consist of screen captures of randomly occurring errors. These images are presented as artworks by the artists. In contrast, glitch-alike artists deliberately manipulate software and hardware using a technique known as databending. These artists intentionally introduce distortions into the visuals by inputting erroneous commands or crashing the programs, creating works that are fully under the artist's control (Jackson, 2011).

Schultz-Figuero (2011) initially defines the glitch as something unexpected. According to him, a glitch seems to originate from the device itself rather than the programmer. He compares the word glitch to error, noting that the latter typically has a clearer and more identifiable cause. Just as accidents are eventually brought under control and transformed into technique, glitches are phenomena whose causes can be explained retroactively. Today, many artists consciously use glitches, and the concept of glitch aesthetics has begun to take shape. The glitch is a form of accident specific to modern technology. It is not intentional, but it is open to randomness. When it occurs, its origin is not immediately apparent and, therefore, should not automatically be interpreted as a programming error.

The first artistic use of glitches emerged during video art performances in Chicago in the 1970s. Over time, the code-based instructions of machines began to carry visual significance, and this phenomenon gradually evolved into a new form of expression. By the 1990s, such digital errors were recognized as part of the material reality of media, forming the foundation of Glitch Art. During this period, Glitch Art emerged as an aesthetic response to the encoding errors encountered in digital music, still or moving images during playback and sampling processes (Betancourt, 2023). The formation of a glitch does not solely rely on the artist. External inputs (such as incorrectly coded syntaxes, unauthorized data leaks, and digital hybridizations), hardware and software (tools carrying functional conflicts), and the viewer (as the actor who manages the processes of perception and interpretation) are also active components in this process. All of these agents operate within overlapping flows that shape the final structure in which the glitch is defined or experienced as a work of art. For this reason, even an intentionally created error can be considered within the scope of Glitch Art. Glitch Art is not merely an individual aesthetic shock or a random malfunction, but rather an artistic genre that manifests as a dynamic and pluralistic metaphor of expression, shaped by the contributions of multiple actors (Menkman, 2011).

Although Vera Molnár is not considered a direct representative of Glitch Art today, her practice can be evaluated within the scope of the "Glitch-alike" aesthetic defined by Moradi. Molnár's controlled distortions created through 1% deviations demonstrate a similar approach rooted in the deliberate production of system-internal errors, employing the concepts of randomness and error as aesthetic tools. This approach can be seen as a precursor to the idea of "reproducing through disruption" found in Glitch Art. The intentional and controlled deviations in her algorithmic works may be considered early examples of the conceptual foundation on which Glitch Art is built. Her works from this period consist of overlapping squares and polygons transformed through distortion. The systematic approach embedded in these structures corresponds to the rational, geometric, and distanced aesthetic that was prevalent in the contemporary art scene. The plotter drawings invite the viewer to focus on the formal properties of the visuals and to decipher the underlying system. However, these works also possess a strong material presence in addition to their computational structure. The thin paper on which the drawings are made retains traces of production, such as perforated edges and the phrase "Job froM MoLnar" at the top of the page. These details spark curiosity about the production process behind the image, encouraging the viewer to question not only the visual itself but also how it came into being (Valyi-Nagy, 2024).

Molnár noted that when she first created computer drawings, she was not yet highly skilled in programming. She stated that the works composed of grid squares filled with vertical and horizontal lines were actually developed from a system she had discovered during childhood. In the early stages of her computer-assisted production, the ability to work depended on whether the computer was available. She began creating works she could not have drawn by hand, generating 25-by-25 square grids with the help of the computer. The Interruptions series, created between 1968 and 1969, belongs to this period. In this series, the artist aimed to generate new forms from a series of regular structures, introducing shapes that connected or abruptly disappeared among the horizontal lines (Ulrich Obrist, 2018).

Figure 5. Vera Molnar, Interruptions. Plotter drawing, 28 x 28 cm. 1969.

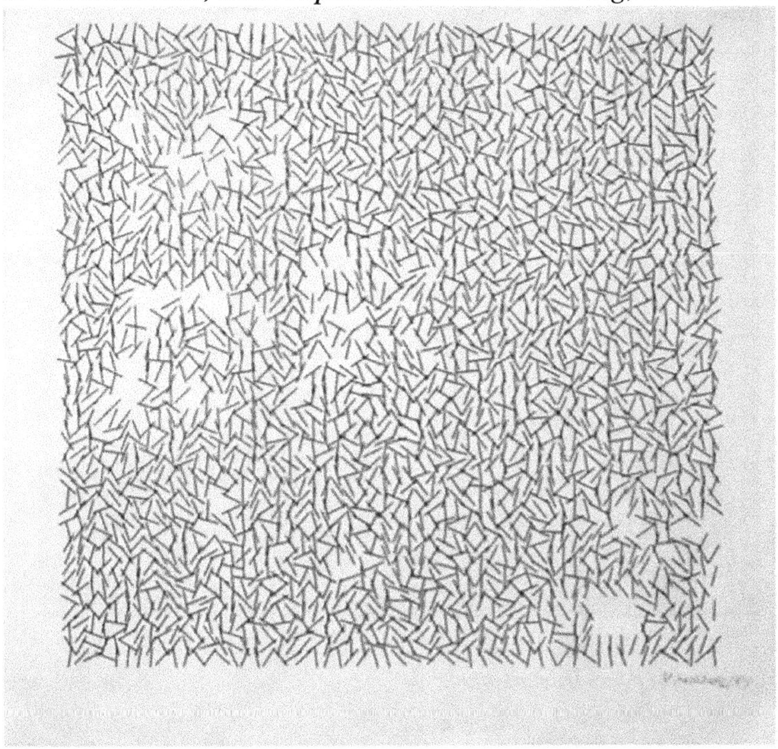

https://dam.org/museum/artists_ui/artists/molnar-vera/interruptions/#lightbox[rel-14884-584302156]-2

In this series, the artist constructs a grid composed of straight lines of equal length. She then assigns a random orientation to each line, creating diagonal and curved forms. Through this method, she aims to generate an effect of chaos upon an otherwise orderly structure. The result is a complex, dense pattern with lines appearing in various directions. Within the composition, randomly occurring voids take shape through the absence of lines and their relationship to the surrounding elements.

Figure 6. Vera Molnar, 1% de désordre, 50 × 65 cm, Plotter drawing, 1974, Artothek

https://how-to-app.de/unordnung.html

In 1974, the artist began to focus more intensely on the square form through the development of the Molnárt System. She constructed her works within grids composed of squares, creating arrangements in which the squares gradually decreased in size along the edges and were symmetrically positioned toward the center. In this system, parameters such as the size of the squares or the number of squares in each row are determined by the artist's preferences. After a while, she aimed to make small interventions within her own set of rules. By altering parameters or making slight adjustments, she began to generate a large number of different outcomes. At times, she removed squares from the grid, shifted the central point, or displaced the corners. She also began to introduce color into the system, integrating hues based on specific values or ratios.

These works were produced using a device called the "Benson Plotter." This machine, equipped with a pen, would replicate the lines defined in the program much like a human hand. The areas where the machine applied more pressure or where lines overlapped created dense markings that lent a painterly quality to the artist's compositions (How-to-App, n.d). Additionally, the artist experimented with attaching a graphite pencil to the machine, as well as with materials capable of producing color; such as blood, fruit juice, or red berries but was ultimately unsuccessful in achieving the desired results (Ulrich Obrist, 2018).

Figure 7. Vera Molnár, 1% de désordre (1% of disorder), 36x55 cm, computer plotter drawing on Benson paper, 1976

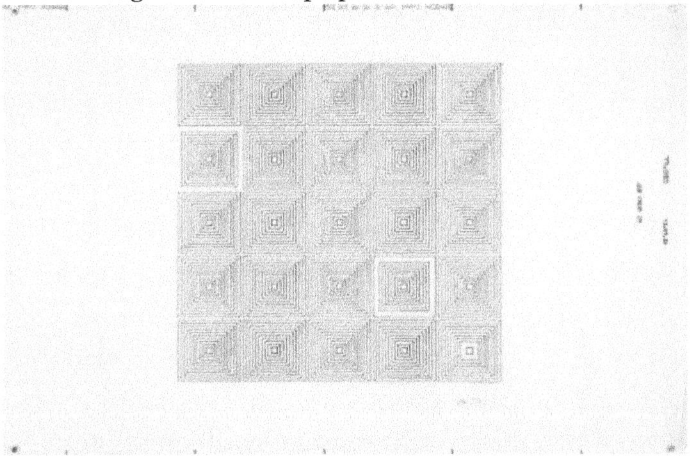

https://news.artnet.com/market/back-room-almine-rech-young-artists-2106572

Molnár's 1% de désordre is among her most significant works, reflecting both her artistic philosophy and the notion of deliberate error. Within a composition based on geometric order, the artist has intentionally introduced errors amounting to 1% of the structure. Through this work, she reveals the relationship between order and randomness, both mathematically and aesthetically. This piece also serves as the foundation of the system she developed, known as the Molnárt System. In an interview, Molnár explains her use of the concept of deliberate error applied through her method of 1% intentional deviation as follows:

> *"I love order, but I cannot bear it. The method I found to live in peace with myself and my surroundings is this: I make orderly structures and then inject so to speak, introduce 1% chaos. Why 1%? Because I like to define things. Maybe it's not even 1%, maybe it's 2%, and it increases with age. And that's not even due to a change in taste but a shift in mental capacity: I make mistakes, I stammer, I mix up words. And maybe that's where the chaos comes from (though maybe I just made this up for the sake of storytelling?). I think it comes from seeing large surfaces of perfectly ordered square grids on the computer screen and, upon realizing that it was technically possible, saying to myself, let's see what happens when I remove one square. And I must have liked it."(Ulrich Obrist, 2018)*

Her statement, "I love order, but I cannot bear it," encapsulates the core idea behind 1% de désordre. Uniform, systematic, and lifeless surfaces disturb her, and by intervening in this artificial order, she seeks to present it as something alive shaped by human hands. This choice may also reflect the reactions she received from her contemporaries at the time. She may have wanted the viewer to notice the faults within order, the visible boundaries of the system, and the human hand behind it.

During this period, when she exhibited her works, she faced significant criticism from her peers. She was accused of dehumanizing art by turning it into a machine-driven process. In response, she argued that computers were invented by humans and not gifted to humanity by God, and that the most human form of art could be made with computers. According to her, every component of a computer is crafted by human hands and intellect (Ulrich Obrist, 2018). In fact, computers are the products of human thought and labor. Creative output generated using them embodies the potential to reveal the imaginative capacities of the human mind. Through her works, Molnár may have sought to demonstrate that computer-based art does not negate the artist or devalue creative labor. Rather, she aimed to show that such works are not soulless or cold, but rather expressions of intuition and aesthetic intention where human intellect and decision-making remain central.

Figure 8. Vera Molnar, (Des)Ordres, plotter drawing, ink on paper, 70 x 70 cm, 1974.

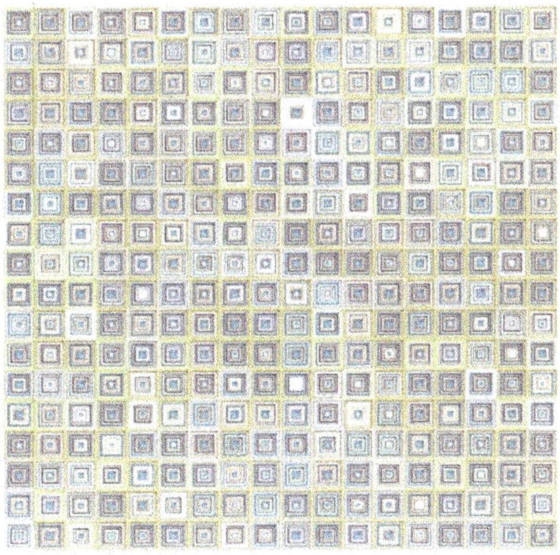

https://dam.org/museum/artists_ui/artists/molnar-vera/des-ordres/

In the (Des)Ordres series, the artist constructs a system composed of overlapping squares, which she disrupts through random interventions, thereby exploring the tension between order and disorder. Within this structure where the squares appear to vibrate Molnár intentionally creates a sense of tension within the orthogonal (right-angled) system. The title of the work is itself a deliberate play on words in French: the expression "désordres" (disorders) and "des ordres" (some orders) suggests a dual meaning, hinting that there may be an underlying logic or structure behind the surface-level chaos (Digital Art Museum, n.d.).

While these works are often interpreted today through the concept of randomness, Molnár did not rely solely on chance. Bayraktar summarizes the artist's perspective on this concept as follows:

"In exploring the relationship between chance and order, Molnár employed iterative production techniques nourished by human intuition and machine interaction. She developed a unique system for refining and selecting visual outputs in real-time dialogue with the machine. By observing visual results, she adjusted parameters and directed the process using subjective judgment. This method is not simply a matter of observing and altering a production; rather, this feedback

loop operates beyond the forms within the images, functioning in the very interaction between the artwork, the artist, and the computer" (Bayraktar, 2024, p. 47).

Molnár's creative process through her investigation of the interplay between structure, deviation, and intervention lays the conceptual groundwork for what would later evolve into the aesthetic of digital distortion. Her approach not only engages with geometric forms and algorithmic systems but also incorporates controlled disruption, intuitive intervention, and artificial randomness within the system itself. In this respect, while her works are not directly categorized as Glitch Art, they should nonetheless be regarded as a key historical threshold that prepared both the formal and conceptual terrain for it.

CONCLUSION

Vera Molnár is one of the pioneering artists who discovered the importance of computer technologies in artistic production in the 1960s. Vera Molnár's algorithmic works represent a significant turning point in redefining the boundaries of the relationship between art and machine at a time when digital technologies were beginning to be incorporated into artistic production. Using simple algorithms in her works, she created systematic compositions and adopted an abstract geometric form of expression based on her early productions. The deliberate errors and deviations applied in her algorithmic productions have made her one of the pioneers of computer art. These deliberate errors and deviations should be seen not only as a formal concern but also as a conceptual intervention. Together with her husband François Molnár, the artist developed the "1% disorder" approach, which she called the Molnárt System, creating small deliberate errors within traditional order and making randomness, intuition, and human intervention visible within the system. At the same time, by questioning the mechanical repetitions of the computer, she argued that the relationship between human and machine in artistic productions also encompassed an intuitive method. This approach can be seen as a precursor to the concepts of "error" and "glitch" that later formed the essence of Glitch art.

Molnár's works are also important in showing how technological tools can be transformed into an artistic language, representing a significant innovation of her time. She regarded the computer not merely as a tool but as an assistant in revealing creativity, bringing her intuition to the forefront in these productions and developing a new form of expression in art. This approach directly overlaps with Glitch art through her works, in which she proposed that aesthetic satisfaction could be achieved even through small errors within a system. In the systems she created, Molnár repeated interventions to understand when the result would be visually aesthetic or acceptable as art, managing this process through intuitive decisions and technical observations. She argued that it was difficult to see various variations in manually produced works and emphasized that such processes were easier to carry out with computers. In her works, not only the outputs of the machine but also the human intellect are prominently featured. Thus, she aimed to make the viewer decipher the logic behind these errors and glitches, creating unexpected emotions and reflections. Similarly, in Glitch art, visual phenomena such as digital crashes and data corruption serve similar purposes.

This research aims to analyze early examples of Glitch art in Molnár's artistic practice. Focusing on the digital works she produced in the 1960s and 1970s, the study interprets how the algorithmic approach in her works intersects with Glitch art. In the research, her works were examined through visual analysis and literature review methods. Her algorithmic works were analyzed both formally and conceptually, and the connection of the "Molnárt System" developed by the artist with Glitch art was explored. The findings reveal that although the artist is not a direct creator of what is now called Glitch art, she should be considered a pioneering figure who laid the historical and intellectual foundations of this art form through her production methods, conceptual approaches, and aesthetic perception. It is believed that her works created through deliberate distortion and randomness can be considered early examples of Glitch art. This approach is seen to have significantly contributed to the development of contemporary Glitch art. Furthermore, by freeing her practice from mechanical repetitions and highlighting human intellect, she is seen as an important guide for contemporary digital art practices. It can also be stated that the artist, by utilizing digital art, transformed the traditional painting surface and adopted an alternative method in this field. As a result, this research reveals that Molnár's works expanded the boundaries between computer art and traditional painting and developed a new approach in terms of aesthetics. Her abstract compositions created through algorithms are pioneering both in terms of integrating technological developments into artistic production and in expanding the possibilities of producing art in collaboration with the machine. Through the "Molnárt System" she developed, the concepts of deliberate distortion, randomness, and error included in the production process can also be considered as indicators of a new aesthetic search. In addition, this research enables a reevaluation of Molnár's art within the context of Glitch art, more clearly revealing her place in digital art.

REFERENCES

Altınyıldız Artun, N. (2016, 6 May). *Dada'nın Makine-İnsanları*. e-skop. https://www.e-skop.com/skopbulten/dadanin-100-yili-dadanin-makine-insanlari/2987

Antmen, A. (2009). *20. yüzyıl Batı sanatında akımlar* (2. bas.). Sel Yayıncılık.

Artun, A. (2021, 29 March). Refik Anadol ve Algoritma Sanatı. e-skop Bülten. https://www.e-skop.com/skopbulten/refik-anadol-ve-algoritma-sanati/6111

Avcı Tuğal, S. (2018). *Oluşum süreci içinde dijital sanat* (1. baskı). Hayalperest Yayınevi.

Bayraktar, K. O. (2024). *Düzeni seviyorum ama ona katlanamıyorum.* Hesaplar ve tesadüfler: Macaristan Ulusal Bankası Koleksiyonundan algoritma sanatı Dora Maurer + Vera Molnar + Gizella Rakoczy sergi kataloğu. Pera Müzesi.

Betancourt, M. (2023). *Glitch theory: Art and semiotics.* Im Pressd.

Ceric, V. (2008). Algorithmic Art: Technology, Mathematics and Art. In *2008 30th International Conference on Information Technology Interfaces* (pp. xx–xx). IEEE. https://doi.org/DOI: 10.1109/ITI.2008.4588386

Daudrich, A. (2016). Algorithmic Art and Its Art-Historical Relationships. *CITAR Journal*, 8(1), Special Issue: xCoAx.

Digital Art Museum. (n.d.). *Vera Molnar – (Dés)Ordres.* https://dam.org/museum/artists_ui/artists/molnar-vera/des-ordres/

Farthing, S. (2024). *Sanatın tüm öyküsü* (G. Aldoğan & F. C. Çulcu, Trans.; 5th5. Basım) Hayalperest Yayınevi.

Fortenberry, D., & Melick, T. (2015). *Tarih boyunca sanat: Dünya sanat tarihinde üsluplar veakımlar*. Yapı Kredi Yayınları.

Galerie Thaddaeus Ropac. (n.d.). *Vera Molnar*. https://ropac.net/gallery-documents/73/

Godfrey, T. (2024). *Çağdaş sanatın öyküsü* (Çev. belirtilmemiş). Hayalperest Yayınevi.

Houghton Mifflin Harcourt. (1992). *The American Heritage Dictionary of the English Language* (3rded.). https://archive.org/details/the-american-heritage-dictionary-of-the-english-language-third-edition-1st-august-1992

How-to-App. (n.d.). *Vera Molnar: Unordnung in der Ordnung*. https://how-to-app.de/unordnung.html

Jackson, R. (2011). *The Glitch Aesthetic* [Master's thesis, Georgia State University]. *ScholarWorks @ Georgia State University*. https://scholarworks.gsu.edu/communication_theses/80

Lepercq, E. (2024, 7 May). *Vera Molnar, Mother of Computer Art, Pioneered the Future of Abstraction*. Artsy. https://www.artsy.net/article/artsy-editorial-vera-molnar-mother-computer-art-pioneered-future-abstraction

Menkman, R. (2011). *Glitch Studies Manifesto*. Academia.edu. https://www.academia.edu/3847007/Menkman_Rosa_2011_Glitch_Studies_Manifesto

Molnar, V. (1975). Toward Aesthetic Guidelines for Paintings with the Aid of a Computerf. *Leonardo*, *8*(3), 185–189. DOI: 10.2307/1573236

Moradi, I. (2004). *Glitch Aesthetics* [Master's thesis]. School of Design Technology, Department of Architecture, The University of Huddersfield.

Obrist, H. U. (2018). Interview: Vera Molnár. In Székely, K. (Ed.), *Bookmarks: Revisiting Hungarian Art of the 1960s and 1970s* (pp. xx–xx). Koenig Books.

Schultz-Figueroa, B. (2011). Glitch/Glitsh: (More Power) Lucky Break and the Position of Modern Technology. *Culture Machine*, *12*, ●●●. https://static1.squarespace.com/static/6317b98c456d53408bb7b7a5/t/631819b3b615f529eecfd284/1662523828020/439-892-1-PB-2.pdf

Smithsonian American Art Museum. (n.d.). *Nam June Paik*. Smithsonian Institution. https://americanart.si.edu/artist/nam-june-paik-3670

Taylor, D. G. (2014). *When the Machine Made Art: The Troubled History of Computer Art*. Bloomsbury Publishing.

Valyi-Nagy, Z. (2024). Between the Lines. *Artforum International, 62*(9).

Wands, B. (2006). *Art of the digital age* (Akınhay, O., Trans.). Akbank Culture and Art Publications. (Original work published 2006)

Wilson, S. (2002). *Information Arts: Intersections of Art, Science, and Technology*. MIT Press.

ADDITIONAL READINGS

Arreola, P., Gardner, C., & Lenz, M. (2024). *Digital art (Victoria and Albert Museum): 1960s–now*. Thames and Hudson Ltd.

Arslan, C. (Ed.). (2021). *Dijital dönüşümün kültür ve sanat üzerindeki yansımaları*. Nobel Bilimsel Eserler.

Dekker, A. (Ed.). (2021). *Curating digital art: From presenting and collecting digital art to networked co-curation*. Valiz.

Demirci, M. E.,Ertan, İ. F. (2024). Algoritmik Sanat Pratikleri ve Örnek Bir Çalışma. Karatay Sanat ve Tasarım Dergisi, 1(1).

Guillermet, A. (2020). Vera Molnar's Computer Paintings, University of Cambridge Jackson, R. (2011, 23 Nov). The Glitch Aesthetic. Georgia State University ScholarWorks @ Georgia State University.

Paul, C. (2016). *Digital art* (3rd ed.). Thames & Hudson.

Reas, C., & McWilliams, C. (2010). *Published by Princeton Architectural Press.*

Taylor, B. (2015). *Art Today*. Laurence King Publishing.

KEY TERMS AND DEFINITIONS

Vera Molnár: Vera Molnár, a pioneer of computer art, created abstract geometric compositions using algorithmic processes and intentional disruptions.

Molnárt System: Molnár's unique method of introducing a 1% randomness into compositions to achieve controlled irregularity.

Glitch Art: An art form that embraces errors and malfunctions in digital or analog systems as an aesthetic expression.

Computer Art: A broad term for artistic works produced or processed using computer technologies.

Algorithmic Art: Art created through predefined rules and algorithms, often supported or executed by computers.

Chapter 8
Digital Art and Sculpture

Mustafa Bulat
http://orcid.org/0000-0002-2192-8508
Atatürk University, Turkey

Gülümser Beyaztaş Özlütürk
Atatürk University, Turkey

ABSTRACT

This study aims to examine contemporary artistic production processes at the intersection of digital art and sculpture. The impact of technological advancements on artistic disciplines has become increasingly evident, particularly in the field of sculpture, where the use of digital tools is now more prominent. Techniques such as 3D modeling, augmented reality (AR), virtual reality (VR), and digital fabrication have fundamentally transformed both material selection and modes of expression in sculpture.Digital sculpture has emerged from the integration of traditional sculpting techniques with digital technologies, offering artists a broader range of expressive possibilities. In this context, the study questions how digital technologies shape artistic creativity, transform the practices of artists, and redefine the dynamics of interaction between the viewer and the artwork.The societal and cultural contexts of digital art and sculpture will be analyzed, and evaluations will be made regarding the current position and potential future of these disciplines in the contemporary art world.

DOI: 10.4018/979-8-2600-0944-4.ch008

INTRODUCTION

Since the beginning, the human being, as a creature of intellect and senses, has ensured its existence by uniting daily life and art under a common roof (Bulat, S., 1999). Artists, inspired by forms in nature, have transformed nature according to their own perspectives by modifying or reinterpreting it while preserving its essence. During this period, debates about art intensified, and the social aspect and functionality of art began to be questioned (Bulat-Bulat and Aydın, 2014). As long as there are no boundaries placed on artists' creative freedom, opposing the fields they have reached or wish to reach, and certainly technological developments, is of no benefit (Bulat, S., 1999). From the last quarter of the 20th century onward, digital programs that began to be used in all areas of art, along with the output methods developed with these programs, have provided new possibilities in the field of sculpture as well(Bulat et al., 2014).

Throughout history, art has undergone continuous transformation in line with societal, cultural, and technological changes. Especially the process of industrialization has significantly influenced the methods of artistic production, modes of expression, and materials used, thereby reshaping aesthetic and conceptual frameworks. The advancement of technology has expanded the boundaries of human intellect and creativity, diversified artistic means of expression, and laid the groundwork for new artistic practices. Forms of artistic production and material usage are directly related to the social and economic dynamics of different periods. In particular, the Industrial Revolution and subsequent technological advances have been among the primary factors radically transforming the processes of art production. This transformation has not only changed the technical infrastructure of art but also restructured aesthetic perceptions, conceptual inquiries, and the social function of art (Bulat, M., 2014). However, the interaction between technology and art has also brought along various ethical and ontological debates. While cultural, social, and scientific developments have made significant contributions to human life, the integration of art with technology has necessitated the reevaluation of concepts such as originality, creativity, and authenticity.

The process of digitalization has changed the dynamics of art production and consumption, and has become a factor that reshapes the relationship between art and society. With the Industrial Revolution, artists began to surpass the limits of traditional production methods by integrating technologies that allowed mass production into artistic practice. With the acceleration of digitalization in the 20th century, this transformation gained momentum, and new artistic forms of expression that surpassed the limitations of analog media emerged. This process transformed the ontological and epistemological structure of art and reshaped production and representation practices in a fundamental way. Especially since the beginning of the 20th century, rapidly evolving social, economic, and cultural changes have deeply affected the structural transformation of art. The mechanization process that began with the Industrial Revolution redefined the relationship of art with traditional materials and techniques, while the spread of digitalization and composite technologies created new possibilities for production and expression for artists. In this context, artists felt the need to continuously renew and transform the form and content of art by integrating the production tools and techniques of the era into their works. Technological advancements have restructured the classical production processes of art, laying the groundwork for intellectual and conceptual approaches beyond the traditional art understanding based on manual skills.This process has enabled art to establish more flexible relationships with the concepts of time and space, thus giving rise to contemporary artistic forms of expression (Coşkun, 2014). In this regard, the interaction between art and technology has been evaluated not merely as a functional transformation, but also as a dynamic process that deeply affects the conceptual structure of art.

Digital art and especially the practice of digital sculpture represent a significant paradigm shift that radically transforms artistic production processes and necessitates the reevaluation of the ontological and epistemological status of the artwork. The digitalization process has surpassed the structure of art based on traditional production techniques and material use, leading to the emergence of new artistic expressions based on data-oriented and algorithmic processes. This transformation has enabled artworks to exist in digital environments rather than as physical representations, allowing them to take on variable and interactive forms.

As a field that questions and redefines the ontological structure of art, digital sculpture practice pushes the boundaries of the material existence of the artwork and foregrounds concepts such as virtual space and digital material. While physical form, material, and spatial installation were considered decisive elements in traditional sculpture practice, digital sculpture has been used by artists as a tool that reconstructs form, space, and perception processes through data, software, and digital environments.

Therefore, digital sculpture art reevaluates fundamental concepts such as permanence,variability, and interactivity of the artwork and demonstrates how art is reshaped in the context of new media and virtual reality.With an information-based approach, digital art also contributes to the redefinition of knowledge production and the artistic creation process. While traditional art production is largely seen as the result of an individual creative process, digital art practice presents a collective and systematic model of knowledge production through data-driven algorithms, AI-assisted production methods, and the artist's interaction with programming tools. Thus, it has transformed both the modes of production and perception of the artwork, making the interaction between art and technology a more dynamic relationship.

In this context, the transformation brought by digital art and the practice of digital sculpture necessitates the reconsideration of the meaning, material, and social function of the artwork within a new epistemological and ontological framework by reconstructing the traditional conceptual frameworks of art. Therefore, the transformation process that art undergoes through digitalization should be evaluated not merely as a technical development but as a fundamental transformation that alters the theoretical structure and perceptual paradigm of art. Throughout history, art has evolved in parallel with technological advancements, undergoing transformations in production practices, modes of expression, and aesthetic approaches. One of the significant stages that this evolution has reached in the contemporary period is digital art. As a practice shaped by the use of digital tools such as computer technologies, algorithms, artificial intelligence, and interactive media, digital art has become a discipline that fundamentally changes today’s artistic production processes. The new expressive possibilities that artistic production has gained through digitalization have necessitated both the reevaluation of aesthetic concepts and the transformation of creative processes. While elements such as physical material and handcrafts were decisive in traditional art understanding, digital art has redefined the materiality and representation of art through data-oriented systems, software-based applications, and virtual environments. In this context, digital art should be considered not only as a technical advancement but also as a phenomenon that transforms the ontological and epistemological status of art, reshaping the processes of production, distribution, and perception.

Art has played a central role in the historical and cultural development processes of societies and has existed as a fundamental element in the formation of collective identity. Artistic productions serve not only as aesthetic expressions but also as cultural heritage that reflects a community's value systems, beliefs, and historical dynamics.The socio-political and economic transformations of societies have continuously influenced the forms and themes of art, giving art the quality of a historical document and ensuring the preservation of cultural identity. Artworks reflect the intellectual and social structures of the periods to which they belong and function as a narrative medium that transcends time. Although many civilizations throughout history have disappeared due to political, economic, or ecological reasons, their artistic productions have continued to exist and transmit their cultural heritage to the present day.The function of art in this context requires its evaluation not merely as an individual or aesthetic creative process but as a discipline that facilitates the preservation of collective memory and historical continuity. Accordingly, the examination of artworks serves as an important epistemological tool in understanding the different periods of the past by offering a comprehensive perspective on a society's history, social structure, and intellectual system.

Throughout history, artists have held a special position within social structures and have played a decisive role in the interaction between the processes of artistic production and social dynamics. Artistic production practices based on individual creativity stand out as one of the fundamental elements that distinguish it from traditional and anonymous cultural formations. While art, as an objective phenomenon, takes shape within certain aesthetic, technical, and conceptual frameworks, it is also shaped by the individual intervention and intellectual orientation of the artist, who is the subject of the creative process (Toptaş, R., 2022).

In this context, the ontological status of the artwork is directly associated with the artist's creative act, and the social role of art reveals how individual creativity is shaped through interaction with cultural transmission processes. Gombrich (1992), likewise, emphasizes that art is a concrete reality created by artists, thereby highlighting the relationship between the subjective creative processes of artistic production and its material representation. The individual intervention of the artist becomes one of the fundamental factors that determine the content and form of the artwork, while this production process is also evaluated within the context of cultural continuity and aesthetic transformation.The production process of art inevitably intertwines with a dynamic of consumption, thereby creating a multidimensional interactional field that determines the economic value of the artwork. Artistic production cannot be reduced merely to the creative practice of the artist; it also exists within an economic ecosystem shaped by viewers, collectors, and actors of the art market.

Artworks, in addition to their aesthetic and conceptual values, transform into economic commodities, thus contributing to the formation of mechanisms of artistic circulation. This reciprocal relationship between production and consumption provides a critical framework for understanding how art is positioned within market conditions and how the institutional structures that determine the value of the artwork operate. In this regard, the connection between art and the economy should not be considered solely as a process of generating material value but also as a system that enables the formation of cultural capital (Uğurlu, 2008, p.249).

When the economic dimension of art is addressed in the context of the dynamics of modern art markets, it is necessary to take into account the decisive influence of elements such as galleries, auction houses, museums, and independent collectors, which determine the circulation of artworks. This interaction between the production and consumption of art contributes to the economic and sociological analysis of art history by functioning as a mechanism that repositions the social function and cultural value of the artwork.Throughout history, art has functioned as one of the fundamental elements shaping societies' sense of identity and understanding of history. Artistic production processes play a determining role not only through aesthetic and conceptual dynamics but also in constructing the cultural identity of a society, thus mediating the preservation of historical continuity. Beyond reflecting the value systems and ideological orientations of the period in which they were created, artworks exist as carriers of collective memory. In this context, the process of artistic production should not be evaluated merely as a creative and individual practice; it should also be considered as a mechanism integrated with economic and social systems. The reciprocal relationship between the production and consumption of art has enabled art to acquire economic value and has created the market conditions that determine the circulation mechanisms of artworks. While artworks undertake a historical role as elements of cultural heritage, they also gain economic value in the art market and become an important component of capital flow. While the artist's individual creativity and the artistic production process determine the ontological and epistemological status of art, they also undergo economic processes driven by market dynamics. In this regard, art possesses a dual identity as both an aesthetic and cultural form of expression and a component of economic systems.

The role of art within economic systems, through institutions such as museums, galleries, auction houses, and collectors, contributes to the integration of artistic production processes into market conditions by determining the material value of artworks. Art should be evaluated not only as a medium of individual creative action and cultural transmission but also as a factor shaping the processes of economic capital production and distribution. In this context, the value of the artwork is defined not only by its aesthetic and conceptual content but also by the economic status it acquires under market conditions.In this respect, the social function of art should be considered in the context of both cultural and economic systems. The processes of artistic production and circulation evolve under the influence of economic dynamics shaped by market conditions, along with the aesthetic and intellectual elements that guide a society's understanding of identity and history. Accordingly, the interaction between the cultural and economic dimensions of art should be evaluated as one of the fundamental factors that determine the place and function of the artwork within society.The influence of contemporary technologies on art has radically transformed artistic practices through the widespread use of digital media and the integration of computational systems into the art production process. Digital art, using digital tools such as computer technologies, artificial intelligence, augmented and virtual reality, expands the traditional boundaries of art while radically redefining art forms based on tangible forms such as sculpture. This interaction between art and technology reconsiders the materiality and spatial relations of art and reveals how digital form creates a transformation in art production.The fundamental elements of traditional sculpture—form, space, and material—are being restructured through digital technologies and enriched with virtual and augmented reality applications, producing new artistic experiences beyond physical space. The transformation created by digitalization in sculpture should be considered not only as a technical innovation but also as an aesthetic and epistemological paradigm shift. The relationship of sculpture with physical materials and spatial positioning is expanded through digital technologies, allowing the artwork to gain an interactive and variable structure.

In this context, examining the impact of digital art on sculpture both technically and conceptually requires addressing the role of digitalization in contemporary art from a more holistic perspective. In digital sculpture art, artists are moving away from traditional production techniques and developing new approaches based on data-driven, parametric design systems and algorithmic processes, thereby reinterpreting the ontological status of sculpture. The transformation undergone during the digitalization process of sculpture challenges concepts such as permanence, tactility, and spatiality of the artwork; replacing the traditional understanding of material with dynamic elements such as data, light, and motion as the fundamental components of art.From this perspective, digital sculpture practice is directly related to the technological transformation of contemporary art and should be evaluated not merely as a technical advancement but as a development that reshapes the theoretical framework of art. The new modes of production and expression acquired through digitalization necessitate understanding the transformed structure of art from both an aesthetic and epistemological standpoint. Accordingly, digital sculpture art should be considered not only in relation to traditional artistic understanding but also as a discipline guiding the artistic production forms of the future.Digital art, as a contemporary art form based on the use of computers, algorithmic systems, and digital technologies, plays a central role in the transformation of artistic production processes. This creative approach, which adopts digital tools as alternatives to the materials and techniques of traditional art, re-evaluates the ontological and epistemological status of art and introduces an innovative dimension to modes of artistic expression. The development of digital art enables the artwork to exist in data-oriented and interactive forms rather than through physical representation; thus, it radically transforms the processes of perceiving and producing art.The new production methods acquired by art through digitalization have become one of the factors shaping the evolution of art both aesthetically and technically. While physical material and form are regarded as defining elements in traditional art practices, digital art restructures these concepts and enables time, space, and material to be addressed in a variable and flexible context. Virtual environments, augmented reality applications, and artificial intelligence-supported production techniques affect both the production and perception processes of the artwork, offering new possibilities to the artist's creative practice.

The transformation of digital art, especially in terms of digital sculpture practice, enables the fundamental elements of traditional sculpture form, space, and material to be restructured through digital environments. Digital sculpture allows for the use of dynamic elements such as data and light instead of physical material, thus reinterpreting the materiality of the artwork. This transformation experienced by sculpture in the process of digitalization should not only be considered as a technical advancement but also as a development that reshapes the theoretical framework and perceptual paradigm of art.As a result, digital art expands the traditional boundaries of art through the opportunities provided by technology and makes unique contributions to contemporary art understanding. The digitalization process of art not only creates a technical transformation in artistic production practices but also restructures the cultural, epistemological, and economic dimensions of art. In this context, digital art should be considered as one of the determining factors shaping the function of art in today's society and the creative practice of the artist, and as a discipline that sheds light on the future directions of art.

The origins of digital art are directly related to the emergence of computer technology, and especially the 1950s and 1960s stand out as the period in which the art world first came into contact with digital tools. During these years, computers were used by institutions with limited access, such as large companies, military research institutions, and academic centers, and could not be directly integrated into the artistic production process. However, the new possibilities offered by computer technology enabled significant steps to be taken toward the transformation of creative processes in the art world and laid the foundations of digital art.In this period, although computer-assisted artistic production methods were limited, artists began to produce visual compositions through mathematical calculations and programmable systems. From the 1960s onward, the interaction between art and technology gradually intensified, and especially computer graphics and algorithmic artistic approaches accelerated the shaping of digital art. The potential of technology to expand artistic expression was handled more systematically by artists in the following years, thus solidifying the place of digital art within the contemporary art understanding.The spread of digital art gained momentum with the advancement of technology and the accessibility of personal computers. The 1980s and 1990s were a critical period in which the production and circulation mechanisms of digital art were shaped, and this process caused a radical transformation in the ontological status and production processes of art. Especially with the emergence of the internet and the development of digital imaging systems, art works moved away from physical representation and began to exist in digital environments, thereby restructuring the aesthetic and conceptual framework of digital art (Toptaş, 2022, p.171).The historical development of digital art is directly connected to the technological transformation of art, and this process is considered not only as a technical advancement but also as a fundamental paradigm shift that changes the conceptual structure and perception methods of art. The origins and development process of digital art offer a critical perspective for understanding the relationship of the contemporary form of art with technology. Sculpture art, as one of the fundamental disciplines in plastic and visual arts with its ability for three-dimensional representation, has undergone significant technical and conceptual transformations throughout history.

This art form, which is as old as human history, was initially shaped using natural materials such as stone, clay, and wood, and was formed through carving techniques, thereby expanding areas of artistic expression. The basic production processes of sculpture art evolved by benefiting from the technological and material possibilities available in each period, and especially with the development of casting technologies in the Middle Ages, it underwent a significant structural transformation. The fundamental elements of traditional sculpture form, space, and material were restructured with the production techniques of each era, and in addition to carving and shaping techniques, casting and assembling methods were integrated into the artistic production process. This process enabled sculpture to become not only an aesthetic object but also an art practice that reflects the cultural identity of societies and preserves historical heritage. The attainment of aesthetic and intellectual depth by sculpture through figurative forms is directly related to production techniques, and technological innovations have been a factor that continuously transforms the artist's creative practice. This transformation has reached a more radical dimension in the contemporary period, especially with the integration of digital technologies into sculpture production processes. Digitalization restructured the traditional understanding of material in sculpture through dynamic elements such as data, light, and motion, and changed the perception of space and form through virtual environments and augmented reality applications. This transformation of sculpture in the context of digital art should be evaluated as a continuation of the technical innovations experienced in previous periods and should be considered as an extension of the evolution sculpture art has undergone throughout history.

Sculpture art, both in historical and contemporary contexts, has been shaped by technical and conceptual transformations and constantly redefines the relationship between materiality and space in artistic production. The evolution that sculpture has undergone throughout history offers an important perspective in understanding how art integrates with technological advancements and how aesthetic concepts undergo change. The effect of digitalization on sculpture art should be evaluated not only as an innovation in production techniques but also as a paradigm that transforms the ontological and epistemological structure of art. In the modern and digital age, sculpture art, through digital production techniques and innovative material uses, necessitates a reevaluation of the ontological and epistemological structure of art both theoretically and practically. While traditional sculpture understanding is characterized by shaping techniques based on physical materials and craftsmanship, the digitalization process has brought new production methods to the artist's creative practice, thereby evolving artistic expression forms into more complex and abstract structures. Computer-aided design systems, parametric modeling methods, and three-dimensional printers have been integrated into the production processes of sculpture art, enabling the emergence of new production practices where physical and digital environments are intertwined. Especially algorithmic design and digital simulations allow the artist to go beyond traditional spatial boundaries, making it possible for production processes to become data-oriented and for dynamic forms to be created. In this context, contemporary sculpture art internalizes the technical and conceptual innovations gained through the digitalization process of art and undergoes a paradigm shift that reshapes the nature of artistic representation. In digital sculpture practice, digital data-based production processes gain prominence instead of physical objects; thus, sculpture becomes a discipline that redefines the concepts of material and space through virtual environments, augmented reality, and interactive systems. Thanks to the flexibility offered by digital technologies, artists go beyond traditional forms and enable sculpture to gain interactive and variable structures independent of physical space. This situation questions the traditional understanding of materiality in art and shows how digital art provides a new epistemological framework in artistic production.

In the modern and digital age, sculpture art, while restructuring production processes through digital technologies, necessitates the interpretation of the changing structure of art both aesthetically and conceptually. The new forms of expression acquired by sculpture art through digitalization allow for a different perspective in addressing the use of material and spatiality in art and should be considered a development that presents new production models and sheds light on the future directions of art within contemporary art understanding. Sculpture art largely preserved the classical structure it acquired during the Archaic period until the beginning of the 20th century, and artists continued to produce works with traditional forms and materials for a long time. However, with the beginning of the 20th century, as art began to interact with different disciplines and new aesthetic understandings developed, a structural transformation process started in sculpture art. Especially the radical rethinking of artistic practices by modernism initiated a process that expanded the conceptual and technical boundaries of sculpture art.

The transformation that took place in the second half of the 20th century caused radical changes in the traditional definition of art and enabled sculpture to go beyond being merely a formal representation. Artists stepped outside traditional forms of expression and benefited from the possibilities offered by different fields of art, developing interdisciplinary production methods. In this process, the use of materials and techniques in sculpture art diversified; industrial materials, ready-made objects, kinetic structures, and installation art were adopted as new forms of expression by artists (Ballı, 2023, p.78).

With the process of digitalization, the evolution of sculpture art has been carried to a more radical dimension, and digital tools such as computer-aided design, algorithmic modeling, augmented reality, and three-dimensional printers have been integrated into artistic practice. These developments changed the relationship of sculpture with spatial and physical representation, offering artists new forms of expression through virtual environments and data-oriented production systemsHere is the word-for-word English translation of your text:The transformation of sculpture from a traditional structure to a digital format should be evaluated as a paradigm shift that questions the ontological and epistemological boundaries of art.

The historical development of sculpture art should be addressed as a process directly connected to the interdisciplinary transformation of art and technological advancements. The conceptual and technical changes experienced in the 20th century have shaped the contemporary forms of sculpture art, and the integration of digital technologies into art is evaluated as a significant development that sheds light on the future orientations of art. Throughout history, sculptors have shaped artistic forms of expression by using traditional materials such as marble, metal, stone, wood, and clay in their production practices. However, with the interdisciplinary structure of contemporary art and the integration of digital technologies into artistic production, sculpture practice has entered a radical transformation process.

Technological developments have become a factor that redefines the artist's creative practice both conceptually and technically, changing the production paradigm of sculpture art. Especially the widespread use of three-dimensional modeling software and computer-aided production techniques allows sculptors to move away from traditional methods and adopt production processes through digital platforms.

Traditional sculpture production includes techniques based on the use of physical space and materials, while the digitization process allows the artist to transcend spatial boundaries and shape works through data-driven design and parametric modeling.In this context, contemporary sculpture art redefines artistic production processes both technically and aesthetically, centering the interaction between physical space and the digital environment. Today, computer-aided software programs enable sculptors to move away from traditional workshop environments and turn to digital sculpture design, allowing the artist to reinterpret their creative practice with new technological tools.Three-dimensional printing technologies, algorithmic modeling, and augmented reality applications encourage artists to create digital sculptures and to develop interactive, variable, and parametric systems in artistic production processes.

This transformation demonstrates that digitization should be evaluated not only as a technical innovation in contemporary sculpture art but also as an ontological and epistemological paradigm shift.

In the modern era, the technological transformation of sculpture art reconstructs the relationship of art with materiality and spatiality, diversifying the artist's creative practice through digital tools.

The new production forms and expressive possibilities gained during the digitization process of sculpture should be considered a decisive development that creates a radical change in both artistic perception and the aesthetic framework, shedding light on the future orientations of art.

As a result of technological advancements, the digitization process has created a transformative shift in sculpture art, just as in many other art disciplines, and has profoundly restructured the production processes.

While traditional sculpture art existed for many years through production techniques based on physical materials and craftsmanship, with the development of digital technologies, these practices have evolved in line with the contemporary art perspective. These technologies, shaped within a multidisciplinary process, change the relationship of sculpture with form, space, and materiality, offering new expressive possibilities to the artist's creative practice. Especially computer-aided design systems, three-dimensional printers, augmented reality applications, and artificial intelligence-based production techniques diversify the production methods of sculpture art and encourage a paradigm shift that requires reconsideration of the ontological and epistemological structure of the artwork.

The traditional perception of form and space in sculpture art transforms into a flexible and dynamic structure during the digitization process, allowing the artist to create their works through digital environments.

This process evolving from physical production to digital design redefines both the conceptual and technical aspects of sculpture. The impact of the digitization process on contemporary sculpture art is not limited to technical innovations, but also transforms artistic forms of expression, allowing the artist to move away from traditional understandings of material. Thanks to data-oriented design processes and the flexibility offered by virtual spaces, sculpture gains structures that transcend the boundaries of physical space and interact with the viewer; thus, production practices and the meaning of art are addressed in a new context. These developments show that digitization is not merely a technical advancement in sculpture art but a theoretical transformation that deeply affects artistic creativity.

In this context, the impact of technological advancements on contemporary sculpture art creates a structure that reconstructs the spatial, material, and representational relations of artistic production.

The integration of digitization into art transforms the artist's creative practice and allows for a reinterpretation of the artwork's connection with physical materiality. Accordingly, digital sculpture art should be evaluated with an interdisciplinary approach within the understanding of contemporary art and considered a fundamental development that defines the future forms of artistic production.

Sculpture art, through its historical process, has evolved in terms of material and technique, becoming a discipline in which the artist continuously re-evaluates methods of shaping physical form.

While traditional sculpture practice is based on creating concrete forms with physical materials such as stone, marble, and bronze, the digitization process adds technological innovations to this production model and transforms artistic creation processes both conceptually and formally.

Digital sculpture transcends the spatial and material limitations of the physical world, allowing the artist to address their aesthetic and technical approaches within a new paradigm. (Bulat, S., 2010)

Computer-aided design (CAD) software, three-dimensional modeling techniques, and augmented reality applications have been integrated into the production processes of digital sculpture art, expanding the artist's ways of representing nature and space. Carving, casting, and shaping techniques used in traditional sculpture art have been brought to a new dimension in the digital environment through parametric modeling, virtual simulations, and interactive systems.In this process, the materiality of sculpture gives way to data-driven designs, and the artist shapes the artwork within digital environments without being dependent on physical space. Digital sculpture practice not only creates a technical transformation but also deeply affects the ontological and epistemological structure of art, redefining the ways in which the artwork is produced and perceived. While perception of form and space is accepted as defining elements in traditional sculpture art, digital technologies enable the creation of variable, interactive, and dynamic structures by distancing artistic production from physical limitations. In this context, the development of digital sculpture art strengthens the interdisciplinary nature of art and introduces new forms of expression to the understanding of contemporary art. Therefore, digital sculpture art has become a discipline that redefines the spatial and material boundaries of sculpture through the integration of technological innovations into artistic production processes.

The role of digitization within the understanding of contemporary art has been addressed not only as a technical advancement but as a fundamental development that shapes the perceptual and conceptual transformation of art. This process reveals a significant paradigm shift that determines the forms of representation of art in the digital age and sheds light on the future directions of sculpture art.

Contemporary art practices maintain the continuity of traditional art forms and preserve the historical and cultural context of art; however, at the same time, they evolve into new production processes and forms of expression under the influence of technological advancements. The digitization process emerges as a factor that transforms the artist's creative practice both technically and conceptually and signals a paradigm shift that radically changes the production models of art. In this context, the widespread use of computer-aided three-dimensional software programs has encouraged the more systematic use of digital technologies in art production and has laid the foundation for the emergence of new artistic forms of expression called digital art and digital sculpture. (Kaya, 2023, p.3) The development of digital art and digital sculpture necessitates a reevaluation of the ontological and epistemological structure of art, enabling the formation of artworks through data, algorithmic processes, and virtual environments instead of physical representation. Computer-aided design (CAD) software, parametric modeling techniques, and augmented reality applications allow the artist to overcome spatial and material limitations and realize the production process through digital platforms. While traditional sculpture art relies on production methods based on the use of physical material, in digital sculpture art, artists create new artistic experiences through virtual spaces, interactive systems, and data-driven designs. This transformation should be addressed not only as a technical advancement but also as a structural change that shapes the theoretical framework and artistic production processes of art. The effect of digitization on contemporary sculpture art expands the artist's aesthetic and conceptual approaches and enables the traditional relationship of art's production process with space, time, and materiality to be addressed in a different context.In this context, digital art and digital sculpture practice should be evaluated as a critical development that transforms the artist's creative process and introduces an interdisciplinary perspective to the understanding of contemporary art.In this context, the role of digital art and digital sculpture within contemporary art practices expands the traditional boundaries of art and ensures that the production processes of art are restructured in line with technological developments.

The digitization of the artistic creation process strengthens the interaction between the physical representation of art and digital environments and should be considered a significant development that determines the future orientations of art. Digital sculpture practice enables artistic creation based on data-driven and algorithmic processes by moving away from traditional production methods based on physical material. Computer-aided design (CAD) software, augmented reality applications, and parametric modeling techniques allow artists to shape their works through digital platforms and transform the spatial representation of art into a structure that transcends the boundaries of physical space. In this context, digital sculpture art expands the formal and conceptual frameworks of traditional sculpture and integrates with new media arts and interdisciplinary production processes.

Thanks to the production opportunities offered by digital technologies, artists construct their artworks not only as physical objects but also as interactive, variable, and parametric structures within virtual environments.

This process, which radically re-evaluates the relationship of sculpture with materiality, transcends the traditional boundaries of concepts such as space, time, and form in art and redefines artistic production both technically and theoretically. The integration of digitization into art redefines the epistemological boundaries of art as a factor that transforms not only the production process but also the perception and interaction forms of art. In this context, digital sculpture art constitutes a critical example showing how technological developments have transformed artistic production processes within the understanding of contemporary art. Artists re-interpret the traditional forms of sculpture through digital tools and develop innovative production techniques that question the spatial and material boundaries of art, thus creating a new form of expression that sheds light on the future directions of art. In this context, digital sculpture practice is evaluated as a dynamic art form that strengthens the interdisciplinary structure of art and expands its aesthetic approaches. The position of digital sculpture art within contemporary art practices should be addressed not only as a technical advancement but also as a conceptual renewal process that transforms the ontological and epistemological structure of the artwork. The digitization process has caused a radical change in the ways in which the artwork is produced and perceived, creating a new artistic paradigm that differentiates the artist's creative intervention and the interaction mechanisms established with the viewer. While in traditional sculpture practice, the artist's direct relationship with physical material is a determining factor, the integration of digital technologies into artistic production has redefined the spatial, material, and conceptual structure of the artwork. Three-dimensional modeling techniques, artificial intelligence-supported design processes, and augmented reality applications allow the artist to radically reinterpret the forms and functions of sculpture. This process not only expands the production techniques of art but also transforms the interaction and experience forms that the artwork establishes with the viewer, allowing it to gain a dynamic and variable structure. The interactive structure of digital sculpture reconsiders the work-viewer relationship, which is defined in a static manner in traditional sculpture art, contributing to the artistic production gaining a performative and process-oriented dimension. Thanks to the flexibility offered by digital tools, artists are able to construct structures based on data, light, and moving elements independently of the limitations of physical space, thus developing new aesthetic and technical approaches that expand the conceptual boundaries of art. In this context, the integration of digital technologies into artistic production points to a paradigm shift that transforms the traditional forms and functions of sculpture art.

As a result, the development of digital sculpture art should be considered not merely as a technical innovation, but as a process that re-evaluates the relationship between art and space, time, and form. Digitization not only questions the use of materials in art but also diversifies artistic modes of representation and offers new ontological perspectives. In this context, digital sculpture practice, gaining an interdisciplinary perspective within the understanding of contemporary art, is evaluated as a defining development that shapes the future directions of art.

Figure 1. Digital Michelango Project Red created by laser scanner the ribbon scans David's face. By analyzing these scans, we found David to be 0.29 mm digitizes with spatial resolution.

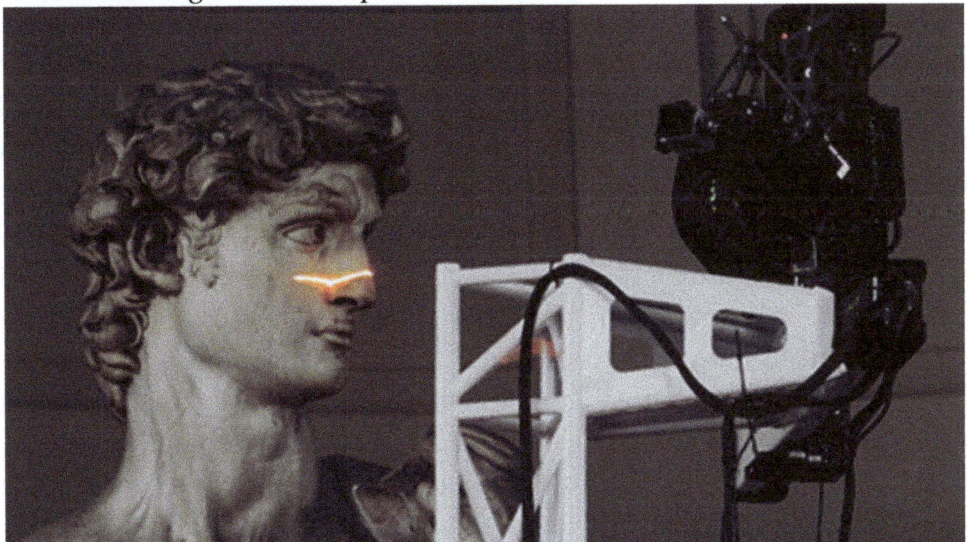

Source: Kaya, A.2023

The process of digitalization has led to the emergence of new methodological approaches in the context of the preservation, examination, and transmission of artworks to future generations. In this regard, developments in digital art and digital sculpture have offered innovative solutions for the preservation of cultural heritage. The Digital Michelangelo Project serves as a concrete example of the interaction between art and technology, enabling the detailed digital transfer of Michelangelo's David sculpture through laser scanning technology, which scans the surface with high precision.

This process facilitates the transfer of the artwork's physical structure to digital platforms, creating a digital model of the surface geometry with a spatial resolution of 0.29 mm, and producing a reference model that contributes to the study of art history. While methods of preserving and examining physical materials in traditional sculpture were once conducted within a limited framework, digital digitization techniques offer a sustainable model that ensures the transmission of artworks to future generations without being affected by physical changes.

With the development of digital art, processes related to the preservation of cultural heritage, archiving of artworks, and reanalysis have created a more comprehensive field of research in art history, supported by technological innovations. Three-dimensional modeling techniques, augmented reality applications, and parametric design systems used in digital sculpture practice create both an aesthetic and epistemological transformation while redefining the relationships between spatial representation of artworks and the digital data environment. The Digital Michelangelo Project stands out in this context as a method that reinforces the role of art in the digitalization process and enables the use of artworks in interdisciplinary studies.

In this context, the Digital Michelangelo Project and similar digitization studies represent a paradigm shift by enabling the transition of art from a physically material-based structure to a digital representation, supporting both art history research and strengthening the sustainability of cultural heritage. In this regard, digital art integrates with the processes of art preservation and archiving, steering an interdisciplinary approach that reevaluates the technical and theoretical structure of artistic production.

Digital art and media arts represent a paradigm shift that moves away from dependency on physical objects in contemporary art practices, enabling the production of works existing in digital environments. While traditional art forms were closely tied to material and physical space for a long time, the process of digitalization has expanded artists' production processes, encouraging the transformation of artistic practice with new materials and expressive techniques. In this context, software, data visualization, and algorithmic processes have become essential tools of art, transforming the artist's creative process into a dynamic structure intertwined with technology.

The development of digital art allows artists to diversify their modes of artistic expression by using data-driven systems and computational methods in their production process. Machine learning algorithms and AI-assisted systems redefine the role of the artist in the creative process, moving the production mechanisms of artworks into an interdisciplinary structure. Particularly, Refik Anadol's data sculptures stand out as an important example of this transformation process, presenting a model that broadens the conceptual framework of art through the processing of environmental and cultural data. Anadol's works not only question the ontological structure of digital art but also highlight the role of data-driven artistic production within the context of contemporary art.

The role of digital and media arts in artistic production should be considered not only as a technical development but also as a theoretical transformation that expands the epistemological boundaries of art. The integration of algorithmic systems into the creative process has allowed artworks to move beyond being static, acquiring interactive and changing structures. This situation has redefined the relationship between art and its audience, as well as the ways in which art is perceived. The interdisciplinary nature of digital art, intersecting with architecture, data science, and AI research, creates a conceptual space that expands the technical and conceptual boundaries of artistic production.

As a result, digital art and media arts offer a critical perspective in understanding the evolving structure of contemporary artistic production. The process of digitalization transforms the relationship between art and physical space, altering the materiality and conceptual framework of artworks, and paving the way for new theoretical approaches regarding the future direction of art. In this context, the interaction between data-driven art practices and machine learning algorithms with art is seen as a defining paradigm shift that expands the ontological boundaries of art.

The role of digital art and digital sculpture in contemporary art practices allows artists to shape their works using algorithmic systems and data visualization methods, rather than relying on physical materials. Anadol's work reconsiders the ontological and epistemological structure of art, ensuring that the artwork transforms into an interactive and dynamic form that goes beyond physical space. This process not only highlights the new modes of production gained by art in the digitalization process but also demonstrates how digital technologies expand the conceptual boundaries of art. (Uğurlu, H., 2008)

Figure 2. Zaha Hadid Architects, Dongdaemun Design Plaza, Seoul, South Korea, 2014

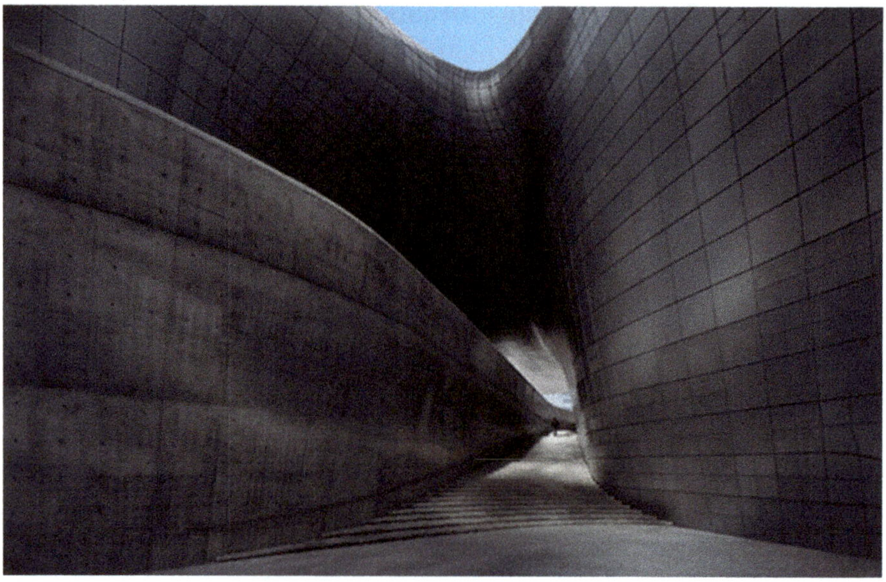

Source: https://www.arkitektuel.com, 2025

This project, which uses the Dongdaemun Design Plaza (DDP) building designed by Zaha Hadid Architects as a canvas, demonstrates how digital technologies are transforming architectural and artistic forms of expression and restructuring the spatial representation of art through digital environments. Anadol visualizes the collective memory of the city of Seoul using AI-supported data processing techniques, presenting the relationship between the city and memory in an artistic format. In this context, *Seoul Haemong* is considered not only a reflection of the technical possibilities of digital art but also of a data-based aesthetic approach.

As a result, the *Seoul Haemong* project reveals how digital art and digital sculpture practices can integrate with architectural space, offering an interdisciplinary model that allows art to be reshaped through data and artificial intelligence technologies. The integration of digitalization into art production transforms the traditional forms and functions of art and redefines the relationship between an artwork's spatiality and materiality. In this context, Anadol's data sculptures should be regarded as a significant paradigm shift, shedding light on the future directions of digital art.

Figure 3. Refik Anadol, "Seoul Haemong"; 2019-2020

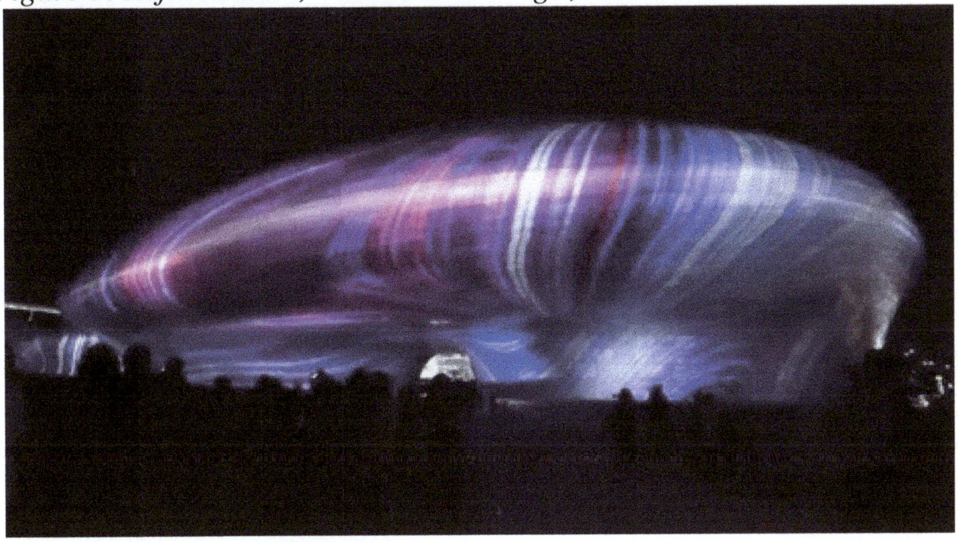

Source: https://www.oggusto.com

Refik Anadol's work *Seoul Haemong* serves as an important example in the field of digital art and digital sculpture, showcasing how data-driven artistic practices can integrate with architectural spaces. While traditional sculpture is based on the use of physical materials and space in the production process, Anadol's work reconfigures artistic representation through artificial intelligence and large datasets, expanding the spatial and conceptual boundaries of digital art.

The increasing use of technology in art has accelerated the transformation of traditional aesthetic concepts, creating profound changes in the production processes and perceptual dynamics of art. The production of artworks using technological tools has allowed aesthetic perception to move from being static to becoming dynamic, variable, and interactive, making it necessary to reconsider the ontological status of the artwork. Especially digital art practices have moved beyond the idea of art as a purely physical representation, developing interactive systems that position the viewer as an active component of the artistic experience.

This transformation in the digitalization process changes the relationship between the artwork and the viewer, taking the artistic experience to an interactive level beyond physical boundaries. Machine learning algorithms, data visualization techniques, and augmented reality applications provide new production methods that expand the artist's creative practice while enabling a rethinking of aesthetic concepts. In traditional art, the viewer was positioned as a passive object of observation, but in digital art, the viewer actively participates in artistic processes, becoming a factor that shapes the dynamic and changing nature of the artwork.

This transformation contributes to the expansion of the perceptual dimension of the artwork, especially in the fields of digital sculpture and media arts, preparing the ground for the formation of new artistic paradigms that extend the ontological boundaries of art. Refik Anadol's data sculptures and algorithmic artistic productions, by engaging the viewer in an interactive process, ensure that the artwork evolves from being a fixed representation to a dynamic structure that changes within data-driven processes. The interactive and process-oriented structure that art gains in the digitalization process offers a critical perspective on understanding new directions in art, both aesthetically and epistemologically.

As a result, the production of art with technological tools enables aesthetic perception to evolve from being fixed to dynamic and interactive, promoting the emergence of new forms of expression in contemporary art. Digital art practices, by positioning the viewer as a component of art, restructure the processes of representation and experience, thus creating an interdisciplinary intellectual space that broadens the ontological and epistemological framework of art.

Generative art, as a new approach that combines randomness and systematic constructs in the art production process, represents a significant transformation that expands the ontological and epistemological boundaries of art. The digitalization process offers the possibility of reshaping traditional production methods with technologies like data manipulation, AI-supported systems, and augmented reality, radically transforming artists' creative practices. Artists, by shaping artistic production within systematic processes through computational algorithms and parametric modeling methods, create a fundamental paradigm shift in the conceptual structure of art (Al, B., 2019, p.78).

In this context, generative art redefines the role of the artist in the creation process, evolving the production process into one primarily based on data-driven and algorithmic systems. While in traditional plastic arts, the direct interaction of the artist with the material was considered a determining element, in generative art practice, the artist's creative intervention combines with AI-supported processes and digital production techniques to create a production structure that is variable and dynamic. The systematic and random components of artistic creation intertwine, allowing the artwork to evolve from being a pre-designed object to an interactive structure shaped through data manipulation.

Generative art practices, directly related to digital art and media arts, strengthen the interactive and changing nature of the artwork while increasing the viewer's participation in the artistic experience. Artists like Refik Anadol, by visualizing collective memory through AI and large data sets, demonstrate how art integrates with data-driven systems. This aspect of generative art encourages the emergence of new theoretical and technical approaches that transcend traditional boundaries of art, bringing artistic production processes into an interdisciplinary framework.

In this context, generative art, by combining randomness and systematic constructs in the production processes, is seen as a critical development that expands the conceptual and technical framework of digital art. Artists, through technological tools like AI and data manipulation, reinterpret the relationship between artistic production and space, time, and materiality, developing new creative practices that define the future directions of art. In this regard, generative art should be considered a determining paradigm shift that strengthens the interdisciplinary and interactive nature of art.

Generative art is an artistic approach that combines randomness and systematic constructs in the art production process using technologies like algorithmic systems, AI, and data manipulation. In this form of art, instead of the artist's direct intervention, works are produced through self-regulating systems according to specific rules and parameters.

At the core of generative art is the shaping of the artwork through algorithms and data sets defined by the artist. In this process, the artist's role emerges as a programmer or system designer, while the artwork takes on a dynamic and variable nature according to the defined parameters. Especially in the context of digital and media arts, generative art, unlike traditional production methods, allows the artwork to acquire a constantly changing and interactive structure.

This form of art, supported by technologies such as machine learning algorithms, generative adversarial networks, and parametric design systems, represents a paradigm shift that expands the ontological and epistemological boundaries of art. The role of generative art in contemporary art, by integrating the artist's creative process with technology, offers an interdisciplinary approach that redefines the production and perception of art.

The interaction between art and technology has reshaped the ontological structure and production processes of art, bringing about fundamental debates on who produces art and how. In traditional art, the artist was considered the subject with creative control over the artwork, but AI-supported artistic production processes are pointing towards a new paradigm that redefines the artist's role by integrating data-driven and algorithmic systems into the production mechanism.

In this context, the shift away from a human-centered creation process toward a shared production practice with machines has led to important philosophical debates in art. AI-supported art production not only changes the artist's traditional creative status but also restructures the epistemological and aesthetic framework of art. The question of whether a work produced by AI can be considered original independent of the artist has become an increasingly important issue in contemporary art theory. Can a form defined by algorithmic processes sustain the subjective creative nature of art? When an artwork is created through a system that operates according to specific rules, how should the artist's individual intervention and artistic intent be defined?

When these discussions are addressed in the context of generative art and AI-supported artistic production, it becomes clear that art is no longer solely about individual creation, but rather has evolved into a multilayered structure shaped by data manipulation, computational systems, and automatic production techniques. AI-based artistic projects, like Refik Anadol's data sculptures, process cultural and environmental data through machine learning algorithms, prompting a rethinking of how artistic form is produced and offering a model that expands the ontological framework of art.

In this context, the relationship between art and technology is encouraging the emergence of new theoretical approaches that transform the creation processes of art. The evolution of art from a human-centered form of expression to one developed through a shared production practice with AI highlights critical questions about who produces art, how it is evaluated, and under which aesthetic parameters it gains meaning. This process should be seen as a paradigm shift that defines the future directions of art and strengthens interdisciplinary intellectual frameworks.

The transformation of art through technological tools is considered a development that broadens the artist's creative process and reshapes traditional aesthetic concepts. However, this transformation not only brings about technical advancements in art production but also lays the groundwork for new ontological and epistemological discussions that alter the social and philosophical meanings of art. The digitalization process represents a paradigm shift that allows art to evolve in form and content, while also transforming the ways in which art is produced and perceived, expanding the cultural and theoretical boundaries of art.

Artists, through technologies like AI, data manipulation, and virtual reality, reinterpret both the material and conceptual structure of art, questioning the definition of the artwork within traditional aesthetic frameworks. AI-supported artistic production processes redefine the role of the artist, moving the creation process from a human-centered practice to a shared production model with machines. In this context, the relationship between the producer and creator of the artwork is re-evaluated; the question of how the subjective creative nature of art is preserved within algorithmic processes is becoming an increasingly important issue in contemporary art theory (Bulut, 2023, p.73).

This transformation also opens up discussions on the ethical dimensions of art and reconsiders how the systems determining the meaning of art are shaped. Algorithmic art is a process that shapes artistic creativity through data-driven systems, offering an alternative framework for creation in contrast to traditional artistic practices where direct artist intervention is decisive. Digital art, through AI-supported production systems, ensures that art functions not only as an aesthetic form of expression but also as a platform for thought. Particularly generative art and data visualization techniques allow art to evolve from being static to becoming dynamic and interactive, thereby changing the way artwork is represented.

In conclusion, the new production methods gained through the digitalization of art are encouraging the formation of new perspectives that question the ontological structure of art, while broadening the aesthetic and theoretical framework of art. AI-supported artistic production processes offer different theoretical approaches to fundamental questions such as who produces art and how it gains meaning, preparing the ground for interdisciplinary intellectual discussions that define the future directions of art. In this context, the interaction between art and technology should be seen as a critical paradigm shift that transforms the production and perception processes of art.

Figure 4. Refik Anadol, "Walt Disney Concert Hall Dreams"; 2018

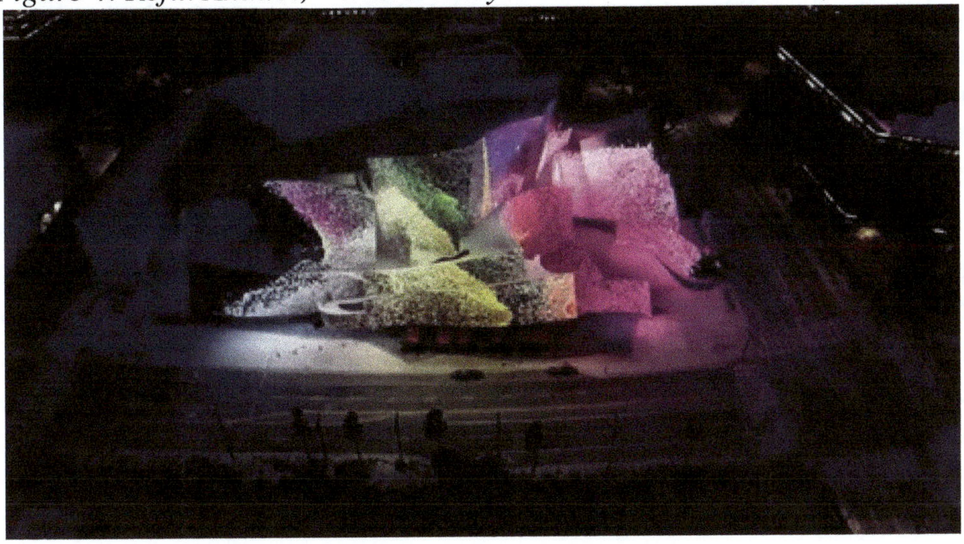

Source: https://www.oggusto.com

Refik Anadol's 2018 project "Walt Disney Concert Hall Dreams" is a groundbreaking work at the intersection of digital art and sculpture. A 45-terabyte dataset from the Los Angeles Philharmonic's digital archives was processed using artificial intelligence algorithms and deep learning techniques, and this data was projected onto the undulating stainless-steel surface of the Walt Disney Concert Hall. This process showcases how digital technologies can integrate with art and architecture.

In this project, Anadol used an AI model that mimics the human brain's dreaming process to create a visual and auditory reinterpretation of past performances. The resulting "data sculptures" were presented both as large-scale projections on the building's exterior and in the interior in an exhibition format where visitors could interact. This serves as an example of how digital art reshapes spatial perception.

"Walt Disney Concert Hall Dreams" demonstrates that digital art is not only an aesthetic form of expression but can also be used as a tool to restructure cultural memory. In this context, Anadol's work is an important reference point for understanding the role of digital art and sculpture in contemporary art practices.

The existence of sculpture in digital art also questions the traditional concepts of art. Digital sculptures, which do not exist as physical objects, require a reassessment of concepts like ownership, authenticity, and permanence. Additionally, digital sculpture production is changing the artist's role; algorithms and AI-assisted design processes add new dimensions to the artist's creative process.

While digital art is fundamentally based on traditional art practices, it is undergoing constant innovation and transformation as it merges with technology. The rapid evolution of computer-based technologies and their adaptation into artistic production processes make it difficult to precisely define the form and structural properties of digital works. This highlights the dynamic and interdisciplinary nature of digital art, while also creating a foundation for new forms of expression that expand the conceptual and aesthetic boundaries of art. In this context, digital art stands out as an ever-evolving paradigm in contemporary art practices.

Digital sculpture applications are based on three main principles: 3D modeling, 3D scanning, and 3D output. These principles optimize the possibilities offered by digital technologies in contemporary art production, signaling a transformation process that reshapes both the technical and aesthetic dimensions of sculpture.

3D Modeling: This is the process of transferring the geometric and physical properties of objects into the digital realm in vector format. This method allows for the creation of a three-dimensional mathematical representation of an object and enables high-precision analysis in the digital environment.

3D Scanning: This refers to the process of creating a digital model by precisely measuring the surface features of a physical object. Scanning techniques play an important role in fields such as the digital preservation of cultural heritage and the digital reproduction of artworks.

3D Output: This is the process of converting digitally created three-dimensional models into physical form. This is typically done through 3D printing, allowing for the transformation of digital works into physical reality.

These three principles form the foundation of digital sculpture applications and represent a paradigm shift that redefines both the aesthetic and production methods of contemporary sculpture (Kaya, A., p. 4, 2023). In this context, digital sculpture has become an essential component of contemporary art, offering artists new forms of expression beyond traditional production methods.

Technological advancements in our time have led the transformation and change of the fundamental elements that make up art and artworks. The global spread of computer and network technologies has made artworks more accessible to broader audiences. Moreover, virtual spaces created through computer programs offer multidimensional innovations in the production process and visibility of artworks.

The interaction between art and technology has become increasingly prominent in our time. Digitalization and computer-assisted production techniques are transforming both the creation process of artworks and the relationship they establish with the audience. In particular, virtual spaces and digital art platforms allow artworks to reach wide audiences independent of physical limitations.

The impact of technology on art is not only limited to accessibility but also has changed the modes of art production. Since the late 20th century, innovations such as digital photography, video art, holograms, and simulation techniques have provided artists with new forms of expression. Today, AI-assisted art production, data visualization, and interactive media are further expanding the boundaries of art.This transformation also questions the traditional concepts of art. For example, since digital artworks do not have a physical presence, concepts such as ownership and authenticity are being redefined. Similarly, as the role of algorithms and automation in the production process increases, the impact on the artist's creative process is also being debated.

In this context, the impact of technology on art is seen not only as a technical transformation but also as a conceptual change. As artists use the opportunities offered by technology to develop new forms of expression, audiences are also discovering new ways to interact with artworks.

The development of digital art has significantly transformed the production processes and conceptual framework of sculpture. While traditional sculpture is shaped by physical materials, digital sculpture is created in virtual environments using 3D modeling techniques. This transformation offers artists new forms of expression and redefines the spatial and material boundaries of sculpture.

Digital sculpture is created using technologies such as computer-aided design (CAD) software, 3D modeling programs, and augmented reality. This process offers artists a freer creative space, independent of physical material limitations. Moreover, sculptures produced in the digital environment can interact with audiences in different ways through virtual exhibitions and interactive platforms.

Throughout history, the fundamental components of art have been interpreted in various ways within aesthetic and cultural contexts, and they have continued to exist as important elements that shape the production process and the meaning of artworks. In traditional art understanding, form, content, and interpretation were seen as the fundamental building blocks of an artwork, and these concepts underwent various transformations in different artistic disciplines.

In traditional sculpture, form materializes through the processing of physical material, while digital sculpture is created using 3D modeling techniques in virtual environments. Computer-aided design (CAD) software, augmented reality, and AI-based production processes have expanded the methods artists use to manipulate form. While abstraction and stylization practices have created transformations in form since ancient times, these processes have become more flexible and dynamic in the digital environment through algorithmic and parametric approaches.

The content of an artwork contains the conceptual and cultural meanings the artist wishes to convey. Digital sculpture, beyond traditional spatial contexts, is transported into virtual worlds, offering new forms of expression. Digital production processes, which are not limited to physical material, are reshaping the position of sculpture within the history of culture and civilization. The interactive and data-driven nature of digital art strengthens the variability of content and the dynamic relationship it establishes with the audience.

An artwork cannot carry meaning on its own; meaning is built through the artist's interpretation and the relationships it forms with the audience. In the practice of digital sculpture, this process has gained a new dimension as the audience directly interacts with the artwork, and the content is reinterpreted in different layers through digital tools. Technologies such as AI, data analytics, and virtual reality are expanding the artist's forms of expression, allowing artistic meaning-making to become more multifaceted.

In this framework, the concepts of form, content, and interpretation play a critical role in understanding the conceptual and technical transformation of digital sculpture. The digitalization process has reshaped the production and consumption mechanisms of art, changing the position of artworks within market dynamics (Uğurlu, H., 2008, p. 250).

The integration of digital technologies into art practice has necessitated a reevaluation of the production methods and conceptual framework of sculpture. Sculptures, traditionally shaped using physical materials, have evolved into a different production process through 3D modeling techniques and algorithms in the digital environment. In this context, the concepts of form, content, and interpretation have been readdressed within digital sculpture, raising new discussions about the ontological and epistemological status of the artwork.

The transformation dynamics of digital art, particularly digital sculpture practice, require a comprehensive reevaluation of art's materiality, its level of interaction, and the relationships it forms with the audience. In this context, formal and conceptual changes are bringing new perspectives to the meaning-making processes, alongside the production processes of artworks.

Digital art, created using innovative techniques such as computer graphics, new media technologies, computer animations, internet art, interactive art, video games, robotics, and biotechnological art methods, has become an important form of expression in contemporary art practices. In this context, this art form, known as "New Media Art," creates new forms of expression through the integration of technology into artistic production and requires a re-evaluation of traditional art concepts.

New Media Art is recognized as a new movement in art, gaining meaning through shared cultural and artistic goals. The possibilities offered by digitalization expand the artist's creative processes and change the ways they interact with the audience. This form of art overcomes the physical space dependence of traditional art and gains existence in digital environments, ensuring that artworks are conceived as dynamic, variable, and interactive structures (Kızılaslan & Kozlu, 2021).

Since ancient times, nature has been seen as the fundamental source of learning and has been accepted as a defining element in shaping artistic production. The idea that aesthetic perfection could be achieved by imitating nature has remained one of the basic principles of art. As knowledge production and accumulation have advanced over time, the human mind, cultural structures, and artistic actions have developed new aesthetic understandings and creative forms, in addition to the beauty offered by nature.

In this direction, the emotional and intellectual effects of nature on humans have shaped the forms of artistic expression, and various theoretical discussions have developed about these effects and their methods of artistic representation. Especially in the context of modern and digital art, extensive research has been conducted on how nature is reinterpreted aesthetically and conceptually, and how it forms a reference point in the artist's creative process. In this context, the reference of art to nature, along with technological tools, is evolving into new forms of expression and is considered one of the fundamental dynamics of contemporary art practices (Kızılaslan & Kozlu, 2021).

With the transformation of technology from a tool in artistic production to a conceptual framework, digital sculpture practice has developed unique approaches to the representation of nature. In contrast to traditional sculpture's physical and material nature, digital sculpture shapes nature as a dynamic, variable, and interactive structure in the virtual environment.

In this transformation, digital tools like algorithms, data visualizations, and AI offer new readings of nature from aesthetic and epistemological perspectives, expanding the artist's creative process. Especially parametric design and generative art techniques provide the opportunity to not only imitate the organic forms of nature but also reproduce its processes within a digital ecosystem. Refik Anadol's data sculptures enable large datasets of nature to be processed artistically, creating both a visual and conceptual transformation.

In this context, digital sculpture is viewed not only as a process of creating a non-physical form but also as a conceptual platform that questions our relationship with nature. While the artist's traditional connection with material is replaced by data, algorithmic processes, and virtual reality elements, the artistic representation of nature evolves from a purely figurative phenomenon to an intersystemic field of interaction.

Traditional sculpture, historically shaped by physical materials like stone, bronze, and wood, developed as an art practice integrating spatial form with conceptual content. However, the integration of digital technologies into art production has radically transformed both the material nature of sculpture and the way it interacts with the audience. Digital sculpture has reinterpreted traditional plastic art concepts through data-driven processes, form manipulations in virtual environments, and interactive experiences, becoming one of the critical components of contemporary art.

Digital sculpture is a form of art that exists in the digital realm, produced through mathematical and algorithmic systems, rather than as a physical mass. In this context, the relationship between traditional sculpture and material and physical space transforms into an interactive and dynamic structure in the digital environment. Artists can now recreate the organic forms of nature or abstract shapes using 3D modeling software, parametric design tools, and AI-supported algorithms.

In this transformation, data-based artistic approaches come to the forefront. Generative art, for example, presents a methodology that intertwines randomness and systematic design processes in sculpture production. Digital sculptures designed through data visualization techniques take shape based on environmental variables (such as climate data, ecological parameters, and human movement) and are defined as dynamic, variable, and interactive structures.

One of the key components of digital art, algorithmic aesthetics, replaces traditional craftsmanship with software processes and parametric manipulations in form production. In this context, artists develop an aesthetic pursuit through coding and data manipulation, rather than manual modeling in sculpture design.

Digital sculptures created through generative design algorithms not only imitate the organic structure of nature but also reproduce its formal processes through mathematical logic. At this point, there are intersections with traditional sculpture in the form production process, but there is a fundamental difference in the design process: instead of sculpting or shaping a material mass, form is created through intersystemic data flow.

For instance, Refik Anadol's data sculptures process environmental and cultural datasets to create algorithmic shapes, thus creating both aesthetic and conceptual transformative processes. The digital sculpture aesthetics seen in the artist's works strengthen the spatial, memory, and interaction-oriented structure of contemporary art.

Figure 5. Refik Anadol, "Machine Memories Are Waiting to Be Discovered", 2021

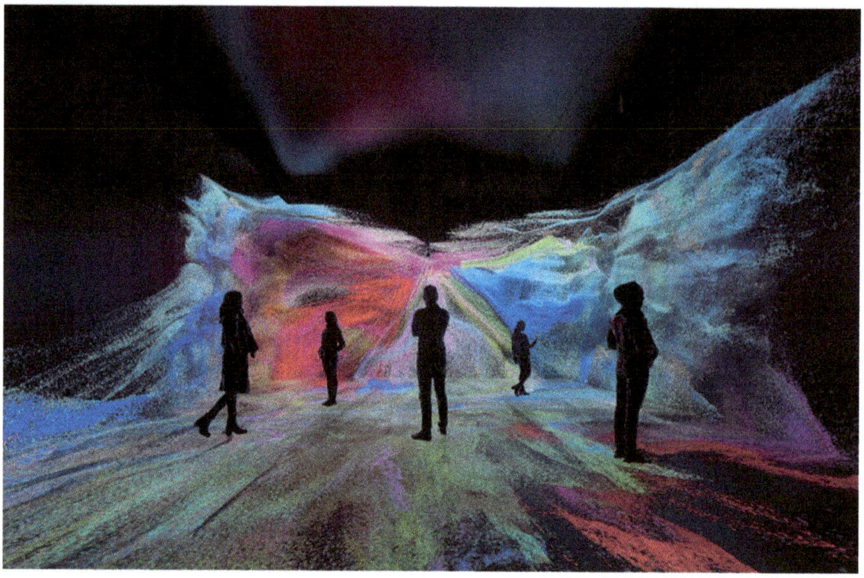

Source:brandlifema.com

Refik Anadol's *Machine Memories: Space* exhibition presents an artistic practice that reinterprets the aesthetic and conceptual dimensions of space exploration using artificial intelligence and data visualization techniques. The exhibition processes data from NASA's public space exploration archives, developing a speculative approach focused on the memory and imagination of machines.

Figure 6. Refik Anadol, "Machine-Memories-Space Exhibition", 2021

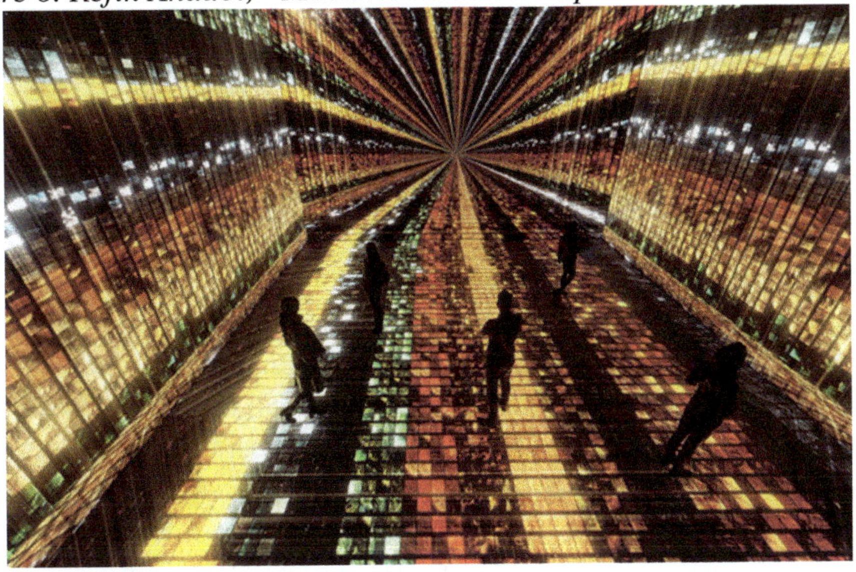

Source:brandlifema.com

Anadol's work transforms large data sets into an artistic form using machine learning algorithms and invites the viewer to explore the unknown layers of space. The exhibition consists of two main sections: Memories and Dreams. While the Memories section involves the creation of dynamic data tables by converting the raw data recorded by space telescopes into pigments, the Dreams section enables artificial intelligence to process this data and produce speculative visual compositions. (Çelenk & Kurak Açıcı, 2022).

In this context, *Machine Memories: Space* is not just an artwork but also an epistemological inquiry focused on data. The exhibition explores the collaborative potential of human-machine interaction, deepening contemporary aesthetics and conceptual trends in digital art.

The passive relationship that traditional sculpture establishes with the viewer turns into an interactive experience in the context of digital art. Digital sculptures produced through augmented reality (AR), virtual reality (VR) and kinetic systems are defined as works of art shaped by the direct intervention of the viewer. This transformation enables the sculpture to evolve from being a static form to a structure that undergoes real-time changes and gains new meanings through individual interactions (Yücel, 2021).

Emerging digital technologies force a rethinking of the spatial position of sculptures, with data flows and interactive forms in virtual environments replacing physical materials. Particularly, integrating digital sculptures with AR applications into physical spaces enables the artwork to exist in both virtual and physical contexts simultaneously.

Digital sculpture emerges as an interdisciplinary mode of expression that redefines the relationship between form, material, and the viewer. Through algorithms, data manipulation, and interactive systems, this new concept of sculpture highlights that technological tools in contemporary art are not only production processes but also conceptual content creators.

In this light, digital sculpture practice reevaluates the relationship between art, material, and space, creating a radical shift in the artistic representation of nature, and immerses the viewer in an interactive experience process. Throughout history, sculpture has undergone transformations in its relationship with space and materiality, with artists expanding three-dimensional forms through various materials and techniques. However, in contemporary art, the influence of digitalization has radically altered the production process of sculpture, with traditional material and form being reinterpreted through the technical and conceptual innovations offered by digital art.

The integration of digital art into sculpture practice does not only offer technical advancements but also creates a new paradigm that expands the ontological and aesthetic framework of art. The significance of digital art in sculpture practice allows artists to enrich their creative processes through data-driven design, 3D modeling, and AI-supported algorithms. While the direct intervention of the artist in physical material is a defining feature in traditional sculpture, in digital sculpture, artists employ virtual environments, AR, and parametric design systems, making production processes flexible and dynamic. This transformation results in a new artistic model where sculptures are not only form objects but also interactive and evolving structures.

The integration of digital technologies into sculpture allows the artwork to transcend spatial and material boundaries, strengthening the interaction between physical space and digital environments. In particular, AI-based artistic projects, such as Refik Anadol's data sculptures, process environmental and cultural data, challenging the traditional boundaries of sculpture and presenting new aesthetic and theoretical approaches that enhance the interdisciplinary nature of art.

The new expressive forms of sculpture gained in the process of digitalization are considered a defining development that illuminates future artistic trends. As a result, the role of digital art in sculpture practice should be viewed not just as a technical progression that transforms production processes, but as a paradigm shift that redefines the ontological and epistemological structure of art.

The process of digitalization in art represents a paradigm shift that profoundly transforms traditional conceptions of art, redefining its mechanisms of production, perception, and interaction. Digital art, through technological tools such as artificial intelligence, data manipulation, and virtual reality, offers new modes of expression that expand the creative processes of artists. Simultaneously, it provides a theoretical framework for questioning the ontological status of the artwork (Erkek, 2020).

This transformation changes the traditional creative status of the artist, turning art production into a collaborative process between humans and machines. Digital sculpture, generative art, and AI-supported artistic production raise questions about how the subjective creative nature of art can be maintained through algorithmic systems. Refik Anadol's data sculptures and algorithmic art projects offer new theoretical approaches that expand the conceptual boundaries of art and reshape both its technical and epistemological dimensions.

The impact of digitalization on art should be considered not only as a technical progression but also as a development that reinterprets the cultural, aesthetic, and social functions of art. Digital art practices strengthen the interactive structure of the artwork by making the viewer an active component, radically changing the way art is experienced. The reshaping of art through machine learning algorithms and parametric modeling methods redefines the artist's role in the creative process and expands interdisciplinary intellectual spaces.

In conclusion, the development of digital art is recognized as a pivotal paradigm shift that illuminates the future directions of art. Through data-driven systems and AI-supported processes, artists are reshaping artistic production and developing new creative applications that continuously expand the ontological and epistemological boundaries of art. The impact of digitalization on art should not only be viewed as a technical transformation but as a conceptual change that reinterprets the meaning and societal function of art.

REFERENCES

Al, B. (2019). Generatif Sanat Kavramı Ve Görsel Sanatlarda Sayısal Yaratıcılık. *Tasarım Enformatiği, 1*(2), 78–91.

Anadol, R. (2020). *Yapay zekâ ve dijital sanat.* Sanat Yayınları.

Anadol, R. (2021, Ekim 15). Dijital sanatın geleceği ve yapay zekâ. Dijital Sanatlar Konferansı, İstanbul, Türkiye.

Anadol, R. (2022, Eylül 20). Refik Anadol'un yapay zekâ projeleri. Refik Anadol Resmi Web Sitesi. https://www.refikanadol.com/projects

Ballı, Ö. (2023). *Günümüz Sanatının Teknoloji Temelli Sanatsal Üretim Ve Sanal Uzam Pratiği: Dijital Heykel.* Akademik Sanat.

Bulat, M. (2014). *Modern sanatta soyutlama.* Atatürk Üniversitesi Yayınları.

Bulat, M., Bulat, S., & Aydın, B. (2014). Bilgisayar Ortamında Üç Boyutlu Tasarım ve Kopyalama, Akademik Sosyal Araştırmalar Dergisi, Yıl: 2, Sayı: 8. *Aralık, 2014*, 548–572.

Bulat, s., (1999). Teknoloji ve Heykel Sanatı, Atatürk Üniversitesi, Güzel Sanatlar Fakültesi Sanat Dergisi, Sayı, 1, S. 133-140.

Bulut, Ş. (2023). Metaverse Ya Da Sanal Gerçeklik Kavramı Ve Sanatçı Refik Anadol'un Çalışmaları. *Cumhuriyet Üniversitesi Fen-Edebiyat Fakültesi Sosyal Bilimler Dergisi, 47*(1), 69–76.

Çelenk, A., & Kurak Açıcı, F. (2022). Tasarımda yeni yaklaşımlar: Refik Anadol ve makine hatıraları. *Akademik Sanat ve Tasarım Dergisi, 17*, 73–86. DOI: 10.34189/asd.2022.17.005

Coşkun, R. (2014). Teknolojinin Olanakları ile Değişen Sanat Alanı. *Sanat Ve Tasarım Dergisi, 6*(6), 76–89. DOI: 10.20488/austd.22705

Kaya, A. (2023). Çağdaş Sanat Formu Olarak Dijital Heykel, Dijital Heykelin Sağladığı Yeni Olanaklar. *Sanat Ve İkonografi Dergisi*, (4), 2–9. DOI: 10.5152/ArtIcon.2023.1226421

Kızılaslan, N., & Kozlu, D. (2021). Teknolojinin ve Dijitalleşmenin Geleneksel Türk Sanatlarına Yansımaları. *Medeniyet Sanat Dergisi, 7*(1), 105–126. DOI: 10.46641/medeniyetsanat.930735

Refik Anadol. (2024, 1 Eylül). Wikipedia. Erişim adresi: https://en.wikipedia.org/wiki/

Tarı, N. (2025, 5 June). artfulliving.com.tr, Deneyselliği Dijitalle Buluşturan 5 Kolaj Sanatçısı, https://www.artfulliving.com.tr/sanat/deneyselligi-dijitalle-bulusturan-5-kolaj-sanatcisi-i-14417

Toprak, A. (2020). *Yapay Zekâ Algoritmalarının Dijital Enstalasyona Dönüşmesi.* Ege Üniversitesi İletişim Fakültesi Yeni Düşünceler.

Toptaş, R. (2022). Türkiye'de Dijital Sanat, Sanatçıları ve Eserleri Hakkında Bir Araştırma. *STAR Sanat Ve Tasarım Araştırmaları Dergisi, 3*(5), 170–186.

Torun, A. (2015). Walter Benjamin, Sanat Eserinin Aurası ve Yeni Medya Sanatı, International Multilingual Academic Journal, Vol. 2, No,1.

Uğurlu, H. (2008). Teknoloji Sanat İlişkisi: Günümüzde Teknolojik Sanatların Amacı. *Uşak Üniversitesi Sosyal Bilimler Dergisi, 1*(2), 247–262. DOI: 10.12780/UUSBD27

Walton, K. L. (2018) Geçirgen Fotoğraflar: Fotografik Gerçekliğin Doğası Üzerine, S.Walden (Ed.), Doğanın Kalemi Üzerine Denemeler (pp.29-67). (H. Yılmaz, Trans.), Espas Yayınları

Yücel, G. (2021). Dijital sanat bağlamında heykel: Yeni medya teknolojileriyle dönüşen form ve izleyici ilişkisi. *Sanat ve Tasarım Dergisi, 12*(2), 45–58. DOI: 10.5281/zenodo.1234567

ADDITIONAL READING

Akın, C. (2015). *Dijital Sanatlarda Etkileşimsellik: Türkiye'de Etkileşimsel Dijital Sanatların Konumu.* Doktora Tezi, Marmara Üniversitesi.

Akkaya, H. M. (2022). *Dijital Çoğaltma Çağında Heykel: Eski Paradigma, Yeni Ufuklar*. Academic Social Resources Journal.

Becer, E. (2019). *Sanatın değişen yüzü: Teknoloji ve estetik*. YKY.

Bingöl, H. (2019). *Heykel Sanatında Dijital Yaklaşımlar*. Yüksek Lisans Tezi, Atatürk Üniversitesi.

Bulat, S. (2010). Teknoloji ve Modern Heykel Sanatı. *Sanat Dergisi, 1*, 133.

Bulat, S., & Bulat, M. ve Aydın, B. (2014). Bauhause Tasarım Okulu. *Atatürk Üniversitesi Sosyal Bilimler Enstitüsü Dergisi.*, *18*(1), 105–120.

Çakmak, S. (2019). Dijital Sanatta Yaratıcı Bir Uygulama Olarak Airbrush Tekniği. İnönü Üniversitesi Sanat ve Tasarım Dergisi, 1(1), 56.

Can, E. (2019). *Seramik Üretim Sürecinde Üç Boyutlu Yazıcıların Kullanımı ve Sanatsal Öneriler*. Sanatta Yeterlilik Tezi, Anadolu Üniversitesi.

Erkek, B. (2020). Dijital sanatın ontolojisi: Yeni medya bağlamında sanatın dönüşümü. İletişim Kuram ve Araştırma Dergisi, 51, 25–46 https://dergipark.org.tr/tr/pub/ikad/issue/56462/763217

Refik_Anadol Anadol, R. (n.d.). Machine hallucinations: Sphere. Refik Anadol Studio. https://refikanadol.com/works/machine-hallucinations-sphere/

KEY TERMS AND DEFINITIONS

3D Modeling: The digital design of three-dimensional forms within a computer environment. It shapes both technical and aesthetic decisions in the pre-production phase of sculpture. Allows the artist to experiment digitally before engaging with physical materials.

Algorithmic Aesthetics: It is the determination of the formal structure of the work of art with algorithms. In digital sculpture, form, movement and interaction are created with codes. The aesthetic decisions of the artist are integrated with the logic of the software.

Digital Transformation: Refers to the shift from analog to digital in artistic production.It transforms the formal, technical, and perceptual structure of sculpture.The artist's tools, interaction with the audience, and creative process are redefined.

Interactivity: It is the physical or digital relationship of the audience with the work. Digital sculpture ceases to be a fixed object and becomes an experiential structure.

Material Simulation: It is the imitation of real materials in a digital environment. Surfaces such as plastic, metal, and stone are visually reproduced in digital sculpture. This process facilitates aesthetic and technical decisions before physical production.

New Media Art: Covers art forms produced and presented with digital technologies. Sculpture becomes interdisciplinary, merging with video, sound, software, and network technologies.

Post-Sculpture: It refers to contemporary approaches that go beyond the traditional understanding of sculpture. Digital tools, time-based media, and conceptual content shape this practice. Sculpture is no longer just a physical object; data, experience, and process.

Compilation of References

44Smartphone Addiction Statistics For 2024 [INFOGRAPHIC]. (2019). Received February 25, 2025, by Slicktext Website: https://Www.Slicktext.Com/Blog/2019/10/Smartphone-Addiction-Statistics/ 4630 On Amending Some Articles of the Law on Intellectual and Artistic Works...—Original Text. (T.Y.). Received March 04, 2025, by LEXPERA Website: http://Www.Lexpera.Com.Tr/Resmi-Gazete/Metin/Fikir-Ve-Sanat-Eserleri-Kanununun-Bazi-Maddelerini-Degistirilmesine-İliskin-Kanun-24335-4630-1

Adorno, T. W., & Horkheimer, M. (2002). *Dialectic of enlightenment*. Stanford University Press.

Ak, H. (2013). *Dijital sanat*. XV. Akademik Bilişim Konferans Bildirileri (s. 978). Antalya: Akademik Bilişim 2013.

Akay, A. (2017). *Sanat bizi seviyor*. Doğu Batı.

Akgül, M. (2017). *Dijitalleşme ve Din*. Marife -Dini Araştırmalar Dergisi, 17(2), 204.

Alav, O. (2001). *Mass Communication and Local Media*. Faculty Bookstore Publications.

Al, B. (2019). Generatif Sanat Kavramı Ve Görsel Sanatlarda Sayısal Yaratıcılık. *Tasarım Enformatiği*, *1*(2), 78–91.

Albayrak, Z. (2016). *Yazının doğuşu ve ilk yazılı belgeler* [The emergence of writing and the first written documents]. İstanbul Üniversitesi Yayınları.

Aldemir, A. (2019). The Intensity of Transparency and Lack of Aura in Social Media. [AKİL]. *Akdeniz University Journal of Communication Faculty*, (32), 54–70.

Altınyıldız Artun, N. (2016, 6 May). *Dada'nın Makine-İnsanları*. e-skop. https://www.e-skop.com/skopbulten/dadanin-100-yili-dadanin-makine-insanlari/2987

Ametordzi, S., & Olalere, F. E. (2024). The effect of digital technology on graphic design ideation output. *IDA: International Design and Art Journal*, *6*(1), 144–156.

Anadol, R. (2021, Ekim 15). Dijital sanatın geleceği ve yapay zekâ. Dijital Sanatlar Konferansı, İstanbul, Türkiye.

Anadol, R. (2022, Eylül 20). Refik Anadol'un yapay zekâ projeleri. Refik Anadol Resmi Web Sitesi. https://www.refikanadol.com/projects

Anadol, R. (2020). *Yapay zekâ ve dijital sanat*. Sanat Yayınları.

Antmen, A. (2009). *20. yüzyıl Batı sanatında akımlar* (2. bas.). Sel Yayıncılık.

Antmen, A. (2012). *20. yüzyıl Batı sanatında akımlar*. Sel Press.

Arslan, C. (2018). *Dijital Yeniden Üretim Çağında Sanat Eseri: "Aura" Kavramının Dijital Sanat Bağlamında Yeniden Değerlendirilmesi*. Art-Sanat.

Artconnect. (n.d.). Sounds of Survival: How Art and Science Are Reviving Coral Reefs. https://www.magazine.artconnect.com/editorial/coral-sonic-resilience

Artun, A. (2021, 29 March). Refik Anadol ve Algoritma Sanatı. e-skop Bülten. https://www.e-skop.com/skopbulten/refik-anadol-ve-algoritma-sanati/6111

Assmann, J. (2011). *Cultural memory and early civilization: Writing, remembrance, and political imagination*. Cambridge University Press. DOI: 10.1017/CBO9780511996306

Avcı Tuğal, S. (2018). *Oluşum süreci içinde dijital sanat* (1. baskı). Hayalperest Yayınevi.

Avcı-Tuğal, S. (2018). *Oluşum süreci içinde dijital sanat.* Hayalperest.

Aydın, B. (2014). Transformation of the Understanding of Privacy in Social Media Platforms. *Istanbul Arel University Journal of Communication Studies, 3*(5), 131–146.

Babacan, M. E. (2016). Social media usage areas and the relationship between addiction. *Addicta : the Turkish Journal on Addictions, 3*, 7–28. DOI: 10.15805/addicta.2016.3.0017

Balcı, Ş., & Baloğlu, E. (2018). Relationship Between Social Media Addiction and Depression: "A Field Research on University Youth". *Galatasaray University Journal of Communication*, (29), 209–234. DOI: 10.16878/gsuilet.500860

Ball, H. (1916). Cabaret Voltaire in Zurich. [Photograph] https://arsenaldeletras.com/2014/06/22/hugo-ball-interpretaciones/

Ballı, Ö. (2023). *Günümüz Sanatının Teknoloji Temelli Sanatsal Üretim Ve Sanal Uzam Pratiği: Dijital Heykel.* Akademik Sanat.

Baloğlu, Ö. Ö. (2023). 6). *Teknolojik Bir Dönüşüm Olarak Dijitalleşme Kavramı ve Etkileri. Sosyal Bilimler Enstitüsü Dergisi, 13*(2), 1191.

Barotti, M. (2025). Coral Sonic Resilience. [Photograph]. https://www.corriere.ca/sculture-sonore-per-rigenerare-i-coralli-e-lartescienza-di-marco-barotti/

Barotti, M. (2019). Clams. [Photograph]. https://www.marcobarotti.com/Clams

Barotti, M. (2025). Buoy. [Photograph]. https://www.corriere.ca/sculture-sonore-per-rigenerare-i-coralli-e-lartescienza-di-marco-barotti/

Barotti, M. (n.d.). Marcobarotti. https://www.marcobarotti.com

Baulrillard, J. (2023). *Consumer Society* (19th ed.). Ayrıntı Publications.

Bayraktar, K. O. (2024). *Düzeni seviyorum ama ona katlanamıyorum.* Hesaplar ve tesadüfler: Macaristan Ulusal Bankası Koleksiyonundan algoritma sanatı Dora Maurer + Vera Molnar + Gizella Rakoczy sergi kataloğu. Pera Müzesi.

Becer, E. (2015). *İletişim ve grafik tasarım* [Communication and graphic design]. Dost Kitabevi.

Betancourt, M. (2023). *Glitch theory: Art and semiotics.* Im Pressd.

Blauvelt, A. (2011). *Graphic design: Now in production.* Walker Art Center.

Bowen, D. (2021). Wilderness. [Photograph]. https://www.dwbowen.com/wilderness

Bowen, D. (2024). Tele-Present Wind. [Photograph]. https://www.dwbowen.com/telepresent-wind

Bowen, D. (2024). Wind sensor on the Perseverance rover. [Photograph]. https://www.dwbowen.com/telepresent-wind

Bowen, D. (n.d.). Dwbowen. https://www.dwbowen.com/

Bozkurt, M. (2012). Medya sanatı. Yılmaz, M. Sanatın günceli güncelin sanatı (pp. 214-256 in).

Bulat, M., (2007). Modern Heykelin Doğuşu, Atatürk Üniversitesi, Güzel Sanatlar Fakültesi Sanat Dergisi, Sayı, 11, S., 83-89.

Bulat, s., (1999). Teknoloji ve Heykel Sanatı, Atatürk Üniversitesi, Güzel Sanatlar Fakültesi Sanat Dergisi, Sayı, 1, S. 133-140.

Bulat, S., (2014).Teknoloji ve Modern Heykel Sanat, Atatürk Üniversitesi G.S.Fak.

Bulat, M. (2014). *Modern Sanatta Soyutlama.* Atatürk Üniversitesi Yayınları, Zafer Ofset.

Bulat, M. (2014). *Modern sanatta soyutlama.* Atatürk Üniversitesi Yayınları.

Bulat, M., Bulat, S., & Aydın, B. (2014). Bilgisayar Ortamında Üç Boyutlu Tasarım ve Kopyalama, Akademik Sosyal Araştırmalar Dergisi, Yıl: 2, Sayı: 8. *Aralık, 2014*, 548–572.

Bulat, S., & Bulat, M. ve Aydın, B. (2014). Bauhause Tasarım Okulu. *Atatürk Üniversitesi Sosyal Bilimler Enstitüsü Dergisi.*, *18*(1), 105–120.

Bulat, S., Yağmur, Ö., & Aydın, B. (2014). Form ve Kompozisyon, Akademik Sosyal Araştırmalar Dergisi, Yıl: 2, Sayı: 6. *Eylül, 2014*, 478–488.

Bulut, Ş. (2023). Metaverse Ya Da Sanal Gerçeklik Kavramı Ve Sanatçı Refik Anadol'un Çalışmaları. *Cumhuriyet Üniversitesi Fen-Edebiyat Fakültesi Sosyal Bilimler Dergisi*, *47*(1), 69–76.

Burke, P. (2001). *Eyewitnessing: The uses of images as historical evidence*. Cornell University Press.

Büyükbaykal, C. (2012). Mass Media and Social Life. *Journal of Family Communication*, *21*, 71–75.

Büyükçorak, M., & Dinç, M. (2020). Psychological Effects of Excessive Use of Social Media and Social Media Usage Characteristics of Turkish Youth. *Psychological Research*, *1*(1), 30–33.

Cai, L., & Jung, E. (2024). The impact of artificial intelligence on the graphic design job market: An analysis of the evolution and opportunities of the designer role. *Psychological Research*, *14*(8), 259–267.

Çakın, İ. (2022). *Dijital Sanat*. Çanakkale On Sekiz Mart Üniversitesi- Fen Edebiyat Fakültesi- Sanat Tarihi Anabilim Dalı-Lisans Bitirmr Projesi.

Çakır, H., & Topçu, H. (2005). Internet as a Communication Language. *Social Sciences Institute Journal*, *19*, 71–96.

Çalışkan, M., & Mencik, Y. (2015). The New Face of the Changing World: Social Media. Academic View Journal, 50, 254-277. Access address: http://www.akademikbakis.org

Çapçıoğlu, İ. (2019). Social Media, 'New Human Type' and Ethical Problems. *1st Congress of Human and Social Sciences Research*.

Çelenk, A., & Kurak Açıcı, F. (2022). Tasarımda yeni yaklaşımlar: Refik Anadol ve makine hatıraları. *Akademik Sanat ve Tasarım Dergisi, 17,* 73–86. DOI: 10.34189/asd.2022.17.005

Ceric, V. (2008). Algorithmic Art: Technology, Mathematics and Art. In *2008 30th International Conference on Information Technology Interfaces* (pp. xx–xx). IEEE. https://doi.org/DOI: 10.1109/ITI.2008.4588386

Cerrah, L. (2016). Social Media and Some Institutional Interactions and Critical Approach to Social Media / Some Institutional Social Media and Interactions and Critical Approach to Social Media. *Atatürk University Social Sciences Institute Journal, 20*(4), 1393–1414.

Çizgen, G. (2007). *Sanat Köprüsü Sırat Köprüsü.* Arkeoloji Sanat Yayınları.

Clottes, J. (2008). *Cave Art.* Phaidon Press.

Çömlekçi, M. F., & Başol, O. (2019). Examining the Relationship Between Social Media Usage Purposes of Young People and Social Media Addiction. *Manisa Celal Bayar University Journal of Social Sciences, 17*(4), 173–188. DOI: 10.18026/cbayarsos.525652

Coronavirus Triggered Digital Addiction [Corporate Site]. (2020). Received February 23, 2025, Sender Https://Www.Yesilay.Org.Tr/Tr/ Website: Https://Www.Yesilay.Org.Tr/Tr/Makaleler/Koronavirus-Dijital-Bagimligi-Teritikledi

Coşkun, R. (2014). Teknolojinin Olanakları ile Değişen Sanat Alanı. *Sanat Ve Tasarım Dergisi, 6*(6), 76–89. DOI: 10.20488/austd.22705

Dachy, M. (2014). *Dada sanatın başkaldırısı* (Türkay, O., Trans.). Yapı Kredi.

Danghad, M. (2021). Study Finds Internet Economy Grew Seven Times Faster Than Total U.S. Economy, Created Over 7 Million Jobs In The Last Four Years. Received February 21, 2025, Posted by IAB Website: Https://Www.İab.Com/News/Study-Finds-İnternet-Economy-Grew-Seven-Times-Faster

Danto, A. C. (2010). *"Sanatın Sonundan Sonra", (Çev. Zeynep Demirsü).* Ayrıntı Yayınları.

Daudrich, A. (2016). Algorithmic Art and Its Art-Historical Relationships. *CITAR Journal*, 8(1), Special Issue: xCoAx.

De Bolla, P. (2012). *Sanat ve estetik.* Ayrıntı.

Digital Art Museum. (n.d.). *Vera Molnar – (Dés)Ordres.* https://dam.org/museum/artists_ui/artists/molnar-vera/des-ordres/

Drucker, J. (2014). *Graphesis: Visual forms of knowledge production.* Harvard University Press.

Drucker, J., & McVarish, E. (2009). *Graphic design history: A critical guide.* Pearson Education.

Dusi, E. (2025, March 6). Ricreato il suono della barriera corallina: aiuterà a rifiorire i fondali marini degradati. https://www.repubblica.it/esteri/2025/03/06/news/suono_barriera_corallina_marco_barotti_universita_padova-424046626/#

Eke, N. P., & Yücel, N. (2023). *Dijital Çağda Sanat ve Sanatçı: Ha: Ar Üzerine bir İnceleme.* Akademik Sanat(20), 79. DOI: 10.34189/asd.2023.20.006

Eliasson, O. (2025). Model for a timeless garden. [Photograph]. Istanbul Modern Art. (Photograph by Özlem Gürpınar, 2025)

Erer, S. (2013). Mass Media and Medical Ethics. *Düzce University Health Sciences Institute Journal, 3*, 24–28.

Ersöz, S., & Askeroğlu, E. D. (2018). *Dijitalleşmenin Etkisinde Dönüşen Sanat ve Kuşaklar Üzerine Bir Çalışma.* İletişim Kuram ve Araştırma Dergisi(47).

Eskilson, S. J. (2012). *Graphic design: A new history.* Yale University Press.

Farthing, S. (2024). *Sanatın tüm öyküsü* (G. Aldoğan & F. C. Çulcu, Trans.; 5th5. Basım) Hayalperest Yayınevi.

Fineberg, J. (2014). *1940'tan günümüze sanat* (G.E. Yılmaz & S. Atay-Eskier, Trans.). Karakalem Kitabevi Press. Fischer- Lichte, E. (2016). *Performatif estetik* (T. Acil, Trans.). Ayrıntı Press.

Flusser, V. (2000). *Towards a Philosophy of Photography*. Reaktion Books.

Fortenberry, D., & Melick, T. (2015). *Tarih boyunca sanat: Dünya sanat tarihinde üsluplar veakımlar*. Yapı Kredi Yayınları.

Galerie Thaddaeus Ropac. (n.d.). *Vera Molnar*. https://ropac.net/gallery-documents/73/

Galloway, A. R. (2004). *Protocol: How control exists after decentralization*. MIT Press. DOI: 10.7551/mitpress/5658.001.0001

Geneste, J. M. (2017). *The Lascaux Cave Paintings: Meaning and Method*. Cahiers de l'Art Préhistorique.

Godfrey, T. (2024). *Çağdaş sanatın öyküsü* (Çev. belirtilmemiş). Hayalperest Yayınevi.

Gülpınar, Ş., & Boyraz, B. (2024). *Sanatın Dijital Çağda Yeniden Tasarlanması: Yapay Zeka Perspektifinden Bir İnceleme*. Yıldız Sosyal Bilimler Enstitüsü Dergisi, 3.

Gülsoy, S. (2020). *Sanat ve Dijitalleşme*. Atatürk Üniversitesi Açık Öğretim Fakültesi.

Hall, S. (1980). Encoding/decoding. In Hall, S., Hobson, D., Lowe, A., & Willis, P. (Eds.), *Culture, media, language* (pp. 128–138). Routledge.

Han, B. C. (2017). *Transparency Society*. Metis Publications.

Hassan, R., & Sutherland, T. (2024). *Medya felsefesi* (Mousavi, S., & Törenli, N., Trans.). Ütopya Press. (Original work published 2023)

Horzum Taylor, I. (2015). Facebook and the being liked motive. *International Journal of Social Sciences and Education Research, 1*(4), 1216–1227. DOI: 10.24289/ijsser.279131

Houghton Mifflin Harcourt. (1992). *The American Heritage Dictionary of the English Language* (3rded.). https://archive.org/details/the-american-heritage-dictionary-of-the-english-language-third-edition-1st-august-1992

How-to-App. (n.d.). *Vera Molnar: Unordnung in der Ordnung*. https://how-to-app.de/unordnung.html

Ingold, T. (2007). *Lines: A brief history*. Routledge. DOI: 10.4324/9780203961155

Ivins, W. M. (1953). *Prints and visual communication*. Harvard University Press.

Jackson, R. (2011). *The Glitch Aesthetic* [Master's thesis, Georgia State University]. *ScholarWorks @ Georgia State University*. https://scholarworks.gsu.edu/communication_theses/80

Jean, G., & Başer, S. (2008). *Yazının tarihi* [History of writing]. Dost Kitabevi.

Kamaruddin, R., & Mazila, Y. (2012). Md. (2012). Selangor Government's "No plastic Bag Day" Campaign: Motivation and Acceptance Level. *Procedia: Social and Behavioral Sciences*, *42*, 205–211. DOI: 10.1016/j.sbspro.2012.04.183

Kardaş, M. (2025). Conspicuous Consumption and Social Appearance Anxiety: A Study on Instagram Women and Female Users (Published master's thesis). Çanakkale Onsekiz Mart University Graduate Education Institute, Çanakkale.

Kaya, A. (2023). Çağdaş Sanat Formu Olarak Dijital Heykel, Dijital Heykelin Sağladığı Yeni Olanaklar. *Sanat ve İkonografi Dergisi*, (4), 2–9.

Kaya, A. (2023). Çağdaş Sanat Formu Olarak Dijital Heykel, Dijital Heykelin Sağladığı Yeni Olanaklar. *Sanat Ve İkonografi Dergisi*, (4), 2–9. DOI: 10.5152/ArtIcon.2023.1226421

Kıran, S., Küçükbostancı, H., & Emre, İ. E. (2020). Investigation of the Effects of Social Media Usage on Individuals. *Journal of Information Technology*, *13*(4), 435–441. DOI: 10.17671/gazibtd.693331

Kiyan, Z. & Dikmen, E. Ş. (2019). "The Role of Social Media in Advertising: A Research on Instagram". İlef Journal, 6(1), 121-146. Doi: https://doi.org/DOI: 10.24955/ilef.554036

Kızılaslan, N., & İsmailoğlu, D. K. (2021). *Teknolojinin ve Dijitalleşmenin Geleneksel Türk Sanatlarına Yansımaları*. Medeniyet Sanat- İMÜ Sanat Tasarım ve Mimarlık Fakültesi Dergisi, 7(1). DOI: 10.46641/medeniyet-sanat.930735

Krause, B. (2008). Anatomy of the Soundscape: Evolving Perspectives. *JAES, 56*(1/2), 73-80. https://www.researchgate.net/profile/Bernie-Krause/publication/257943187_Anatomy_of_the_Soundscape_Evolving_Perspectives/links/00b4952668ef8dfbf5000000/Anatomy-of-the-Soundscape-Evolving-Perspectives.pdf

Kuçuradi Philosophy and Human Rights Foundation (Director). (2019). ETHICAL VALUES AND EDUCATION Part 1. Received Date Sender Https://Www.Youtube.Com/Watch?V=İpmm5cydeyy

Künüçen, H. H., & Samur, S. (2021). *Dijital Çağın Gerçeklikleri: Sanal, Artırılmış, Karma ve Genişletilmiş Gerçeklikler Üzerine Bir Değerlendirme*. Yeni Medya Hakenli, uluslararası, e-Dergi(11), 40. doi:DOI: 10.34189/ymd.2021.11.003

Lepercq, E. (2024, 7 May). *Vera Molnar, Mother of Computer Art, Pioneered the Future of Abstraction*. Artsy. https://www.artsy.net/article/artsy-editorial-vera-molnar-mother-computer-art-pioneered-future-abstraction

Lupton, E., & Miller, J. A. (1996). *Design writing research: Writing on graphic design*. Phaidon.

Manovich, L. (2001). *The Language of New Media*. MIT Press.

Margolin, V. (2002). *The politics of the artificial: Essays on design and design studies*. University of Chicago Press. DOI: 10.7208/chicago/9780226518374.001.0001

McLuhan, M. (1964). *Understanding Media: The Extensions of Man*. McGraw-Hill.

Meggs, P. B., & Purvis, A. W. (2016). *Meggs' History of Graphic Design* (6th ed.). John Wiley & Sons.

Menkman, R. (2011). *Glitch Studies Manifesto*. Academia.edu. https://www.academia.edu/3847007/Menkman_Rosa_2011_Glitch_Studies_Manifesto

Meron, Y. (2022). Graphic design and artificial intelligence: Interdisciplinary challenges for designers in the search for research collaboration. In Lockton, D., Lenzi, S., Hekkert, P., Oak, A., Sádaba, J., & Lloyd, P. (Eds.), *Proceedings of DRS2022 International Conference* (pp. 1–12). Design Research Society. DOI: 10.21606/drs.2022.157

Mirzoeff, N. (1999). *An Introduction to Visual Culture*. Routledge.

Molnar, V. (1975). Toward Aesthetic Guidelines for Paintings with the Aid of a Computerf. *Leonardo*, *8*(3), 185–189. DOI: 10.2307/1573236

Moradi, I. (2004). *Glitch Aesthetics* [Master's thesis]. School of Design Technology, Department of Architecture, The University of Huddersfield.

Moran, J. C. (1971). The development of the printing press. *Journal of the Royal Society of Arts*, *119*(5177), 281–293.

Mullen, L. (2008). Cave art and the origins of typography. *Visual Communication Quarterly*, *15*(1–2), 6–16. DOI: 10.1080/15551390801914546

Nomonov, B. (2022). Printing in Europe and the global spread of literacy. *European Studies Review*, *34*(1), 88–102.

Obrist, H. U. (2018). Interview: Vera Molnár. In Székely, K. (Ed.), *Bookmarks: Revisiting Hungarian Art of the 1960s and 1970s* (pp. xx–xx). Koenig Books.

Örs, M. (2022). *Dijital Sanatın Tarihi ve Güncel Sanat Eserlerine Yakından Bakış*. 1-2. İzmir, Türkiye.

Özselçuk, S. (2023). A critical review on the use of artificial intelligence algorithms in the context of digital art: Refik Anadol's 'Machine Memoirs: Space' exhibition. *International Journal of Economic and Administrative Academic Research, 3*(1), 1–21. https://dergipark.org.tr/tr/download/article-file/4266984

Öztürk, R. (2020). "Proteophobia" in the Context of Zygmunt Bauman's Understanding of Morality.

Ozturk, Y. (2021). The relationship between active social media use and depression and self-esteem: a foundation university student sample (Published master's thesis). Istanbul Gelisim University Graduate Education Institute, Istanbul.

Ozturk, Ş. (2015). Ethical Issues in Social Media. *Selcuk Communication, 9*(1), 287–311. DOI: 10.18094/si.57598

Paul, C. (2003). *Digital art*. Thames & Hudson Ltd.

Pelù, M. (2025, March 18). Sculture sonore per rigenerare i coralli: è "l'artescienza" di Marco Barotti. [Rapporto]. Corriere Canadese. https://www.corriere.ca/sculture-sonore-per-rigenerare-i-coralli-e-lartescienza-di-marco-barotti/

Poynor, R. (2003). *No more rules: Graphic design and postmodernism*. Yale University Press.

Rathus, L. F. (2013). Understanding art (10th Ed.). Usa: Wadsworth, Cengage Learning.

Read, H. (2020). *Modern sanatın felsefesi* (Kök, E., & Orgun, H., Trans.). Hayalperest.

Refik Anadol. (2024, 1 Eylül). Wikipedia. Erişim adresi: https://en.wikipedia.org/wiki/

Rodriguez, C. (2023). AI in graphic design: Here to help or replace us? [Master's thesis, Liberty University]. Liberty University Institutional Repository.

Sağlam, N. (2024). TikTok Usage Habits of Generation Z in the Context of Uses and Gratifications Theory (Published master's thesis). Uşak University Graduate Education Institute, Uşak.

Sağlamtimur, Z. (2010). *Dijital Sanat.* Anadolu Üniversitesi-Sosyal Bilimler dergisi, 218.

Şan, E. (2024). Sanat felsefesinin hikayesi: Mağara resimlerinden dijital imajlara.

Schafer, M. R. (1994). *Our sonic environment and the soundscape the tuning of the world.* Destiny Books. (Original work published 1977)

Schmandt-Besserat, D. (2014). *How writing came about.* University of Texas Press.

Schultz-Figueroa, B. (2011). Glitch/Glitsh: (More Power) Lucky Break and the Position of Modern Technology. *Culture Machine, 12*, •••. https://static1.squarespace.com/static/6317b98c456d53408bb7b7a5/t/631819b3b615f529eecfd284/1662523828020/439-892-1-PB-2.pdf

Şengünalp,C.,(2019). Çağdaş Sanatta İntihal ve Sermaye İlişkisi, Sosyal Araştırmalar Dergisi, 7, (88), S., 140-151.

Siyanbola, A., Omolola, A., & Adeyemi, A. (2021). Visual communication in prehistoric societies. *International Journal of Anthropology, 13*(2), 45–58.

Smithsonian American Art Museum. (n.d.). *Nam June Paik.* Smithsonian Institution. https://americanart.si.edu/artist/nam-june-paik-3670

Social, W. A. (2024, January 31). Digital 2024. Received December 26, 2024, by We Are Social UK Website: Https://Wearesocial.Com/Uk/Blog/2024/01/Digital-2024/

Solak, Ö. (2022, Aralık). *Dijital Sanatlar- Dijital Edebiyatlar.* Söylem Filoloji Dergisi(15), 387. doi:DOI: 10 29110/soylemdergi

Soydan, B. (2023). New Media and Social Media: Ethical Problems and Solution Approaches. *New Media Electronic Journal*, *7*(3), 198–215. DOI: 10.17932/IAU.EJNM.25480200.2023/ejnm_v7i3002

Sunlu, U., Lök, A., Küçükdermenci, A., Kırtık, A., & Kurtay, E. (2023). *Midyelerin biyolojik arıtma özelliklerinin İzmir Körfez'inde uygulanabilirliği projesi raporu.* İzmir Kalkınma Ajansı 2022 Yılı Teknik Destek Programı, İzmir. https://izka.org.tr/wp-content/uploads/pdf/midyelerin-biyolojik-aritma-ozelliklerinin-izmir-korfezine-uygulanabilirligi.pdf

Suvay Eker, H. (2022). How Social Networks Benefit from Big Data: Facebook and Twitter. *Journal of International Management*, *5*(1), 118–130. DOI: 10.33721/by.983553

Tarhan, P. D. N. (2000). YOUNG PEOPLE WHO RESEMBLE EACH OTHER WITH AESTHETIC SURGERY. Date of Arrival March 21, 2025, Posted by Nevzattarhan.Com Website: Https://Www.Nevzattarhan.Com/Estetik-Ameliyatla-Birbirine-Benzeyen-Gencler.Html

Tarı, N. (2025, 5 June). artfulliving.com.tr, Deneyselliği Dijitalle Buluşturan 5 Kolaj Sanatçısı, https://www.artfulliving.com.tr/sanat/deneyselligi-dijitalle-bulusturan-5-kolaj-sanatcisi-i-14417

Taylor Swift Nude Deepfake Goes Viral On, X. Despite Platform Rules. (2024, January 26). Received February 24, 2025, Posted by Https://Www.Nbcnews.Com/Tech/Misinformation/Taylor-Swift-Nude-Deepfake-Goes-Viral-X-Platform-Rules-Rcna135669

Taylor Swift's Deepfake Porn Sparks AI Debate. (2024, February 1). Received May 05, 2024, Posted by Euronews Website: Https://Tr.Euronews.Com/Kultur/2024/01/29/Taylor-Swiftin-Pornografi-Deepfake-Goruntuleri-Abdde-Yapay-Zeka-Tartismalarini-Ilevlendir

Taylor, D. G. (2014). *When the Machine Made Art: The Troubled History of Computer Art.* Bloomsbury Publishing.

Tinguely, J. (1960). Homage to New York. [Photograph]. https://www.moma.org/calendar/exhibitions/3369

Toprak, A. (2020). *Yapay Zekâ Algoritmalarının Dijital Enstalasyona Dönüşmesi*. Ege Üniversitesi İletişim Fakültesi Yeni Düşünceler.

Toptaş, R. (2022). Türkiye'de Dijital Sanat, Sanatçıları ve Eserleri Hakkında Bir Araştırma. *STAR Sanat Ve Tasarım Araştırmaları Dergisi, 3*(5), 170–186.

Toptaş, R. (2022). *Türkiye'de Dijital Sanat*. Sanatçıları Ve Eserleri Hakkında Bir Araştırma, Sanat ve Tasarım Araştırmaları Dergisi.

Torun, A. (2015). Walter Benjamin, Sanat Eserinin Aurası ve Yeni Medya Sanatı, International Multilingual Academic Journal, Vol. 2, No,1.

Turhan, Ö. (2006)." Bilgisayar teknolojilerinin Heykel Sanatına Sağladığı Yeni Olanaklar:

Turkish Language Association Presidency Ethics Guide. (2015) Access address https://tdk.gov.tr/wp-content/uploads/2016/11/TDK-Etik-Rehberi .pdf

Turkish, D. W. (Director). (2020). Philosopher Kuçuradi: Human Relationships Are Harder Than Going to Mars - DW Turkish. Received Date From Https://Www.Youtube.Com/Watch?V=SQ7soJHTZ9g

Turner, B. S. (2019). *Beden ve toplum sosyal teoride arayışlar* (Kaya, İ., Trans.). Nobel.

Uçar, E. (2004). *Görsel kültür ve iletişim* [Visual culture and communication]. İletişim Yayınları.

Uğurlu, H. (2008). Teknoloji Sanat İlişkisi: Günümüzde Teknolojik Sanatların Amacı. *Uşak Üniversitesi Sosyal Bilimler Dergisi, 1*(2), 247–262. DOI: 10.12780/UUSBD27

Valyi-Nagy, Z. (2024). Between the Lines. *Artforum International, 62*(9).

Vargün, Ö. (2023). *Teknoloji ve Sanatın Dönüşümü: Dijital Sana*t. *Journal of Art, 6*(1), 176. DOI: 10.31566/arts.1968

Vidal, J. (2012, September 3). 'A great silence is spreading over the natural world'. The Guardian. https://www.theguardian.com/environment/2012/sep/03/bernie-krause-natural-world-recordings#comments

Walton, K. L. (2018) Geçirgen Fotoğraflar: Fotografik Gerçekliğin Doğası Üzerine, S.Walden (Ed.), Doğanın Kalemi Üzerine Denemeler (pp.29-67). (H. Yılmaz, Trans.), Espas Yayınları

Wands, B. (2006). Art of the digital age. Londra: Thames and Hudson.

WANDS, B. (2021). *Dijital Sanat sergi Küratörlüğünün 25 Yılı:1993-2018*. GSF Sanat Dergisi, 1-2.

Wands, B. (2021). *The Engagement of Digital Art With Contemporary Art*. Sanat ve İnsan, 215.

Wands, B. (2006). *Art of the digital age* (Akınhay, O., Trans.). Akbank Culture and Art Publications. (Original work published 2006)

Wands, B. (2006). *Dijital çağın sanatı* (Akınhay, O., Trans.). Renk Ayrımı.

Weeks, M. (2024). *Dakikalar içinde felsefe* (Özeren, M. M., Trans.). Kronik.

Wilson, S. (2002). *Information Arts: Intersections of Art, Science, and Technology*. MIT Press.

World's First. 'Cybercrime Index' Ranks Countries by Cybercrime Threat Level | Oxford University. (2024, April 10). Received March 16, 2025, From Https://Www.Ox.Ac.Uk/News/2024-04-10-World-First-Cybercrime-Index-Ranks-Countries-Cybercrime-Threat-Level

Yağmur, Ö.,(2018). Heykel Sinestik Düşünmek, Ordu Üniversitesi Sosyal Bilimler Araştırmalar Dergisi, 8, (3), S., 691-697.

Yıldırım, O., & Ayan, V. M. (2024). *From Twitter to X: Evaluation of the Change in Ownership Structure in Social Media on the X Platform*. İlef Journal., DOI: 10.24955/ilef.1432738

Yıldırım, S. (2021). The Phenomenon of Showing Off in Social Media and the Consumption of the Sacred. *Iğdır University Journal of Social Sciences*, *28*, 125–143.

Yılmaz, M. (2013). *Modernden postmoderne sanat*. Ütopya Press.

Yücel, D. (2012). *Dijital Teknolojiler Ekseninde Değişen Sanat ve Kurumlar*. Genç Sanat.

Yücel, G. (2021). Dijital sanat bağlamında heykel: Yeni medya teknolojileriyle dönüşen form ve izleyici ilişkisi. *Sanat ve Tasarım Dergisi*, *12*(2), 45–58. DOI: 10.5281/zenodo.1234567

Yüksel, İ., & Aşan Yüksel, O. (2024). Sanatta yapay zeka devrimi: Yaratıcılığın yeni boyutları. *Sanat & Tasarım Dergisi*, *14*(2), 261–285. DOI: 10.20488/sanattasarim.1602572

Zou, X., Zhang, W., & Zhao, N. (2024). From fragment to one piece: A survey on AI-driven graphic design. *Journal of LaTeX Class Files*, *14*(8), 1–16.

About the Contributors

Murat Han Er completed his undergraduate studies in the Graphic Design Department at Atatürk University. He earned his Master's degree from the Photography Department of the Faculty of Fine Arts at Atatürk University and his Doctorate from the Photography Department of the Faculty of Fine Arts at Mimar Sinan Fine Arts University. In 2005, he began working as a Research Assistant in the Photography Department at the Faculty of Fine Arts at Atatürk University. Between 2010 and 2015, he worked in the Photography Department at Mimar Sinan Fine Arts University. He currently serves as an Associate Professor in the Photography Department of the Faculty of Fine Arts at Atatürk University. The artist has participated in numerous exhibitions both nationally and internationally and has received various awards.

Basri Gençcelep worked as a research assistant in Atatürk University, Fine Arts Faculty, Graphic Design Department. From 2013 to 2018, he worked as a research assistant in Mimar Sinan Fine Arts University, Faculty of Fine Arts, Department of Photography. He had completed his Proficiency in Art at 2017 in Mimar Sinan Fine Arts University, Faculty of Fine Arts, Department of Photography. From 2018 he started giving lectures as an Assistant Professor in Atatürk University, Fine Arts Faculty, Graphic Design Department. He had taken part in national and international art events and projects.

***

Gülümser Beyaztaş Özlütürk continues her academic and practical studies in sculpture in Erzurum. Her work focuses on the reinterpretation of cultural objects within the artistic context, exploring material diversity and formal studies. Through an interdisciplinary approach, she aims to expand the boundaries of artistic expression by focusing on alternative materials.

Bulat Serap completed her Master Thesis entitled "Stone Ornaments on İshakpaşa Palace in Doğubeyazit" at the Deaprtment of Art History for the Institute of Social Sciences Ataturk University 1996- She started to work as a research assistant at the Department of Sculpture in the Faculty of Fine Arts, Atatürk University. 1996-Atatürk University, Faculty of Fine Arts, he started working as a research assistant in the Department of Sculpture. 1990-94- She graduated from the Department of Sulpture in the Faculty of Fine Arts.

Nurevşan Karaduman Başcı was born in 1998 in Erzurum, Türkiye. Following her primary and secondary education, she began her undergraduate studies in the Department of Graphic Design at Atatürk University, Faculty of Fine Arts, in 2016 and graduated in 2020. In the same year, she commenced her master's degree at Atatürk University, Institute of Fine Arts, which she successfully completed in 2023. She is currently pursuing her Proficiency in Art (equivalent to a doctoral-level program) at the same institute.

Burcu Toğrul was born in Erzurum in 1981. He completed his primary, secondary, and high school education in Erzurum. He graduated from Atatürk University, Faculty of Fine Arts, Department of Traditional Turkish Handicrafts in 2005 and from Uşak University, Institute of Social Sciences, Traditional Turkish Handicrafts in 2017. He began his education in the Atatürk University, Faculty of Fine Arts, Plastic Arts, Proficiency in Art Program in 2024. Since 2018, he has been working as a lecturer at Ağrı İbrahim Çeçen University, Doğubayazıt Ahmed-i Hani Vocational School, Handicrafts Program.

Index

A

C

D

E

G

H

I

L

M

N

P

S

T

V

www.ingramcontent.com/pod-product-compliance
Ingram Content Group UK Ltd.
Pitfield, Milton Keynes, MK11 3LW, UK
UKHW051039091026
15624UKWH00011B/548

9 798260 009444